assen

P9-BXZ-390

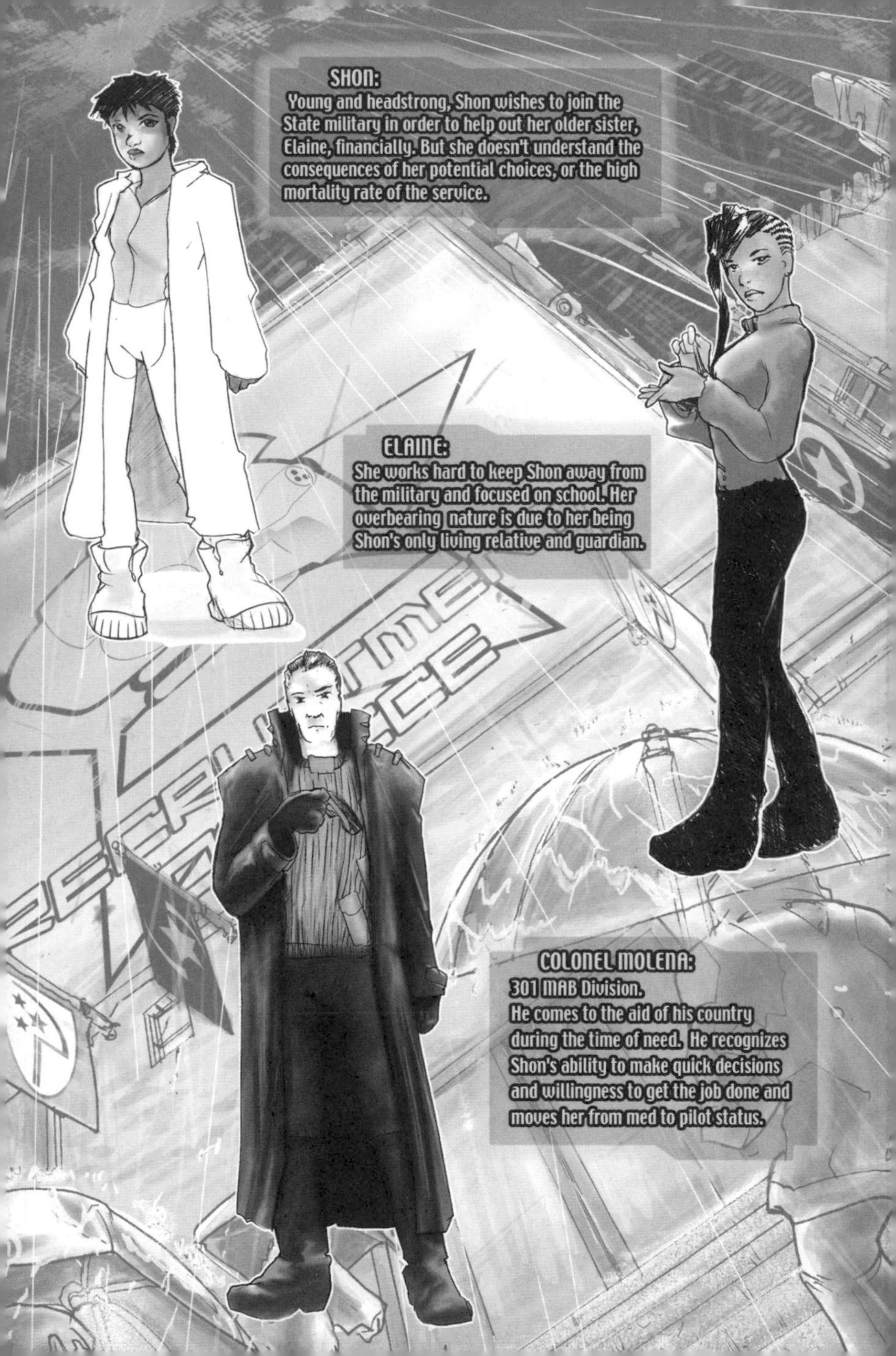
SHON:
Young and headstrong, Shon wishes to join the State military in order to help out her older sister, Elaine, financially. But she doesn't understand the consequences of her potential choices, or the high mortality rate of the service.
ELAINE:
She works hard to keep Shon away from the military and focused on school. Her overbearing nature is due to her being Shon's only living relative and guardian.
COLONEL MOLENA:
301 MAB Division.
He comes to the aid of his country during the time of need. He recognizes Shon's ability to make quick decisions and willingness to get the job done and moves her from med to pilot status.

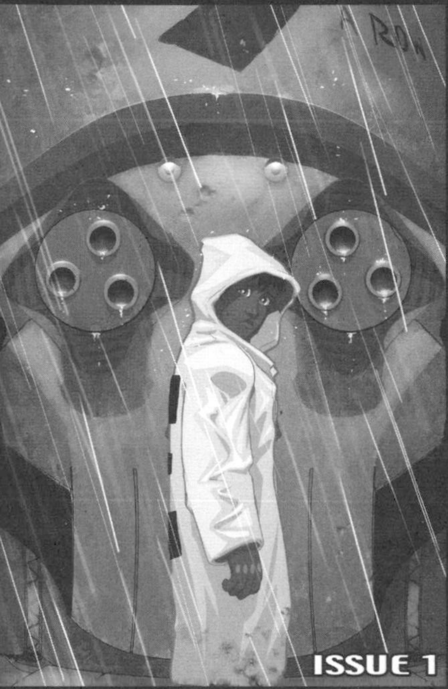
ISSUE 1

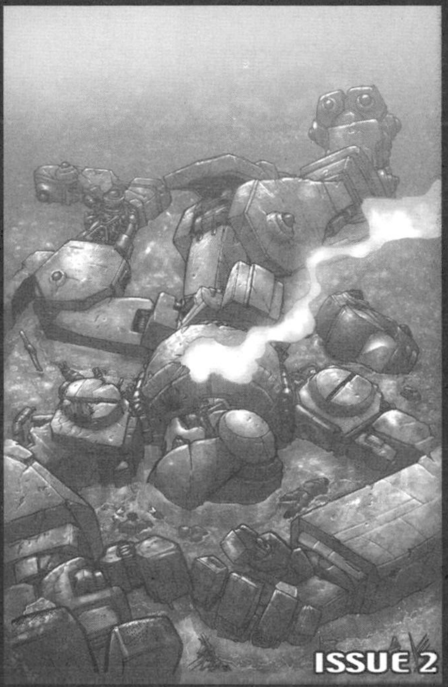
ISSUE 2

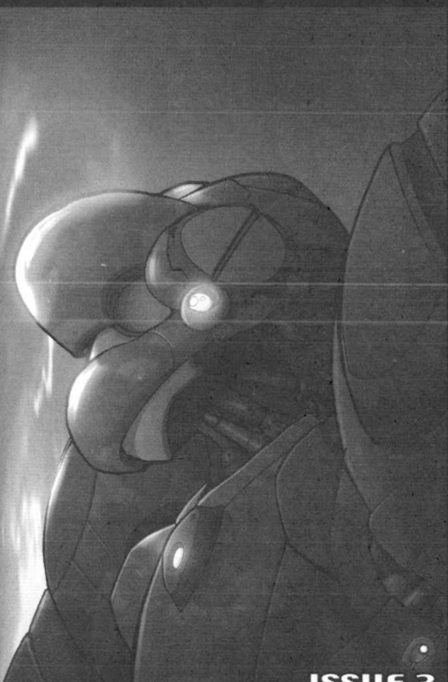
ISSUE 3

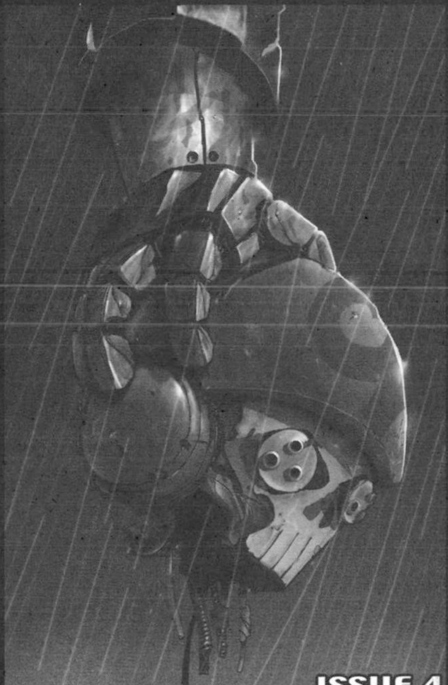
ISSUE 4

assembly

Creator - Sherard Jackson
Graphic Designer - Sherard Jackson
Cover Design - Guru e-FX
Layout - Paul Kilpatrick

Editor in Chief - Jochen Weltjens
President of Sales and Marketing - Lee Duhig
Art Direction - Guru e-FX
VP of Production - Rod Espinosa
Publisher - Joe Dunn
Founder - Ben Dunn

Come visit us online at www.antarctic-press.com

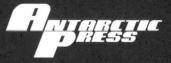

Antarctic Press

Assembly Pocket Manga Volume #1 by Sherard Jackson
An Antarctic Press Pocket Manga

Antarctic Press
7272 Wurzbach Suite 204 San Antonio, TX 78240

Collects *Assembly* issue 1-4
First published in 2003 by Antarctic Press.

Assembly Pocket Manga Volume 1, June 2004.

"We're so broke we can't even afford to pay attention."

ISBN: 1-932453-51-2

Printed and bound in China by Sung Fung Offset Binding Co. Ltd.

VOLUME 1

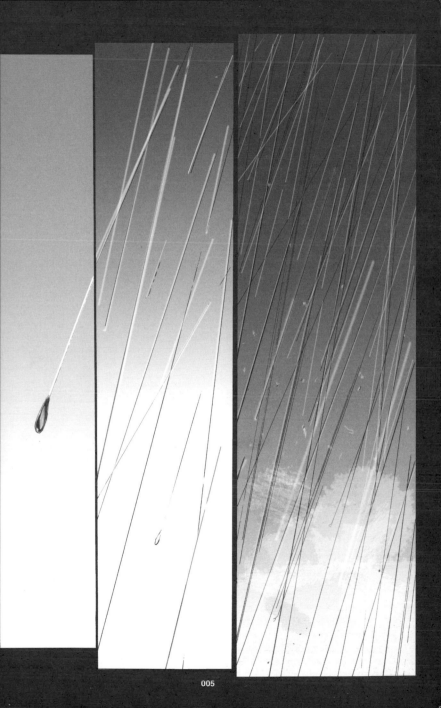

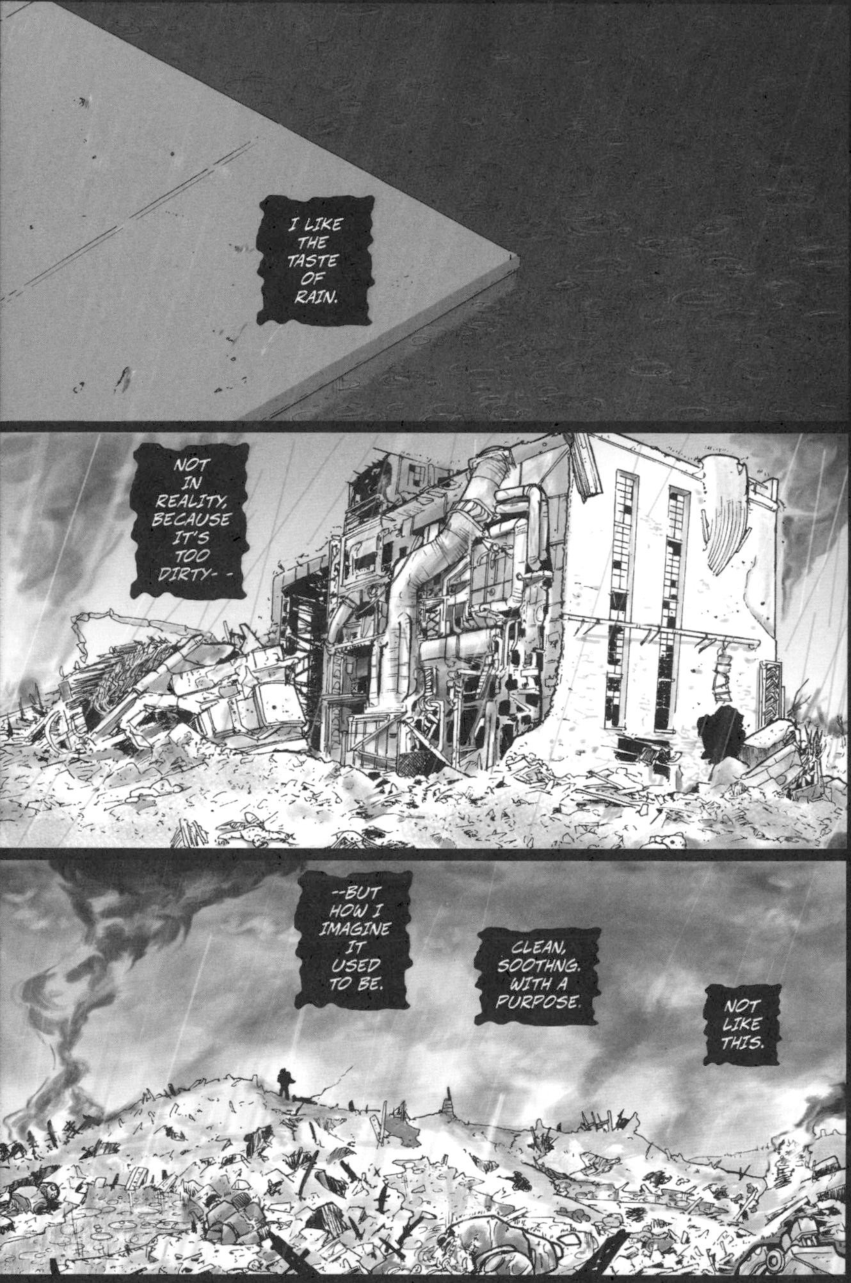
I LIKE THE TASTE OF RAIN.
NOT IN REALITY, BECAUSE IT'S TOO DIRTY- -
--BUT HOW I IMAGINE IT USED TO BE.
CLEAN, SOOTHNG. WITH A PURPOSE.
NOT LIKE THIS.

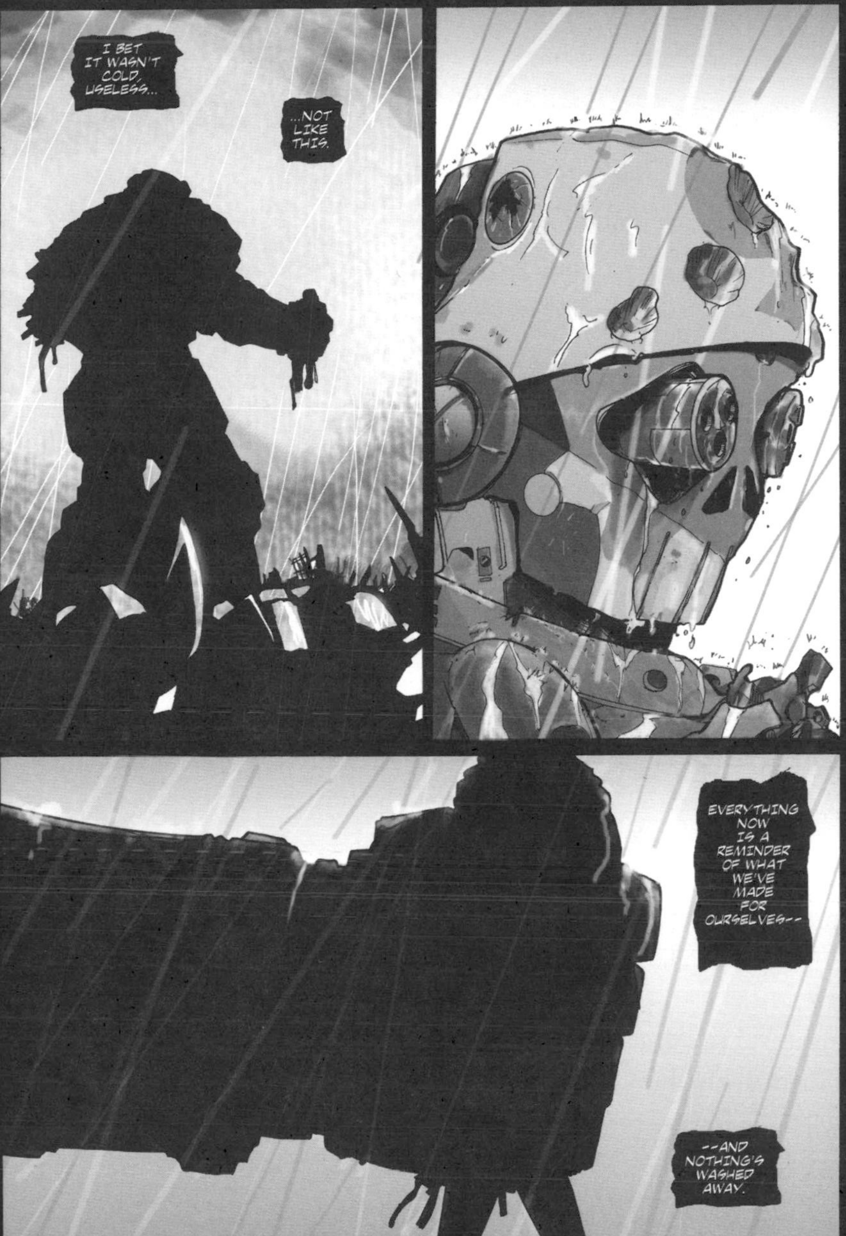
I BET IT WASN'T COLD, USELESS...
...NOT LIKE THIS.
EVERYTHING NOW IS A REMINDER OF WHAT WE'VE MADE FOR OURSELVES--
--AND NOTHING'S WASHED AWAY.

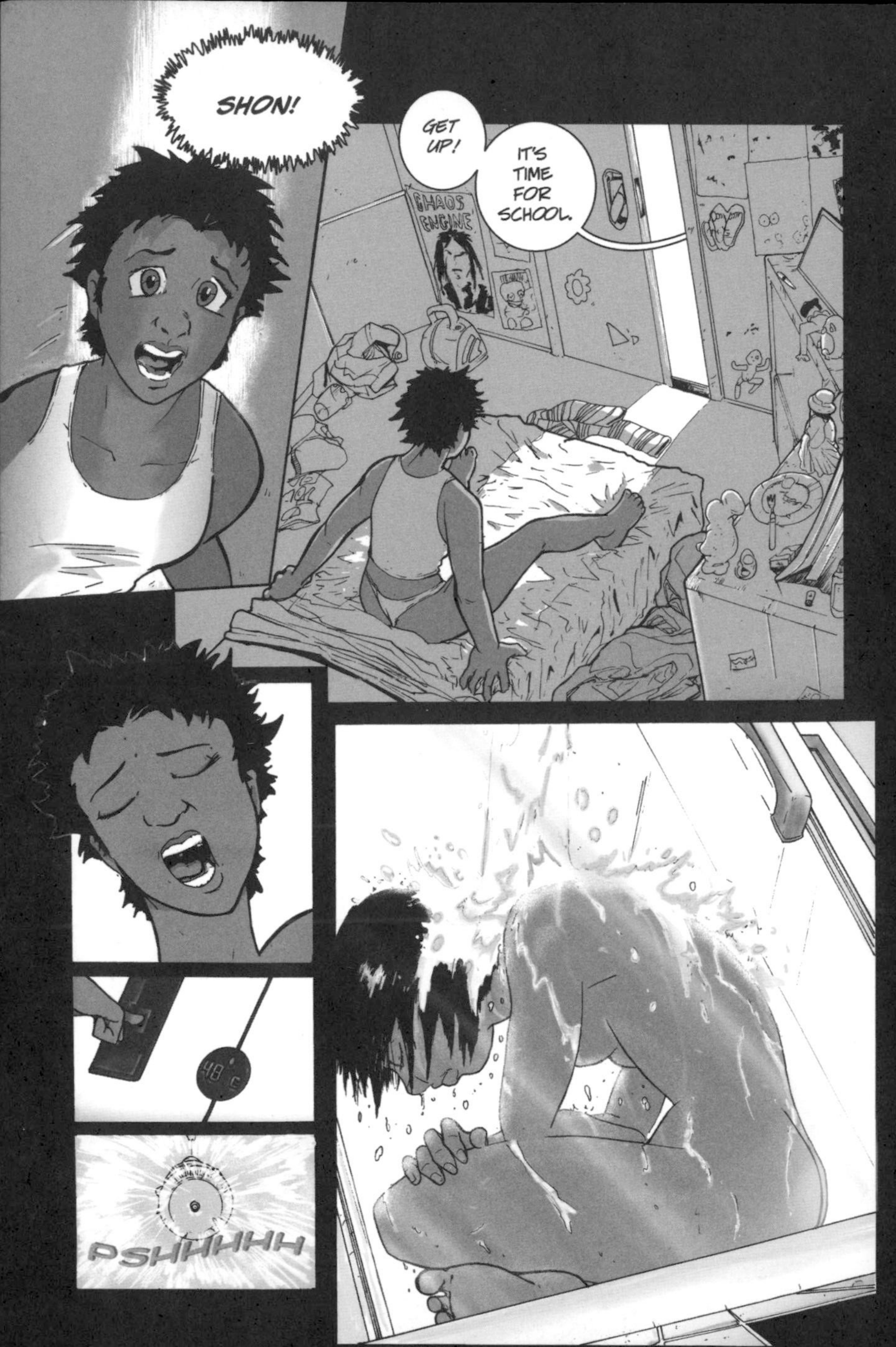
SHON!
GET UP!
IT'S TIME FOR SCHOOL.
CHAOS ENGINE
PSHHHHH

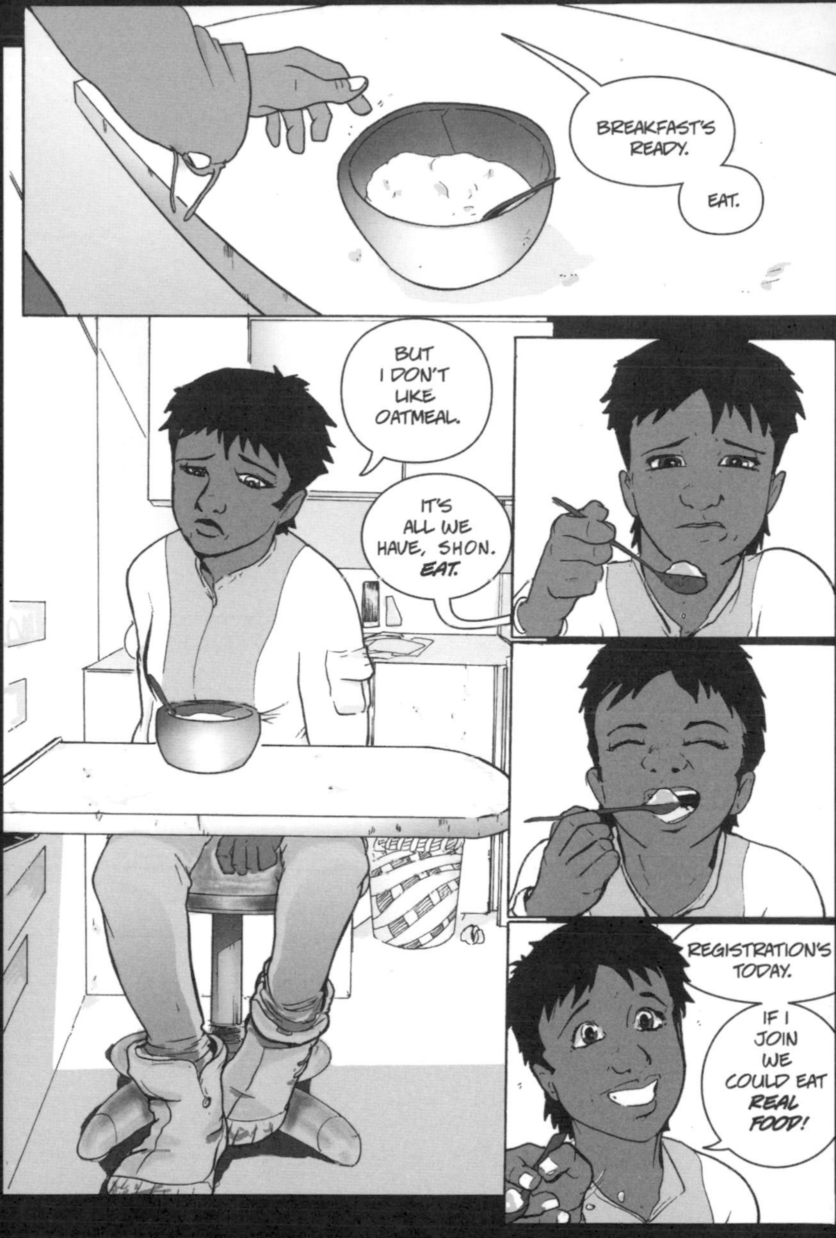
BREAKFAST'S READY.
EAT.
BUT I DON'T LIKE OATMEAL.
IT'S ALL WE HAVE, SHON. EAT.
REGISTRATION'S TODAY.
IF I JOIN WE COULD EAT REAL FOOD!

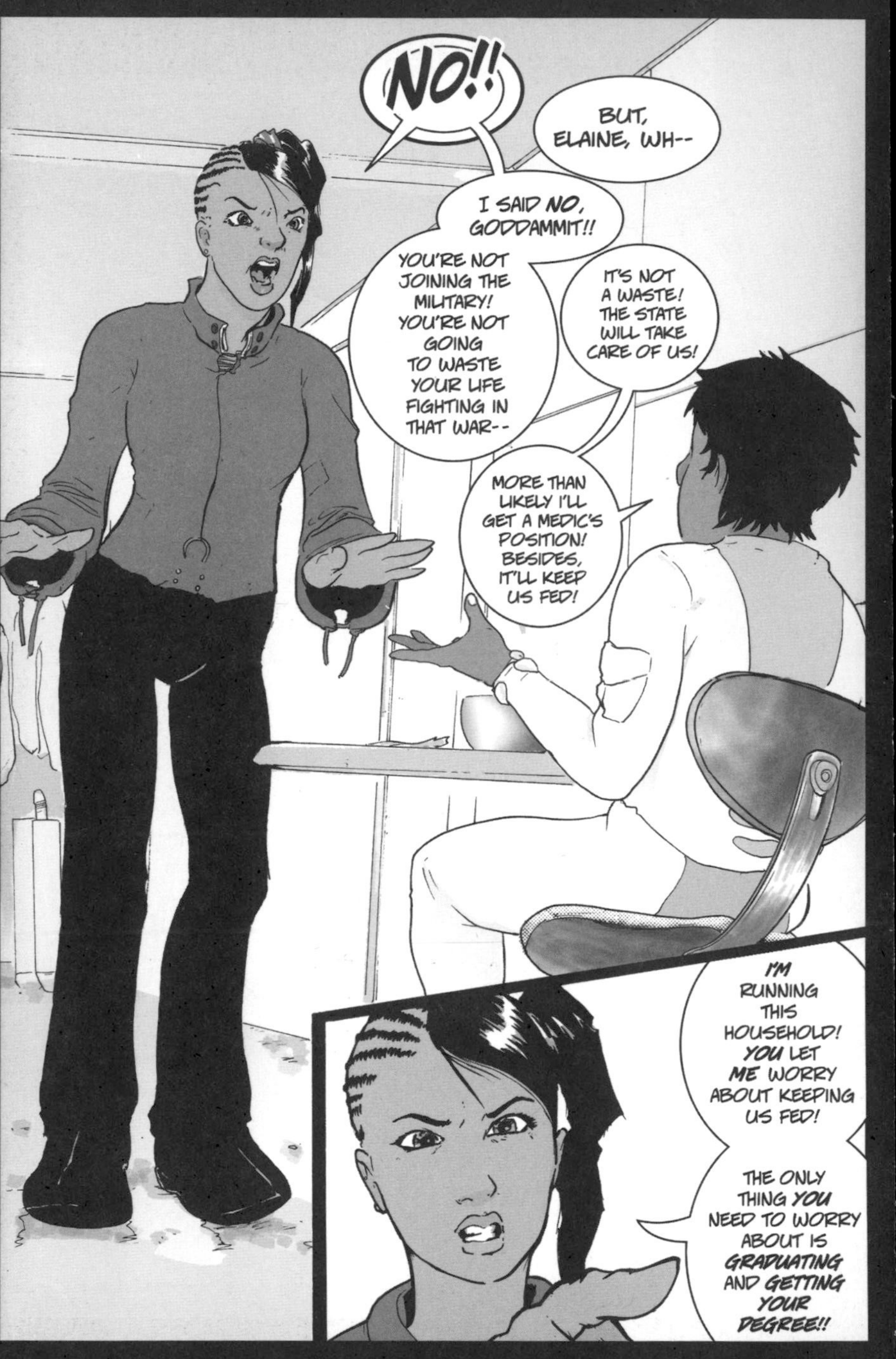
NO!!
BUT, ELAINE, WH--
I SAID NO, GODDAMMIT!!
YOU'RE NOT JOINING THE MILITARY! YOU'RE NOT GOING TO WASTE YOUR LIFE FIGHTING IN THAT WAR--
IT'S NOT A WASTE! THE STATE WILL TAKE CARE OF US!
MORE THAN LIKELY I'LL GET A MEDIC'S POSITION! BESIDES, IT'LL KEEP US FED!
I'M RUNNING THIS HOUSEHOLD! YOU LET ME WORRY ABOUT KEEPING US FED!
THE ONLY THING YOU NEED TO WORRY ABOUT IS GRADUATING AND GETTING YOUR DEGREE!!

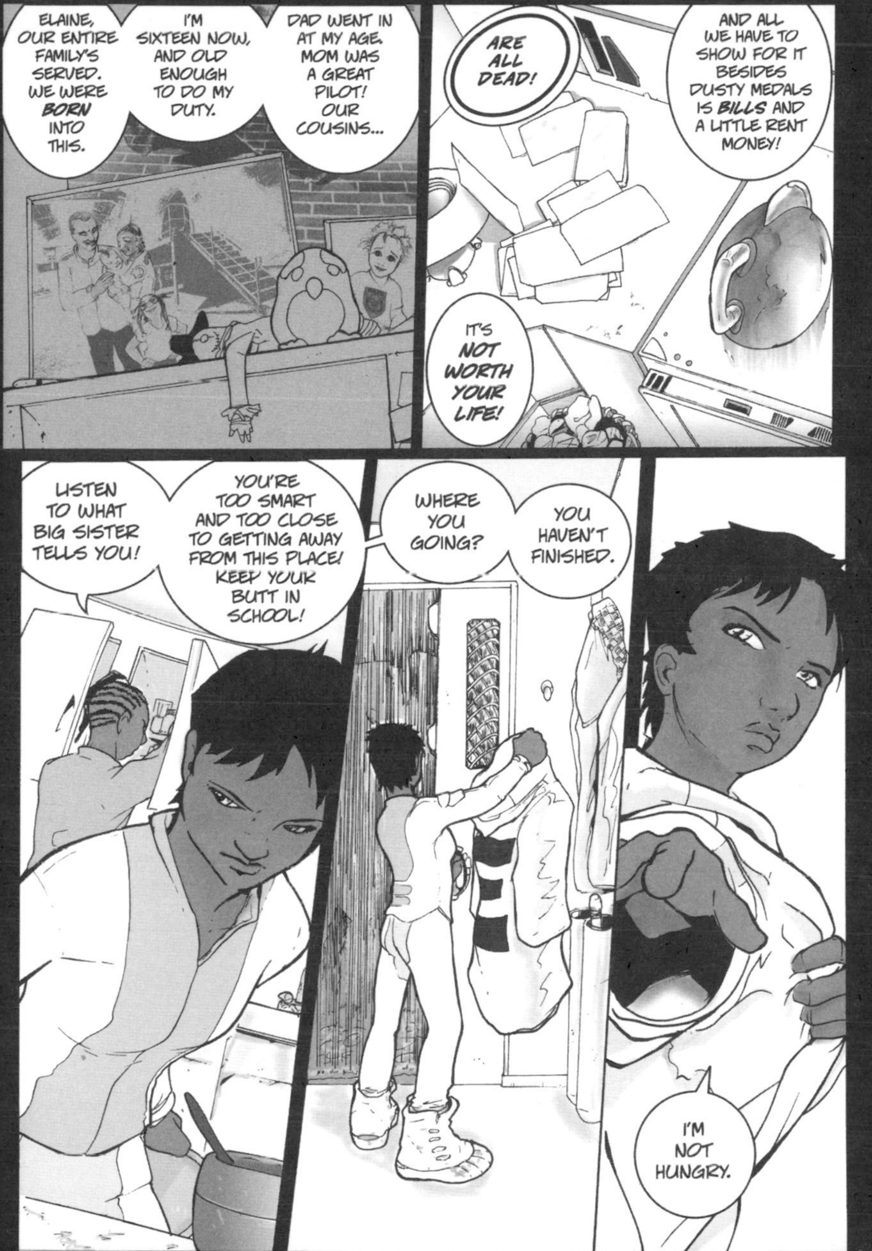
ELAINE, OUR ENTIRE FAMILY'S SERVED. WE WERE BORN INTO THIS.
I'M SIXTEEN NOW, AND OLD ENOUGH TO DO MY DUTY.
DAD WENT IN AT MY AGE. MOM WAS A GREAT PILOT! OUR COUSINS...
ARE ALL DEAD!
AND ALL WE HAVE TO SHOW FOR IT BESIDES DUSTY MEDALS IS BILLS AND A LITTLE RENT MONEY!
IT'S NOT WORTH YOUR LIFE!
LISTEN TO WHAT BIG SISTER TELLS YOU!
YOU'RE TOO SMART AND TOO CLOSE TO GETTING AWAY FROM THIS PLACE! KEEP YOUR BUTT IN SCHOOL!
WHERE YOU GOING?
YOU HAVEN'T FINISHED.
I'M NOT HUNGRY.

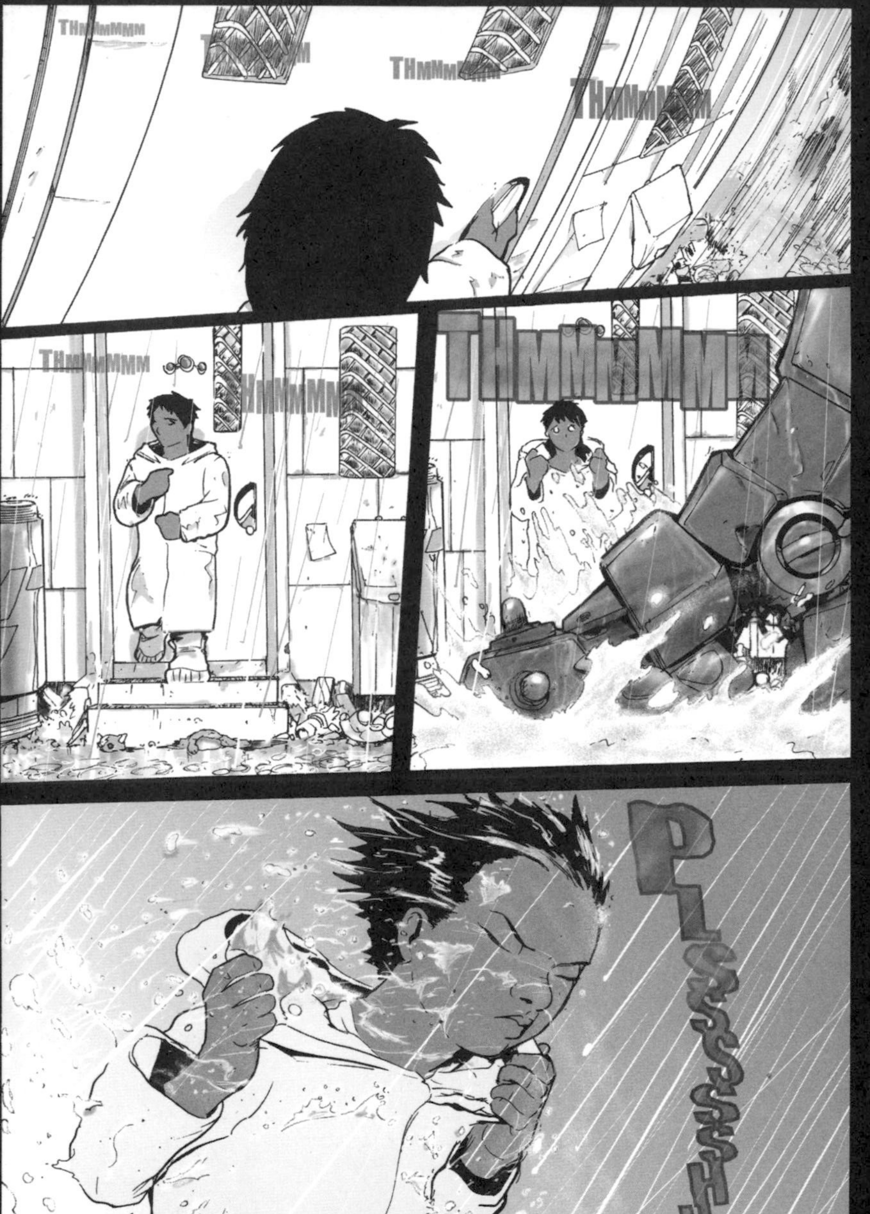
THMMMMM
THMMMMM
THMMMMM
THMMMMM
THMMMMM
HMMMMM
THMMMMMM
PLSSSSSH

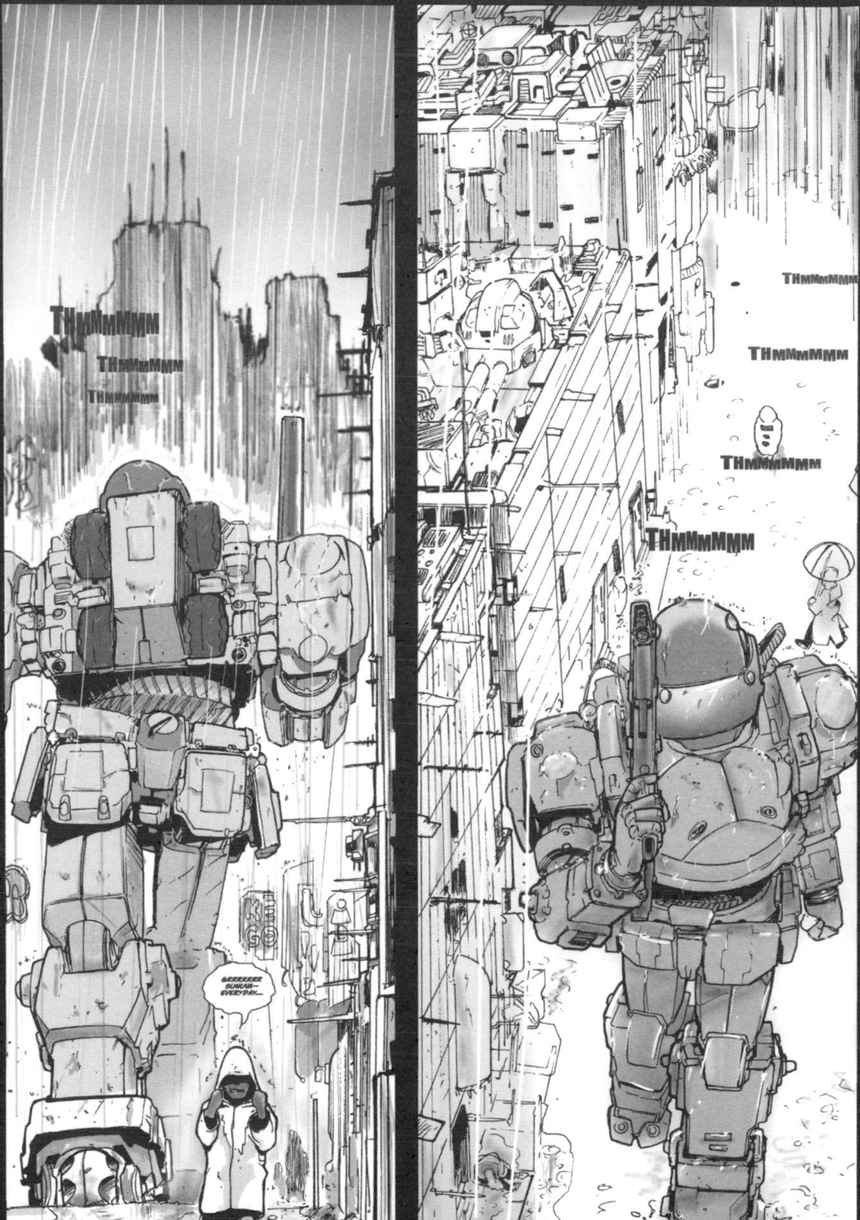
THMMMMMM
THMMMMMM
THMMMMMM
GRRRRRRR SUMMAH— EVERYDAY...
THMMMMMM
THMMMMMM
THMMMMMM
THMMMMMM

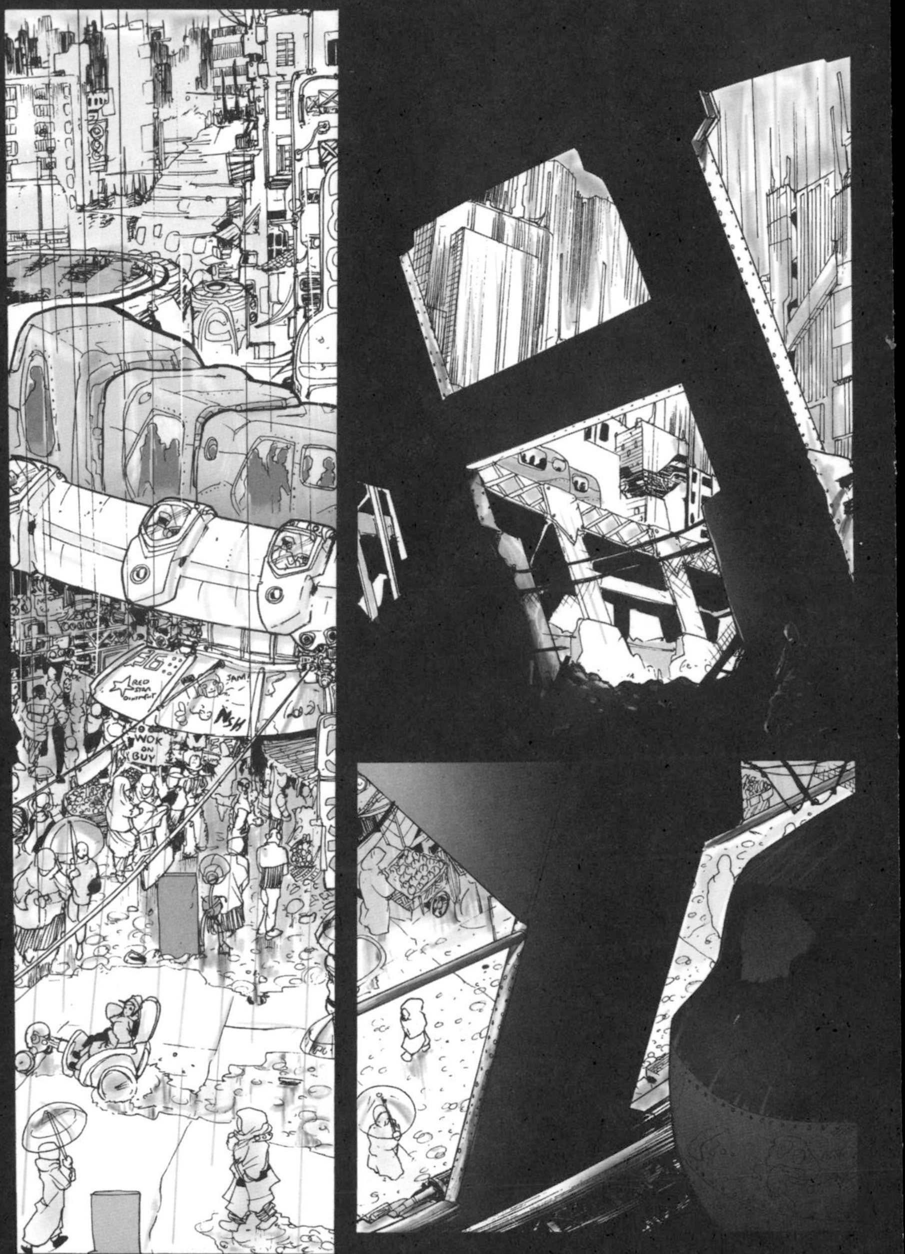
36
RED STAR DISTRICT
SAM!
NSH
WOK ON BUY

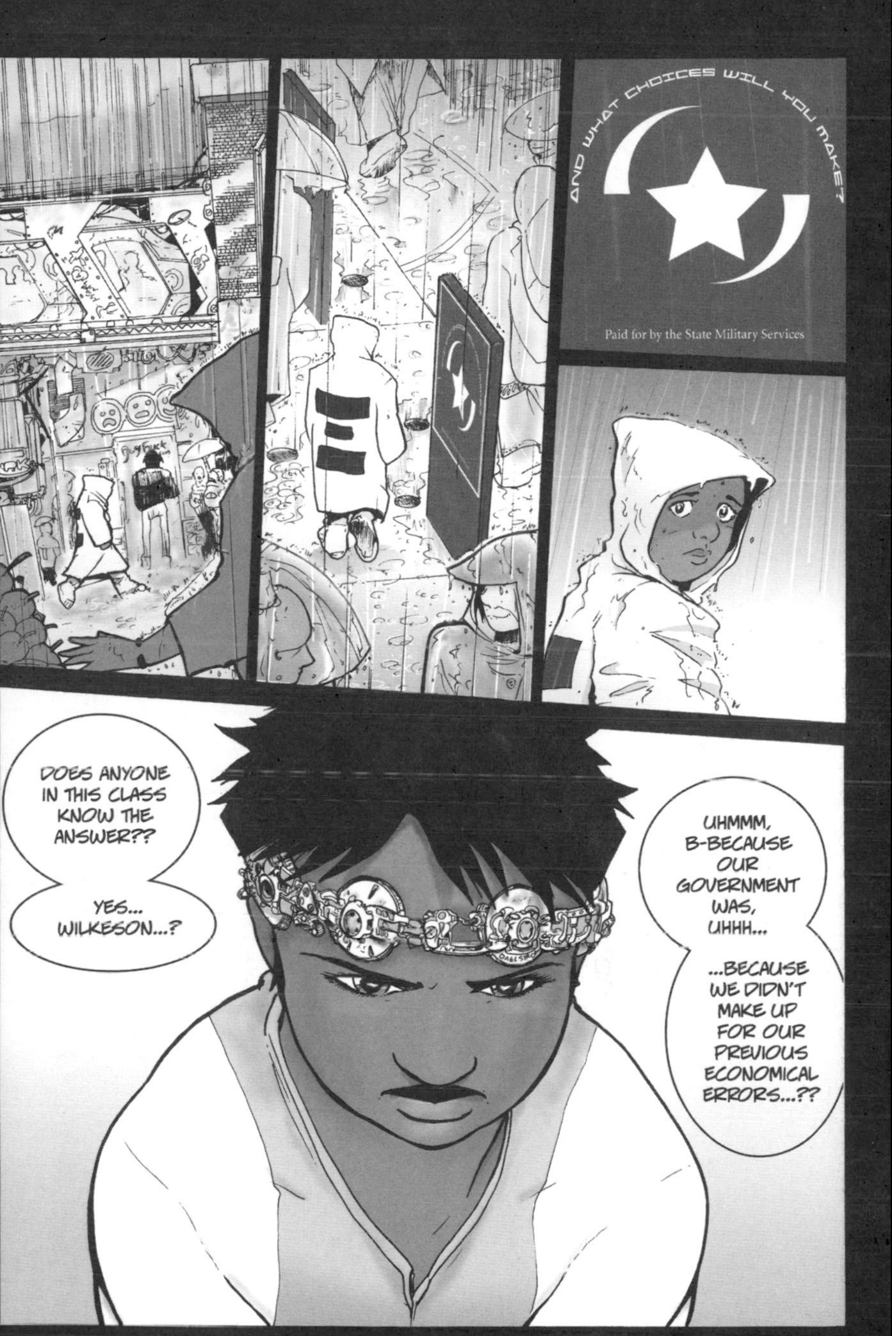
AND WHAT CHOICES WILL YOU MAKE?
Paid for by the State Military Services
DOES ANYONE IN THIS CLASS KNOW THE ANSWER??
YES... WILKESON...?
UHMMM, B-BECAUSE OUR GOVERNMENT WAS, UHHH...
...BECAUSE WE DIDN'T MAKE UP FOR OUR PREVIOUS ECONOMICAL ERRORS...??

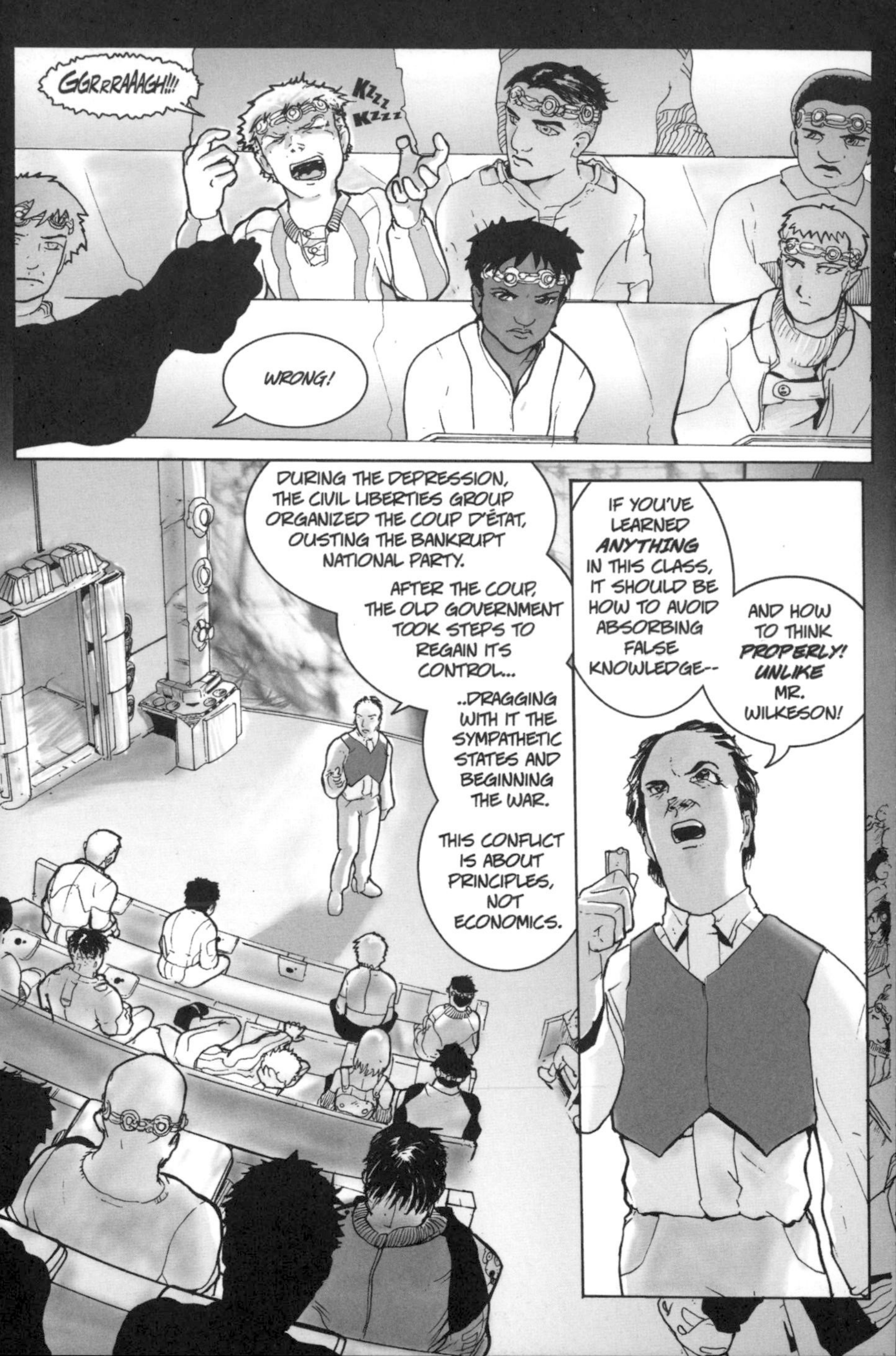
GGRRRAAAGH!!!
KZZZ KZZZ
WRONG!
DURING THE DEPRESSION, THE CIVIL LIBERTIES GROUP ORGANIZED THE COUP D'ÉTAT, OUSTING THE BANKRUPT NATIONAL PARTY.
AFTER THE COUP, THE OLD GOVERNMENT TOOK STEPS TO REGAIN IT'S CONTROL...
..DRAGGING WITH IT THE SYMPATHETIC STATES AND BEGINNING THE WAR.
THIS CONFLICT IS ABOUT PRINCIPLES, NOT ECONOMICS.
IF YOU'VE LEARNED ANYTHING IN THIS CLASS, IT SHOULD BE HOW TO AVOID ABSORBING FALSE KNOWLEDGE--
AND HOW TO THINK PROPERLY! UNLIKE MR. WILKESON!

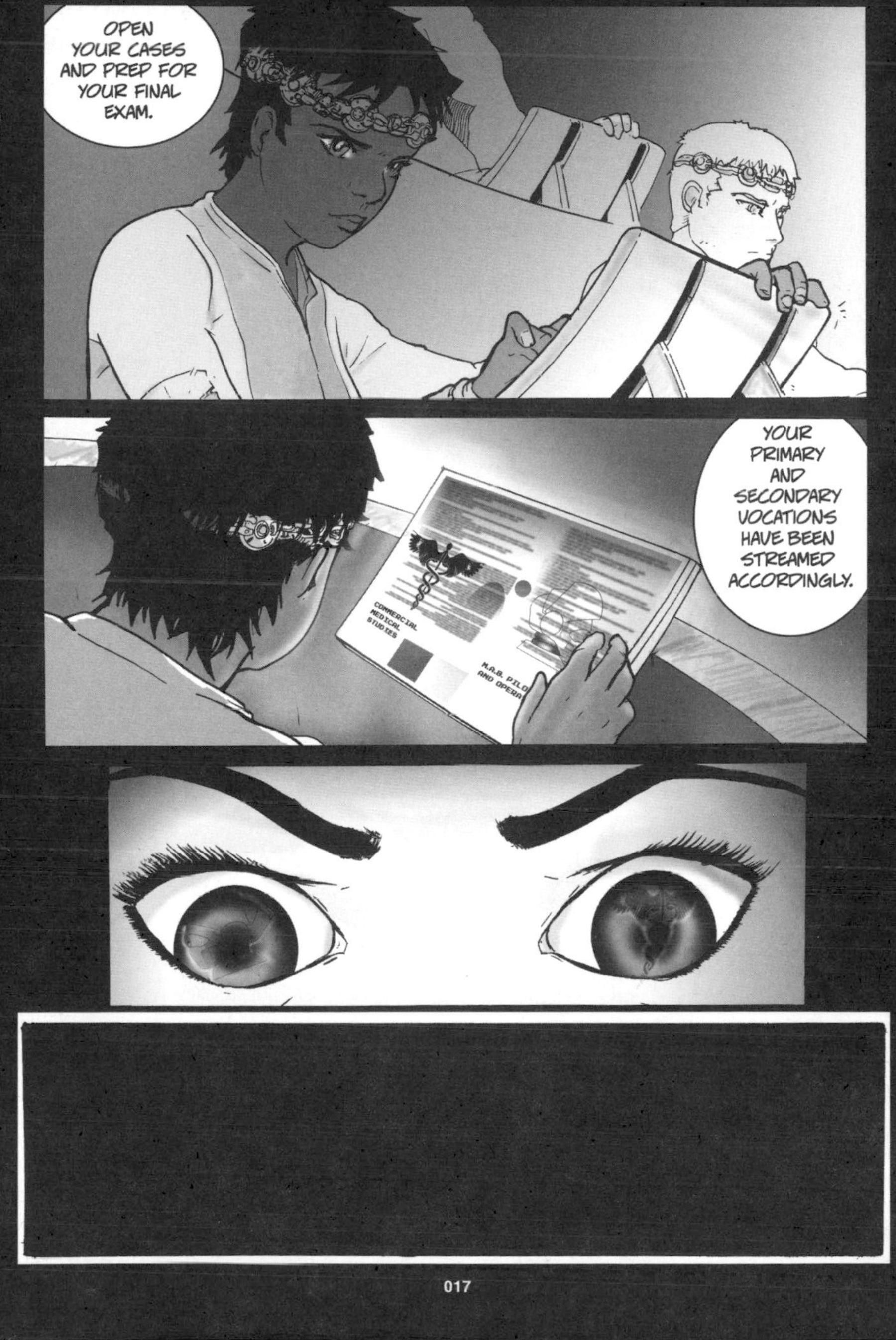
OPEN YOUR CASES AND PREP FOR YOUR FINAL EXAM.
YOUR PRIMARY AND SECONDARY VOCATIONS HAVE BEEN STREAMED ACCORDINGLY.
COMMERCIAL MEDICAL STUDIES

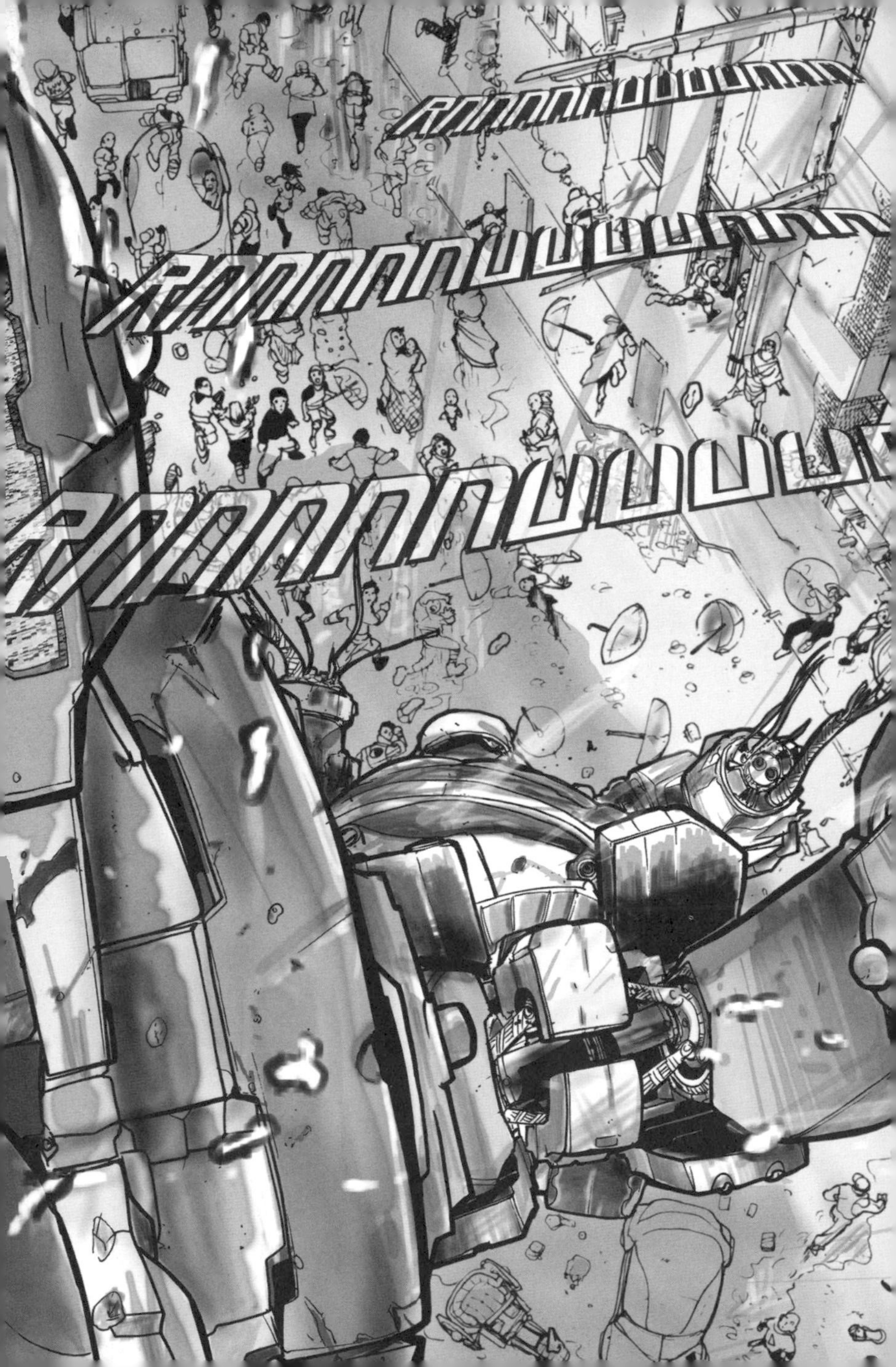
RAAAAAUUUUAAAA
RAAAAAUUUUAAAA
RAAAAAUUUUU

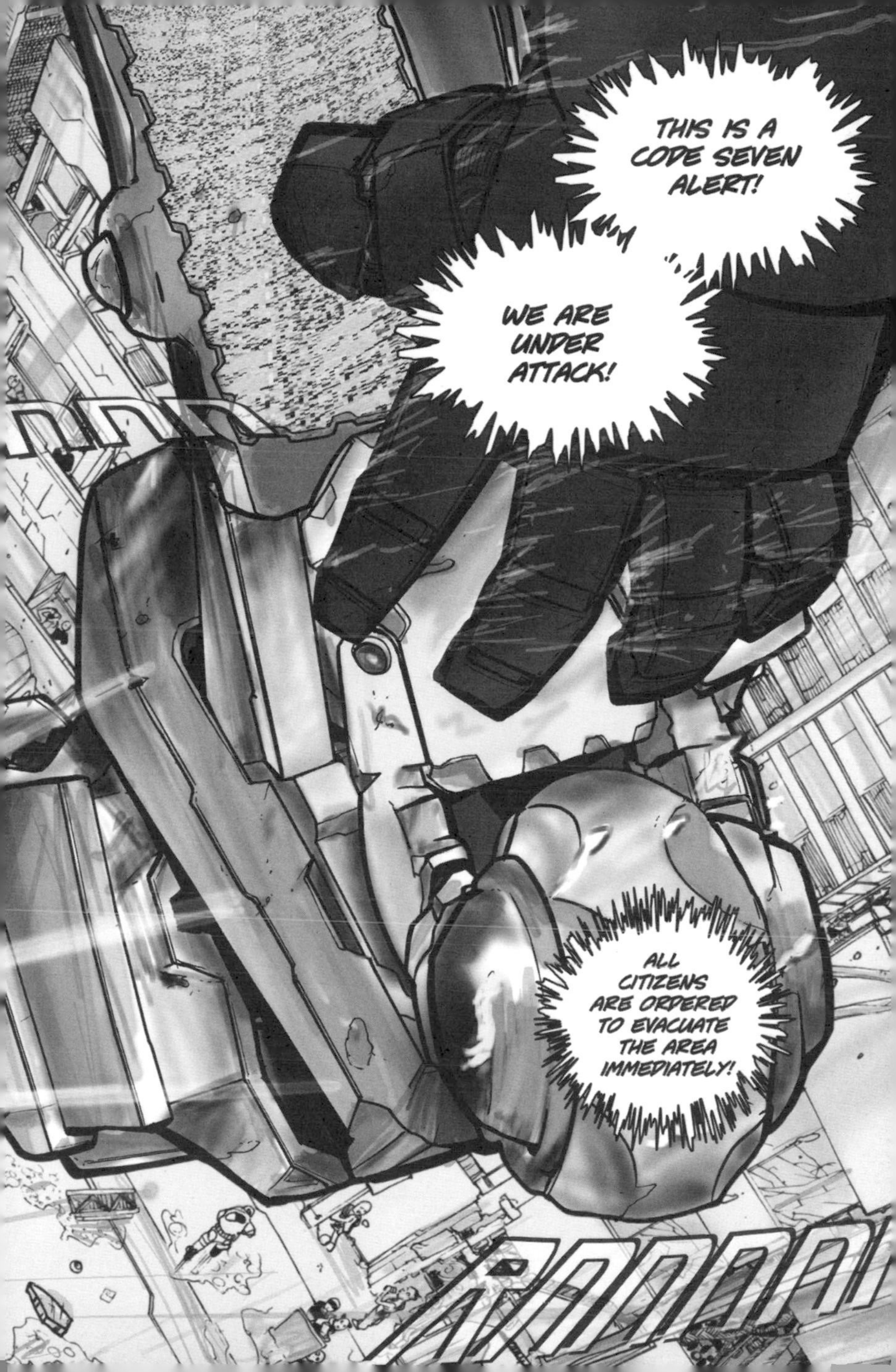
THIS IS A CODE SEVEN ALERT!
WE ARE UNDER ATTACK!
ALL CITIZENS ARE ORDERED TO EVACUATE THE AREA IMMEDIATELY!

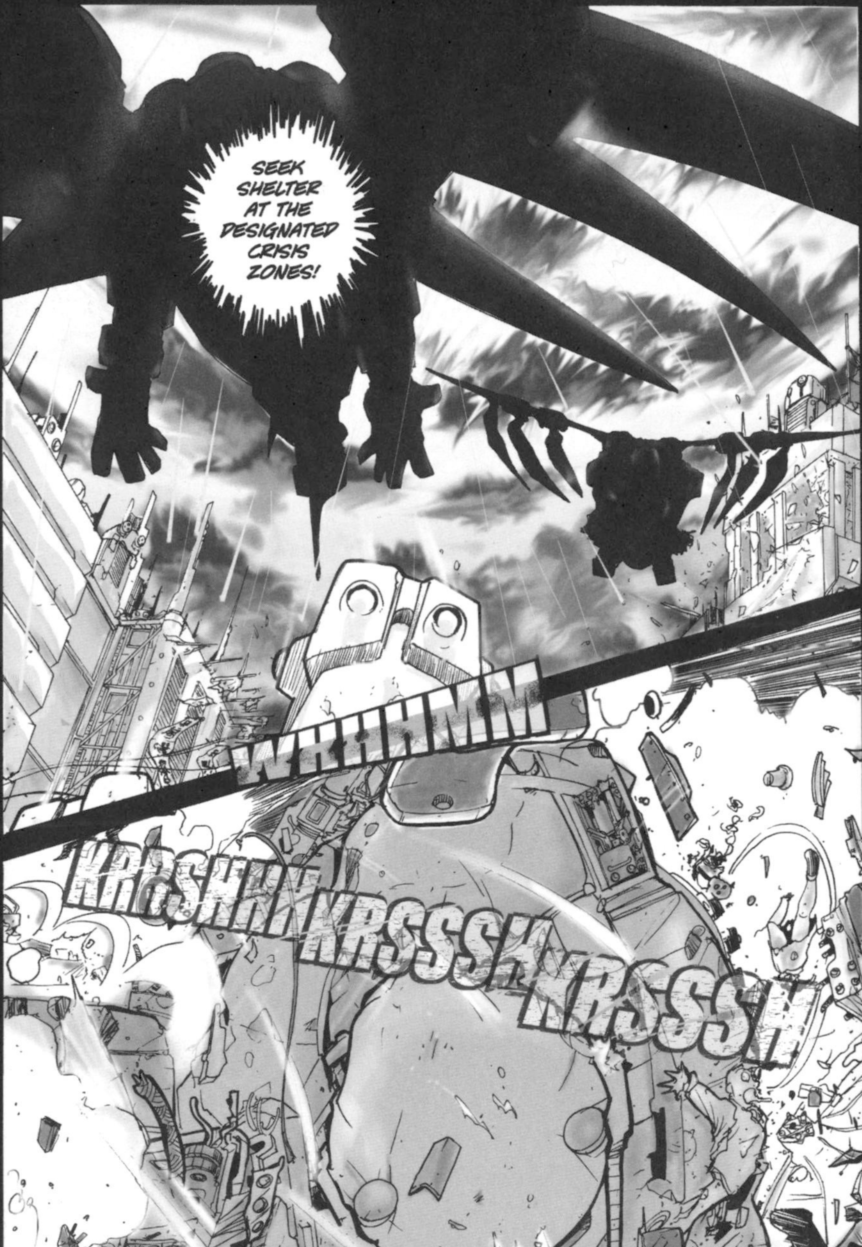
SEEK SHELTER AT THE DESIGNATED CRISIS ZONES!
WHHHMM
KRRSHHH KRSSSH KRSSSH

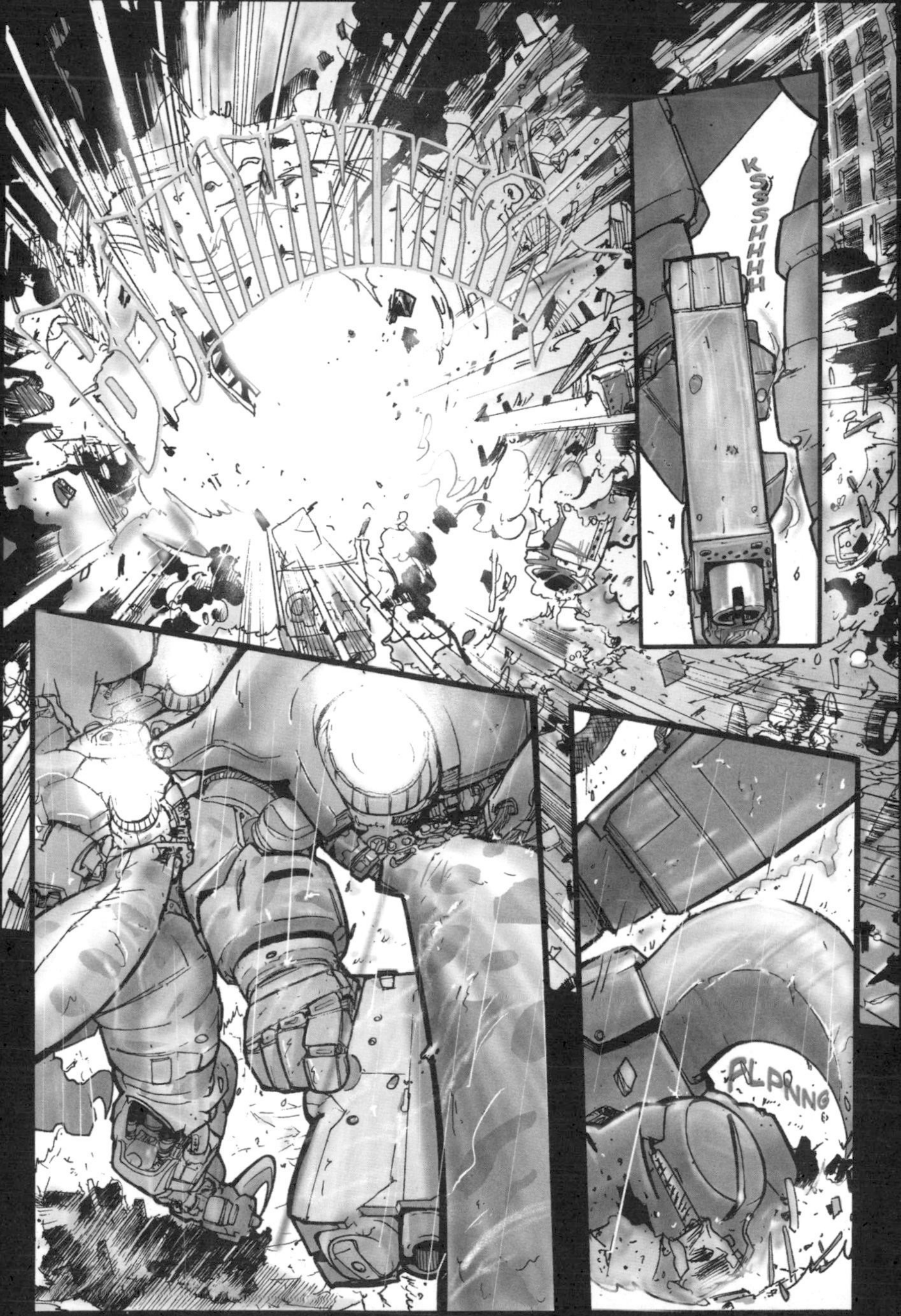
KSSSHHHH

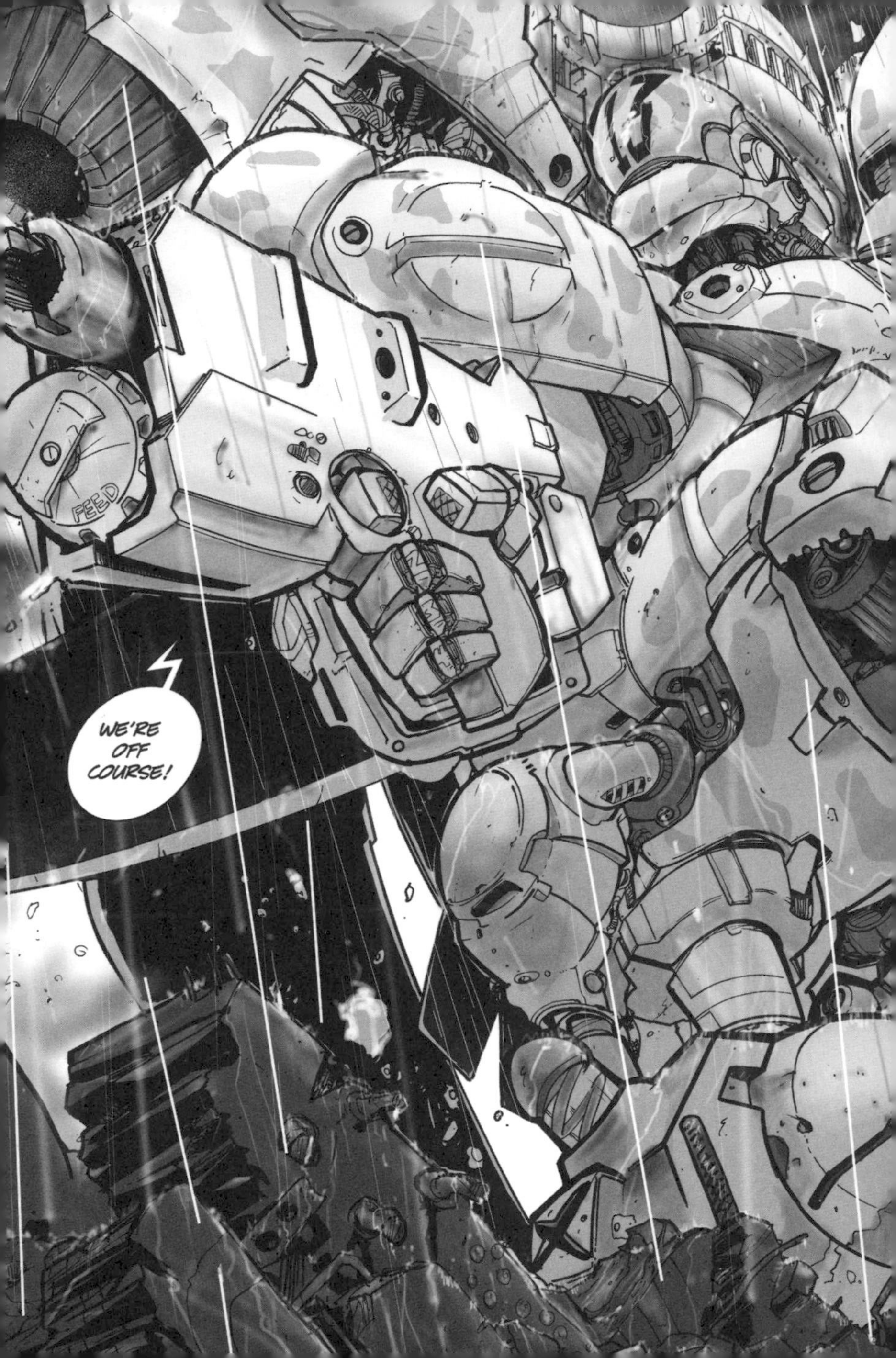
FEED
WE'RE OFF COURSE!

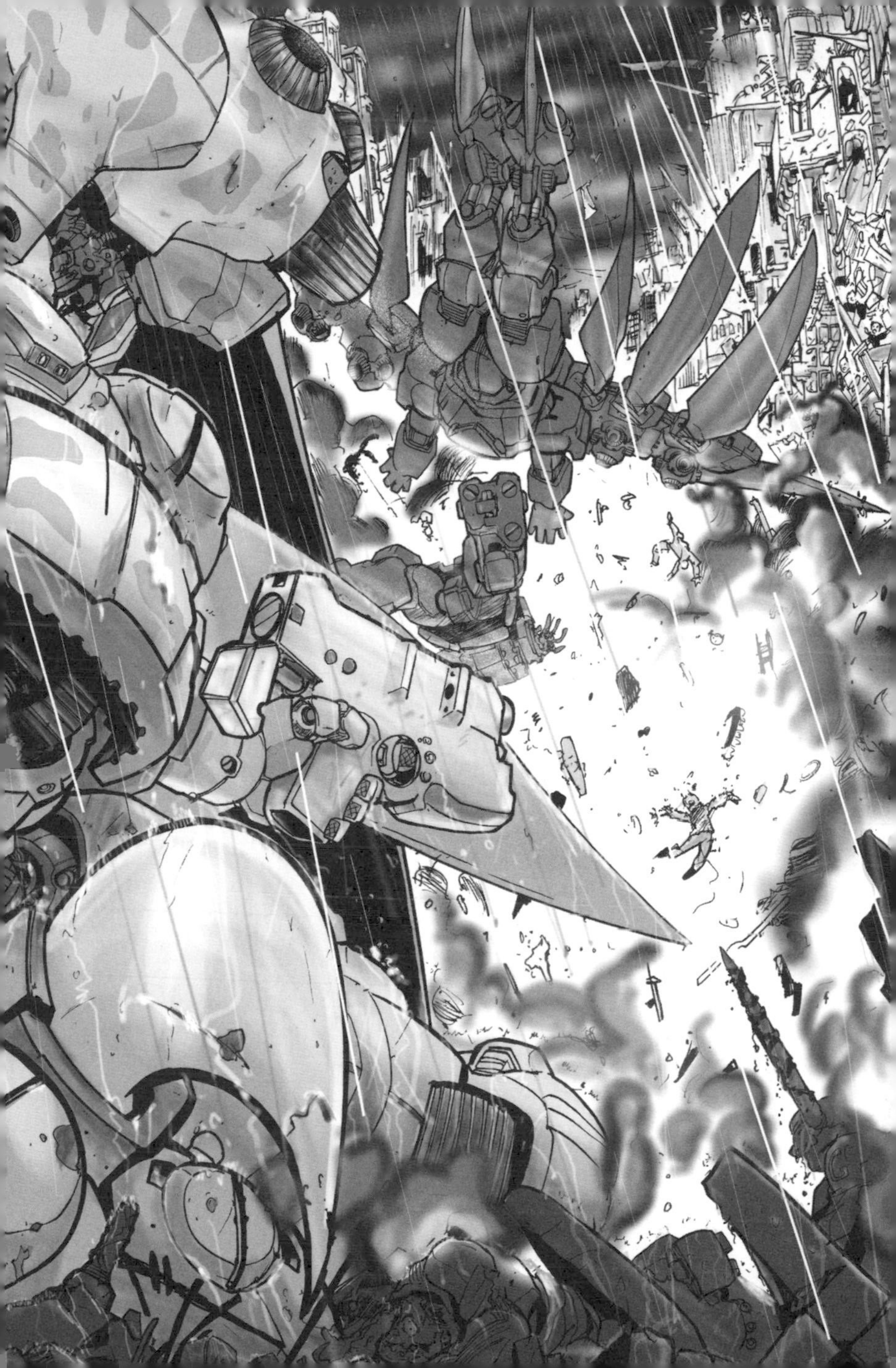

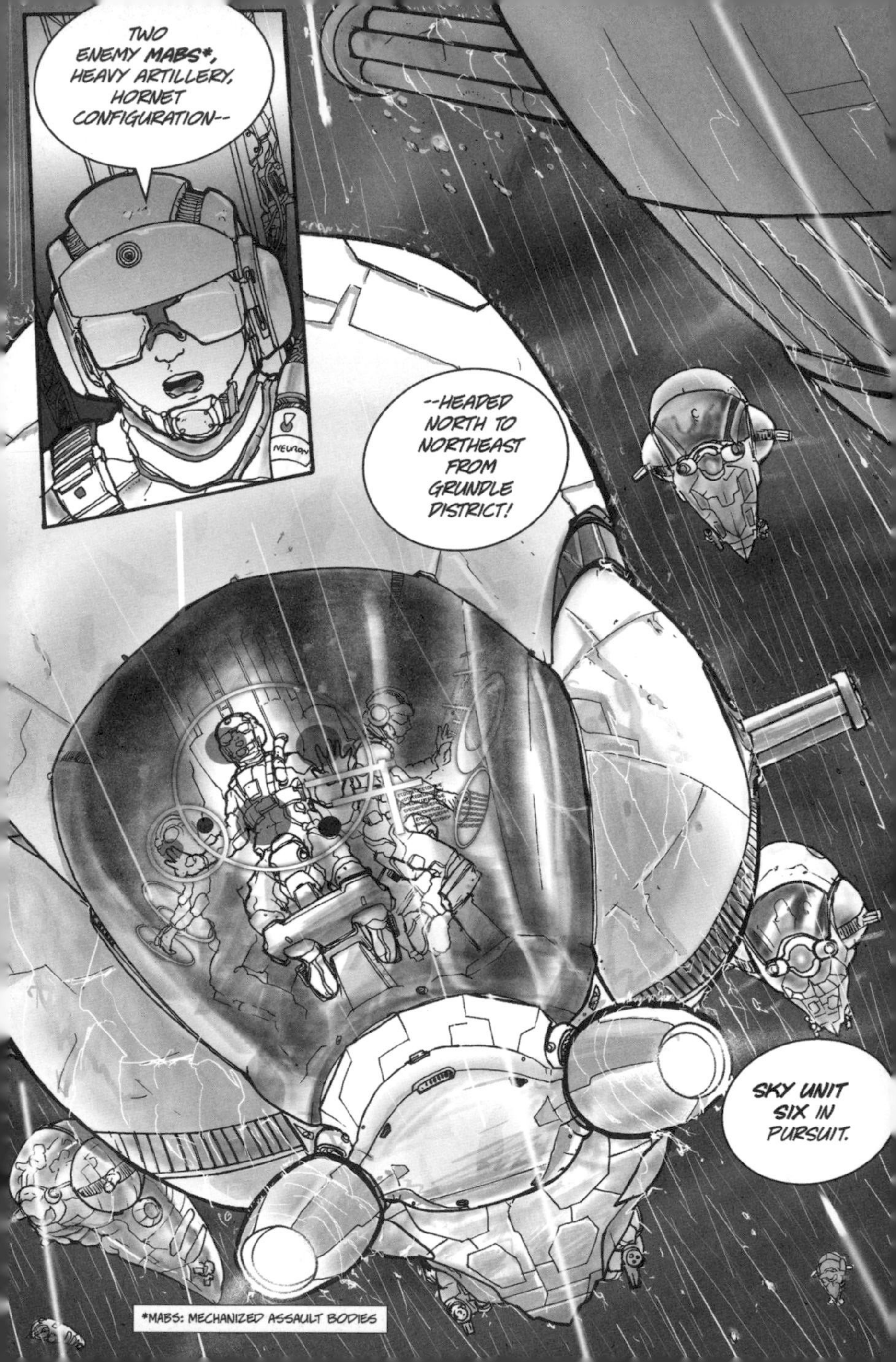
TWO ENEMY MABS*, HEAVY ARTILLERY, HORNET CONFIGURATION--
NEURON
--HEADED NORTH TO NORTHEAST FROM GRUNDLE DISTRICT!
SKY UNIT SIX IN PURSUIT.
*MABS: MECHANIZED ASSAULT BODIES

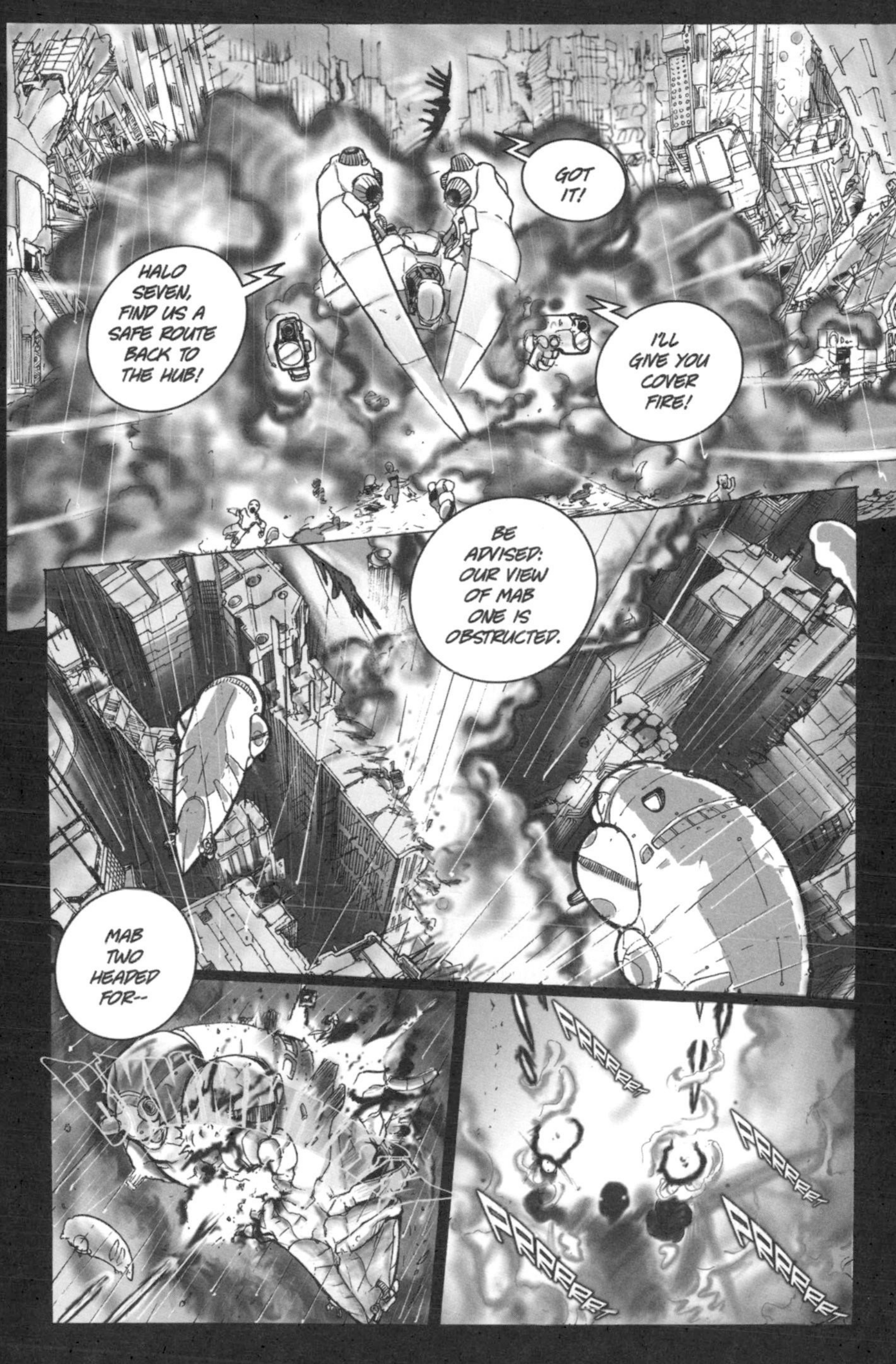
GOT IT!
HALO SEVEN, FIND US A SAFE ROUTE BACK TO THE HUB!
I'LL GIVE YOU COVER FIRE!
BE ADVISED: OUR VIEW OF MAB ONE IS OBSTRUCTED.
MAB TWO HEADED FOR--
FFRRRRRT
FFRRRRRT
FFRRRRRT
FFRRRRRT

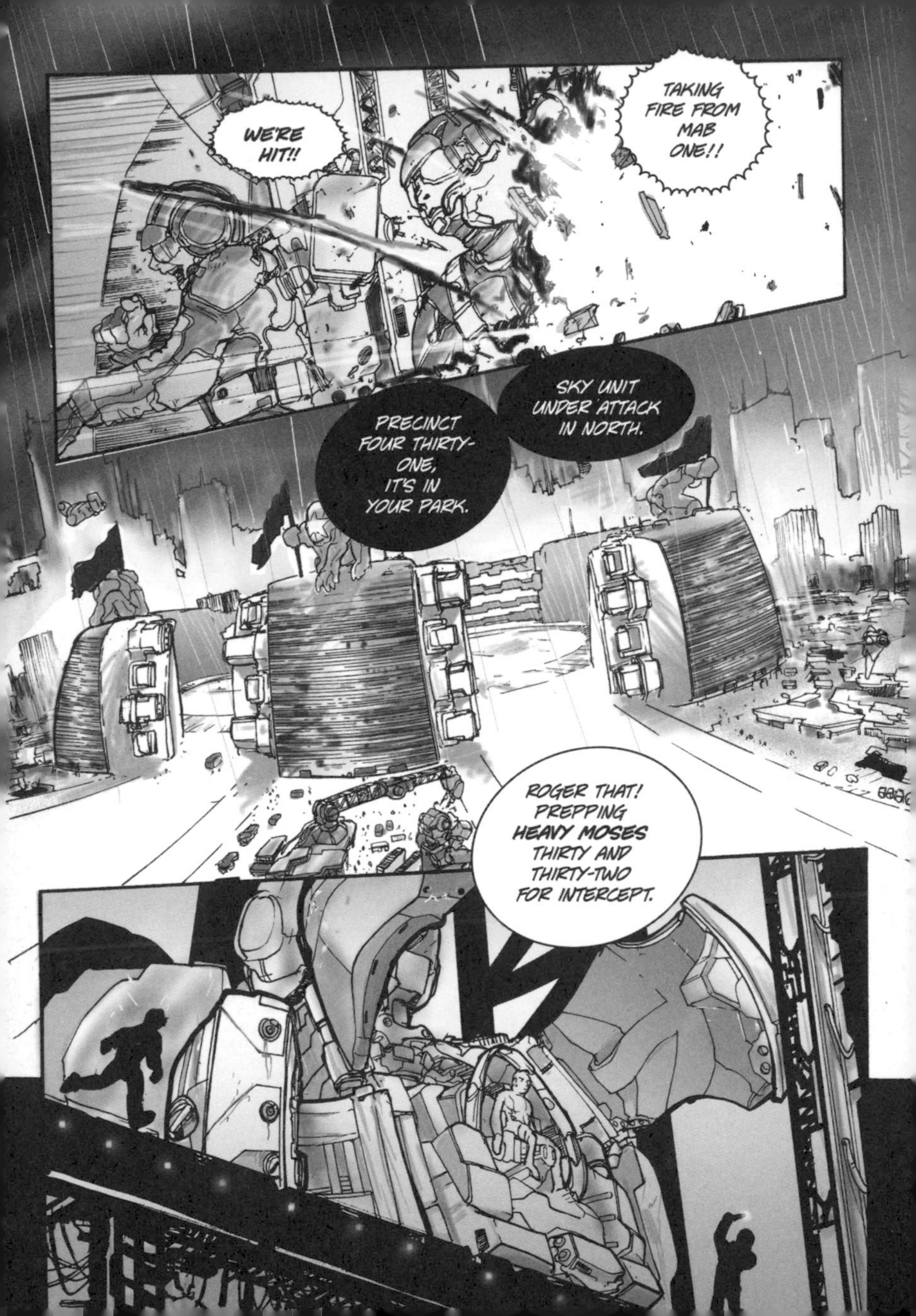
WE'RE HIT!!
TAKING FIRE FROM MAB ONE!!
SKY UNIT UNDER ATTACK IN NORTH.
PRECINCT FOUR THIRTY-ONE, IT'S IN YOUR PARK.
ROGER THAT! PREPPING HEAVY MOSES THIRTY AND THIRTY-TWO FOR INTERCEPT.

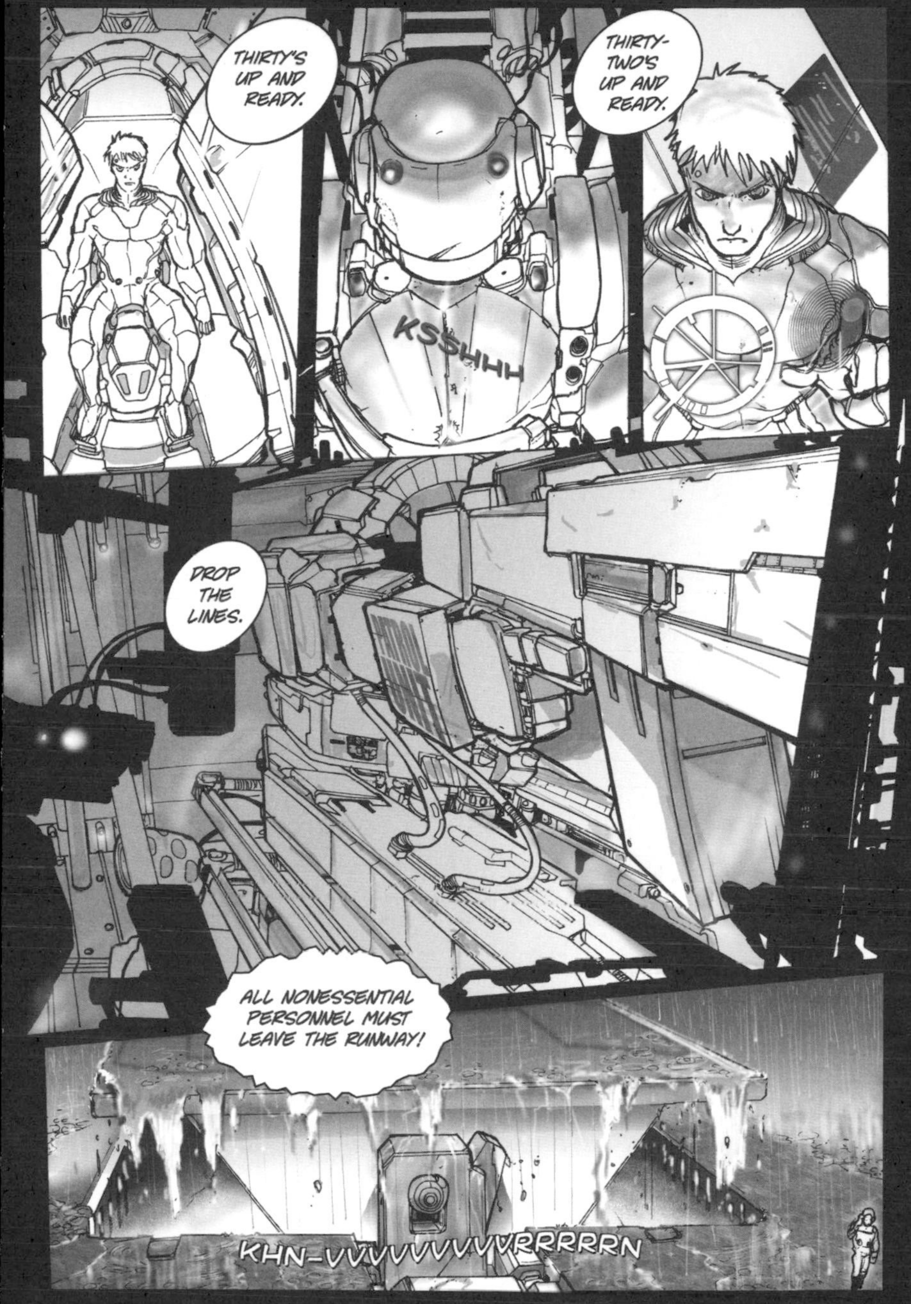
THIRTY'S UP AND READY.
KSSHHH
THIRTY-TWO'S UP AND READY.
DROP THE LINES.
ALL NONESSENTIAL PERSONNEL MUST LEAVE THE RUNWAY!
KHN-VVVVVVVVVVRRRRRN

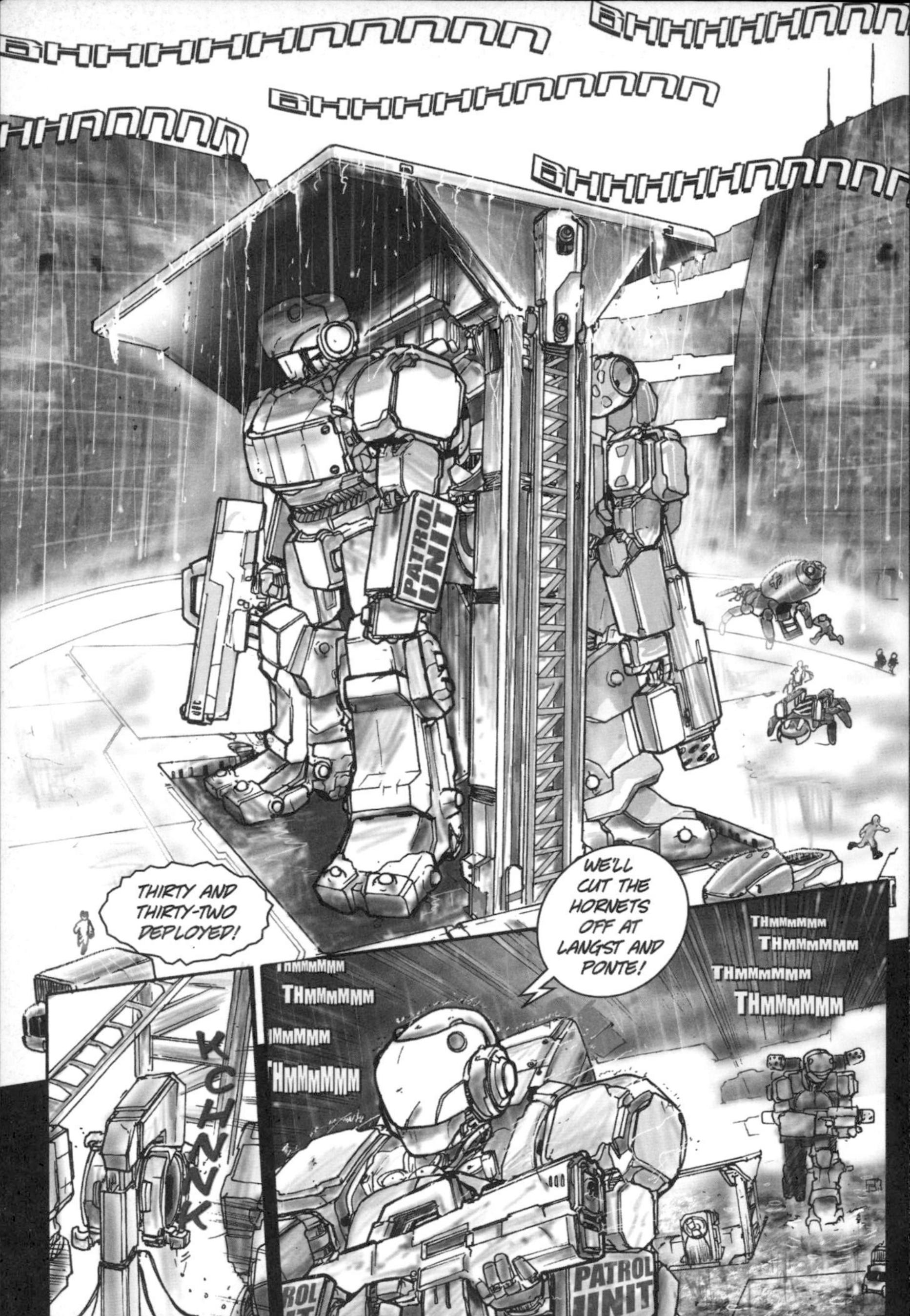

BHHHHHHHnnnnnnn
BHHHHHHHnnnnnn
BHHHHHHHnnnnnnn
HHnnnnnn
BHHHHHHnnnnnn
PATROL UNIT
THIRTY AND THIRTY-TWO DEPLOYED!
WE'LL CUT THE HORNETS OFF AT LANGST AND PONTE!
THMMMMMM
THMMMMMM
THMMMMMM
THMMMMMM
THMMMMMM
THMMMMMM
MMMMM
THMMMMMM
KCHNNK
PATROL UNIT
ROL UNIT

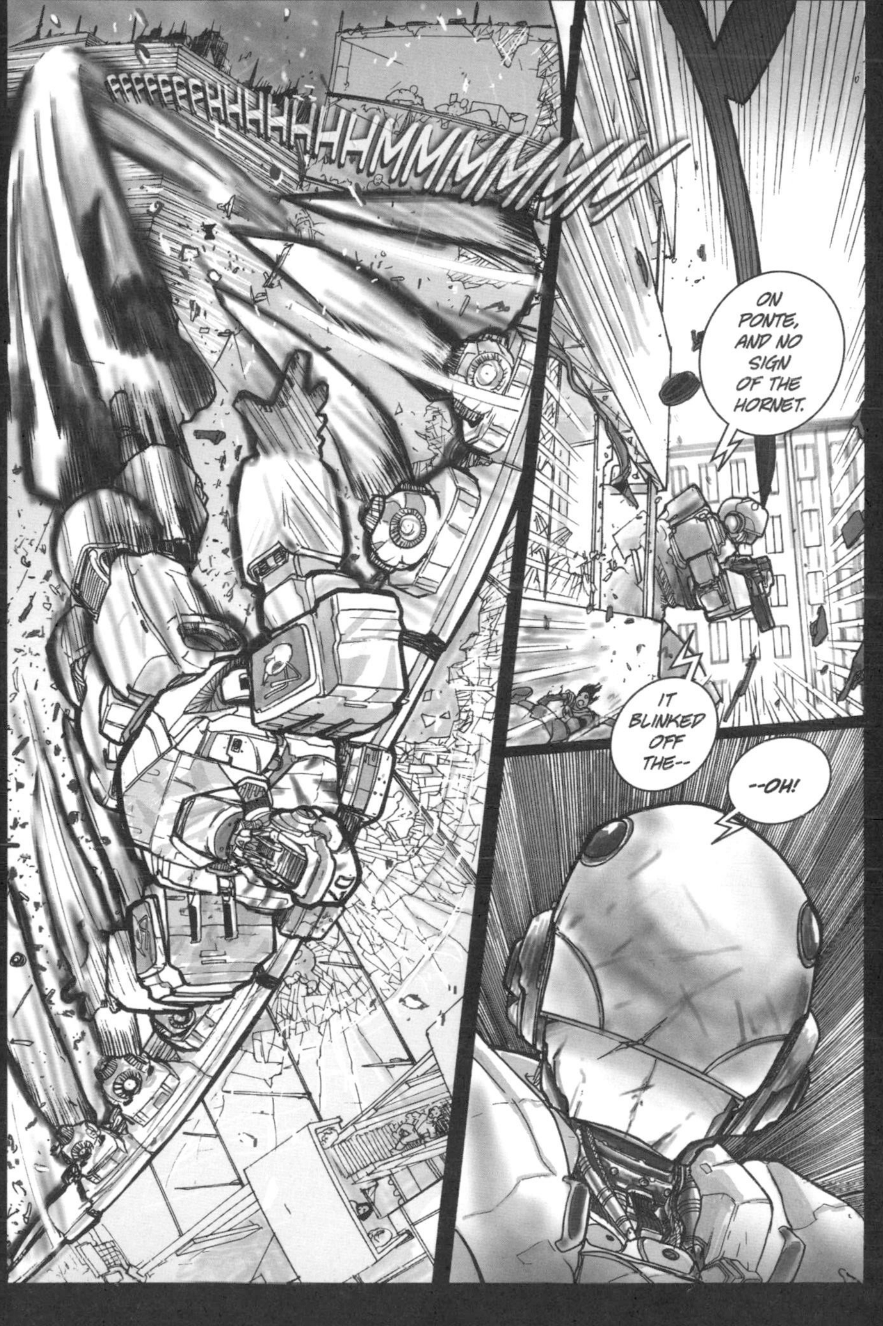
ON PONTE, AND NO SIGN OF THE HORNET.
IT BLINKED OFF THE--
--OH!

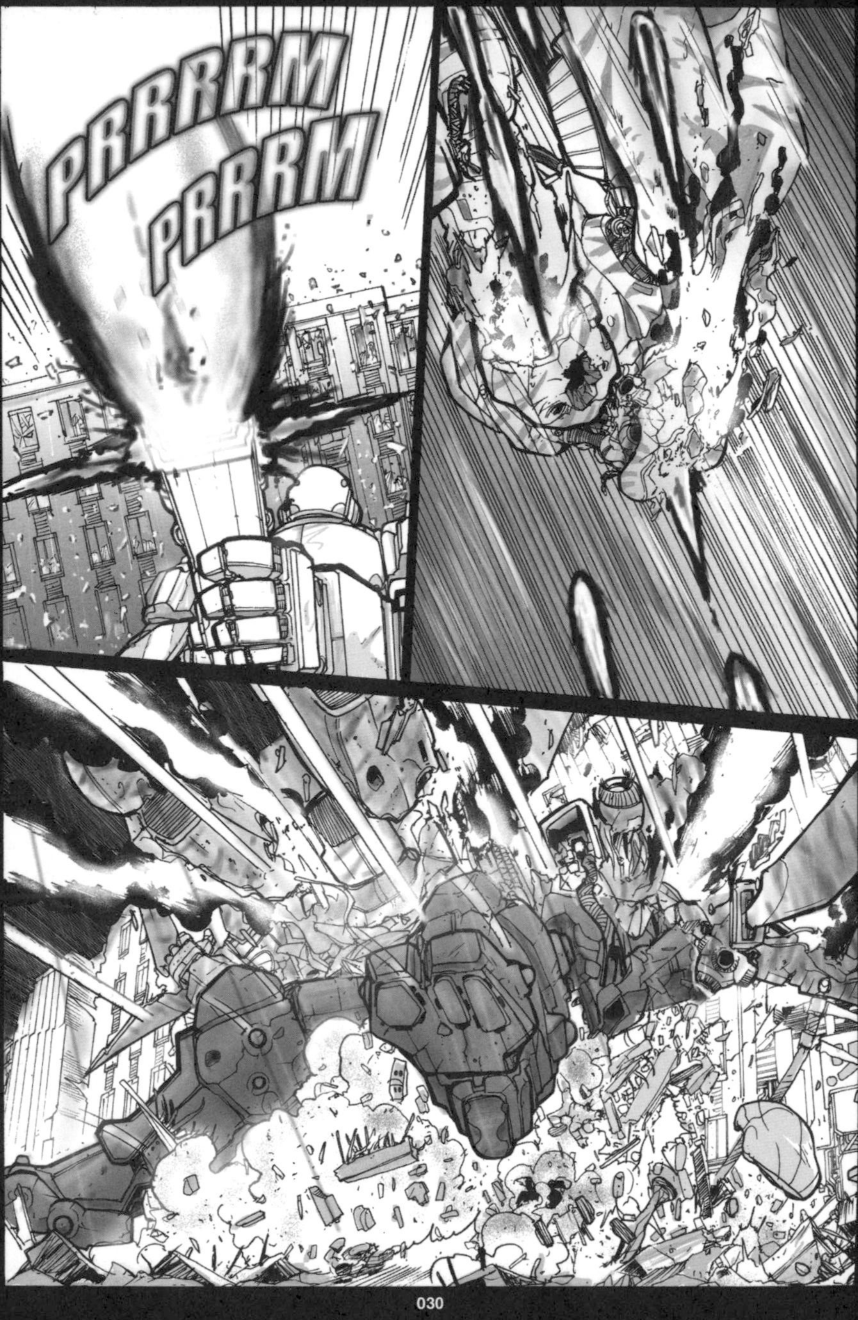
PRRRRM
PRRRM

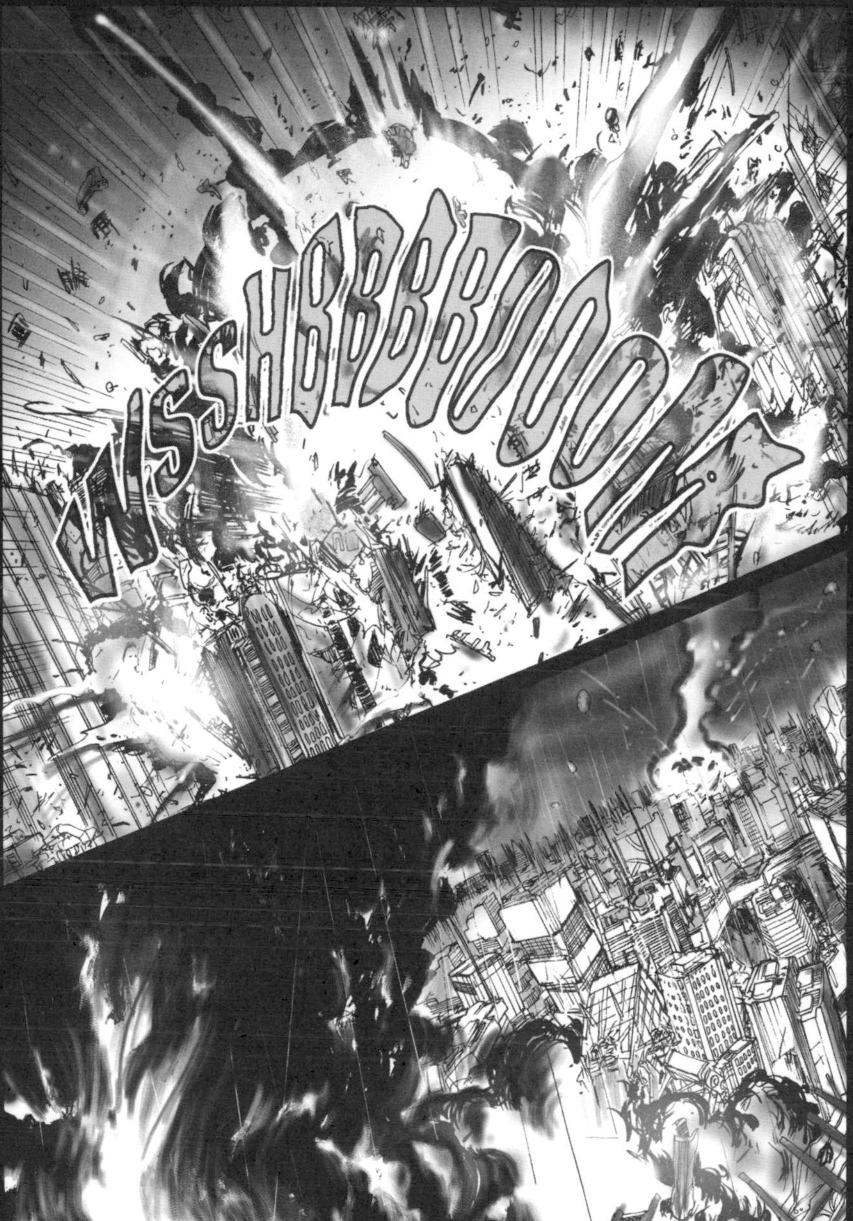
WSSHBBBROOOM!

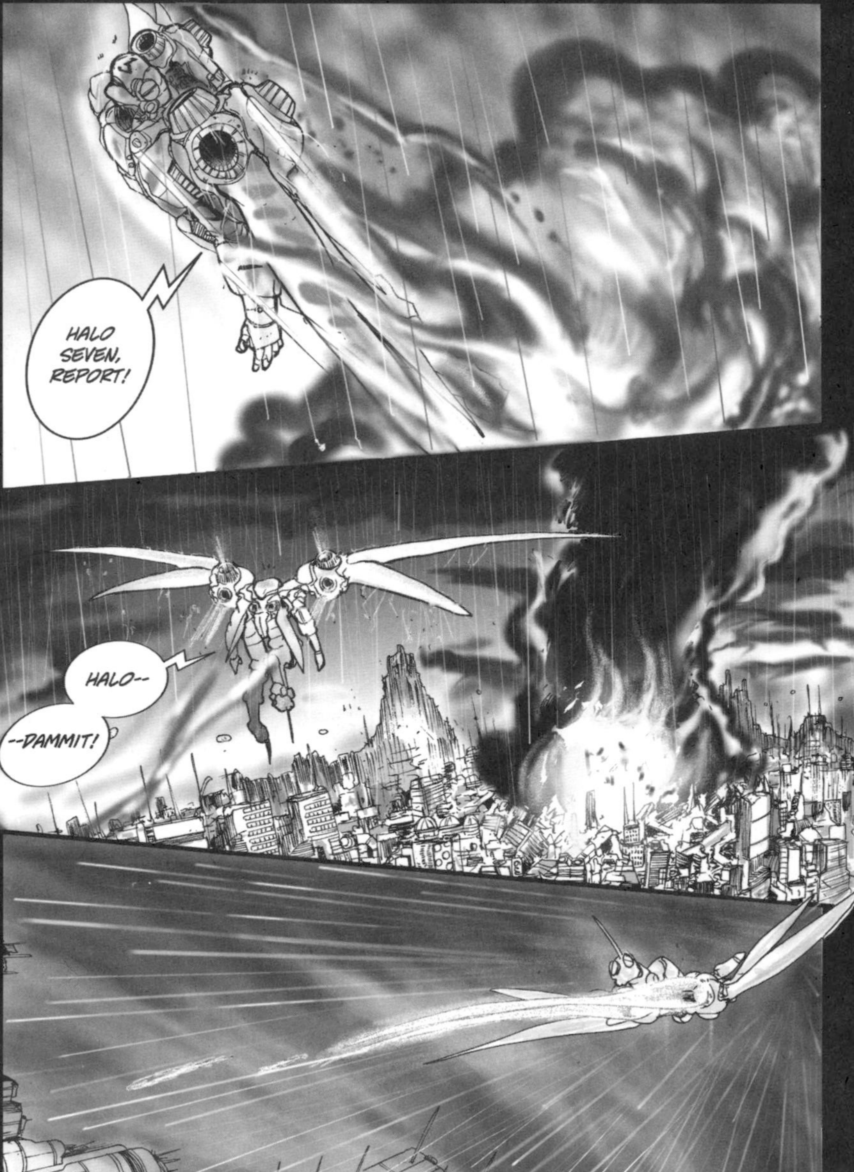
HALO SEVEN, REPORT!
HALO--
--DAMMIT!

SPECIAL REPORT
SN N

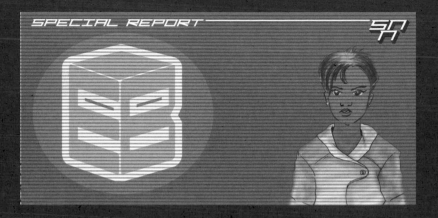

"FOUR HUNDRED DEAD AND TWO THOUSAND INJURED IN AN UNPROVOKED ATTACK ON OUR COUNTRY'S SOVEREIGNTY. IT IS BELIEVED THAT AGENTS SYMPATHETIC TO THE CAUSE OF THE **EASTERN BLOC** CONDUCTED THIS SHAMELESS ACT OF TERRORISM, MIDDAY, IN THE GRUNDLE BUSINESS DISTRICT. THE PLS HAS BEEN IN A STATE OF WAR WITH THE BLOC FOR OVER THREE DECADES, BUT THE SPARSE CONFLICTS WERE ALWAYS CONFINED TO THE NEIGHBORING COUNTRIES.

SPECIAL REPORT
SN N

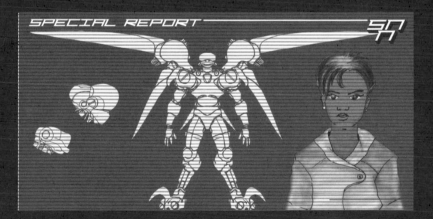

"THE TWO MECHANIZED ASSAULT BODIES WERE REPORTEDLY FROM THE **HORNET'S NEST**, A MERCENARY ORGANIZATION THAT, UNTIL NOW, HAD SHOWN NO MALICE TOWARDS THE STATE. IT IS BELIEVED THEY WERE HIRED BY THE BLOC TO CONDUCT THE ATTACKS IN THE CITY TO SWAY PUBLIC OPINION AGAINST THE ADMINISTRATION'S POLICY ON THE CONTINUING WAR.

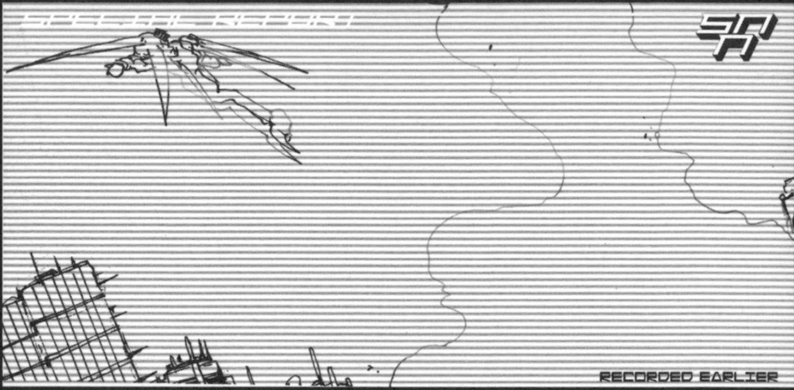
RECORDED EARLIER

"BEFORE THIS INCIDENT, THEIR ILLEGAL OPERATIONS NEVER INCLUDED STATE TARGETS FOR FEAR OF A SWIFT, BLINDING COUNTERATTACK. THE HORNETS' ORGANIZATION DIRECTOR ISSUED A STATEMENT SHORTLY AFTER, SAYING: "THESE TWO INDIVIDUALS ACTED ON THEIR OWN ACCORD. IT IS THE NEST'S PREROGATIVE TO ACCEPT SORTIES OF VARYING FINANCIAL GAIN, HOWEVER, STATE-ASSOCIATED TARGETS WERE NEVER CONSIDERED A PREREQUISITE. WE GRIEVE FOR YOUR LOSSES."

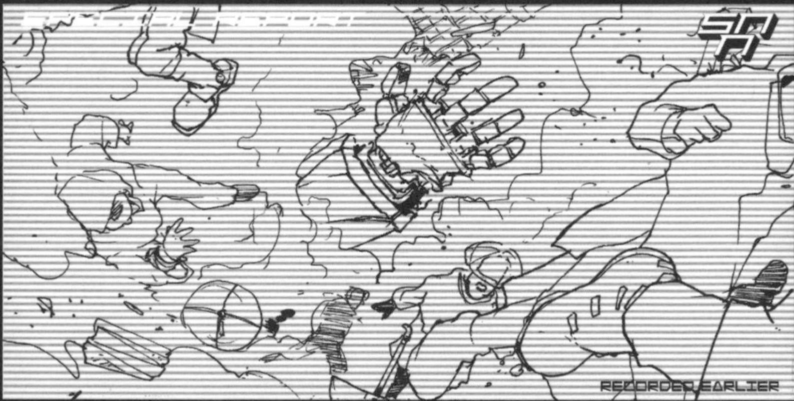
RECORDED EARLIER

"SECURITY CHIEF DIASON CALLED THE STATEMENT "A BAD JOKE WITH AN INSULTING PUNCH LINE."

THE MINISTRY IS CONSIDERING A MEASURE THAT WOULD CALL FOR MILITARY ACTION IN THE **COMFORT ZONE**, THE DEMILITARIZED AREA BETWEEN THE STATE AND BLOC ALLY COUNTRY, **MECHADO**, TO EXTERMINATE ALL NEARBY MERCENARY NETWORKS.

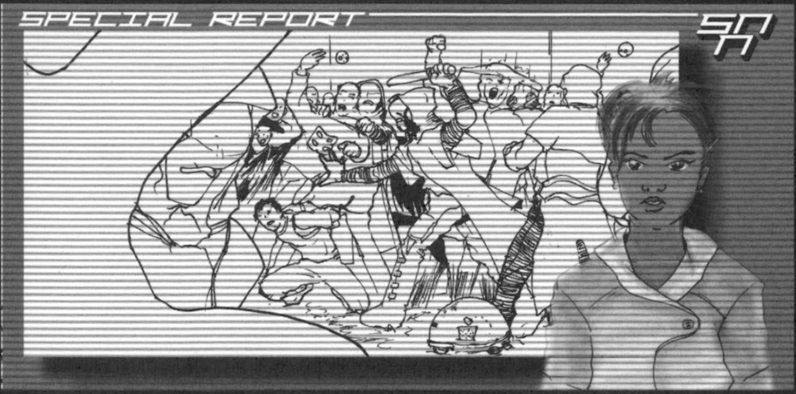
SPECIAL REPORT
SNN

"OUTSIDE THE DEFENSE MINISTRY, POLICE DISPERSED A MOB OF OVER EIGHT HUNDRED BLOC AND OLD GOVERNMENT SYMPATHIZERS RALLYING IN FAVOR OF THE ATTACKS. THE MISINFORMED MOB CALLED FOR THE DEMISE OF OUR GREAT ADMINISTRATION, CLAIMING THE STATE IS RESPONSIBLE FOR PERSECUTING FINANCIALLY BEREFT, TRUE DEMOCRATIC COUNTRIES. NINETY-THREE WERE ARRESTED.

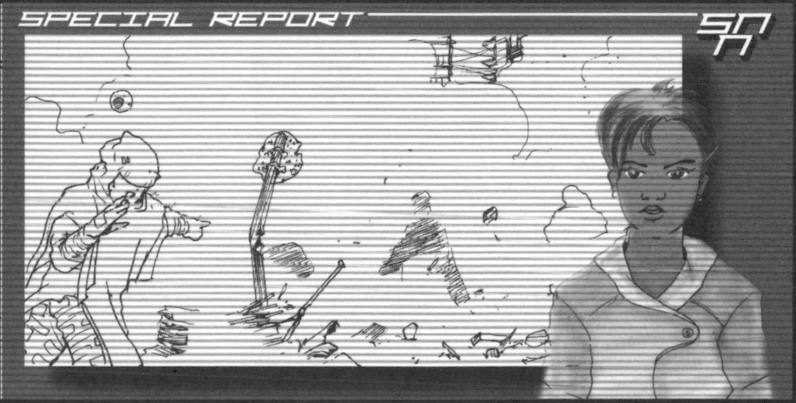
SPECIAL REPORT
SNN

"IN THE WAKE OF THE ATTACK, THE SEARCH CONTINUES FOR POTENTIAL SURVIVORS WHO MAY BE TRAPPED UNDERNEATH THE DEBRIS. AS THE MILITARY AND STATE PLANNING MINISTRY FURTHER THEIR INVESTIGATION OF THIS TRAGEDY, WE WILL CONTINUE TO BRING YOU UP-TO-THE-MINUTE REPORTS".

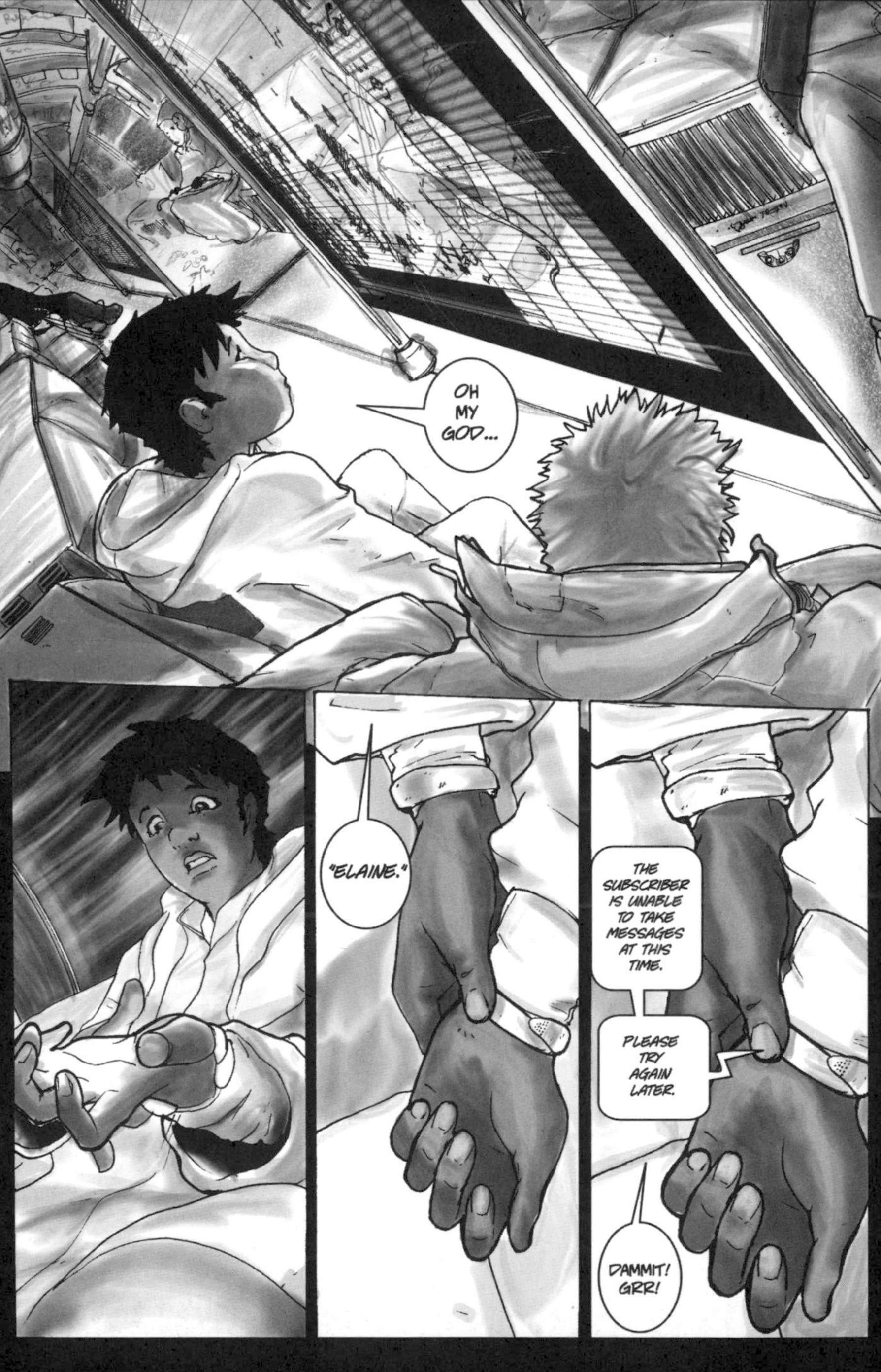
OH MY GOD...
"ELAINE."
THE SUBSCRIBER IS UNABLE TO TAKE MESSAGES AT THIS TIME.
PLEASE TRY AGAIN LATER.
DAMMIT! GRR!

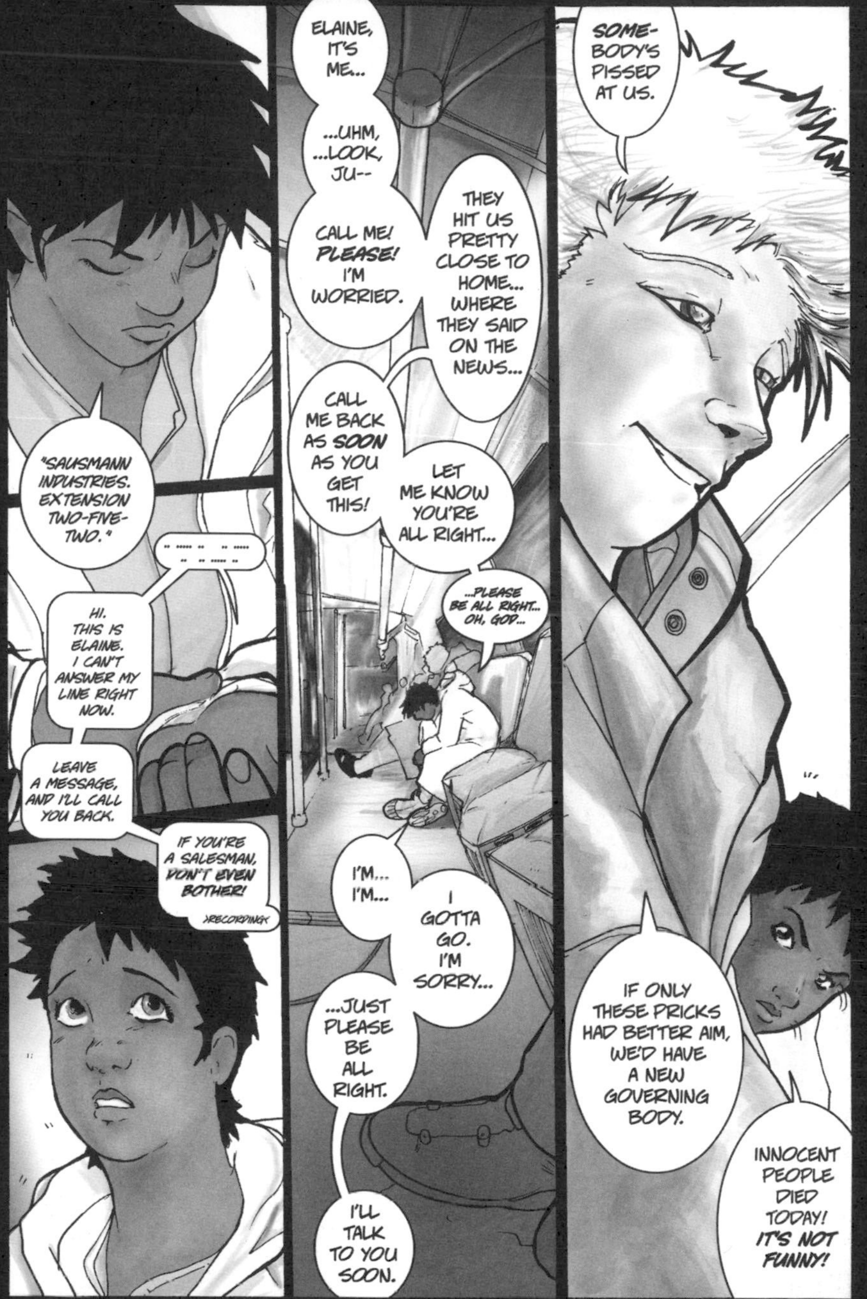
"SAUSMANN INDUSTRIES. EXTENSION TWO-FIVE-TWO."
HI. THIS IS ELAINE. I CAN'T ANSWER MY LINE RIGHT NOW.
LEAVE A MESSAGE, AND I'LL CALL YOU BACK.
IF YOU'RE A SALESMAN, DON'T EVEN BOTHER!
>RECORDING<
ELAINE, IT'S ME...
...UHM, ...LOOK, JU--
CALL ME! PLEASE! I'M WORRIED.
THEY HIT US PRETTY CLOSE TO HOME... WHERE THEY SAID ON THE NEWS...
CALL ME BACK AS SOON AS YOU GET THIS!
LET ME KNOW YOU'RE ALL RIGHT...
...PLEASE BE ALL RIGHT... OH, GOD...
I'M... I'M...
I GOTTA GO. I'M SORRY...
...JUST PLEASE BE ALL RIGHT.
I'LL TALK TO YOU SOON.
SOME-BODY'S PISSED AT US.
IF ONLY THESE PRICKS HAD BETTER AIM, WE'D HAVE A NEW GOVERNING BODY.
INNOCENT PEOPLE DIED TODAY! IT'S NOT FUNNY!

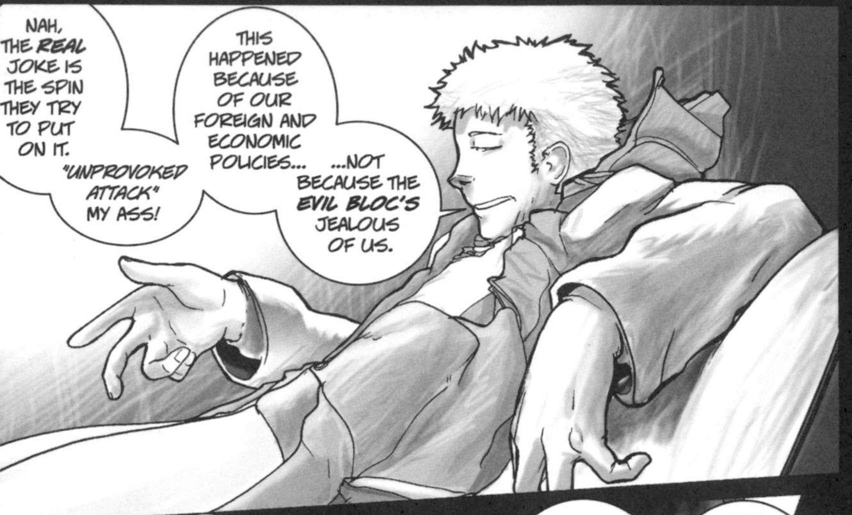

NAH, THE REAL JOKE IS THE SPIN THEY TRY TO PUT ON IT.
"UNPROVOKED ATTACK" MY ASS!
THIS HAPPENED BECAUSE OF OUR FOREIGN AND ECONOMIC POLICIES...
...NOT BECAUSE THE EVIL BLOC'S JEALOUS OF US.

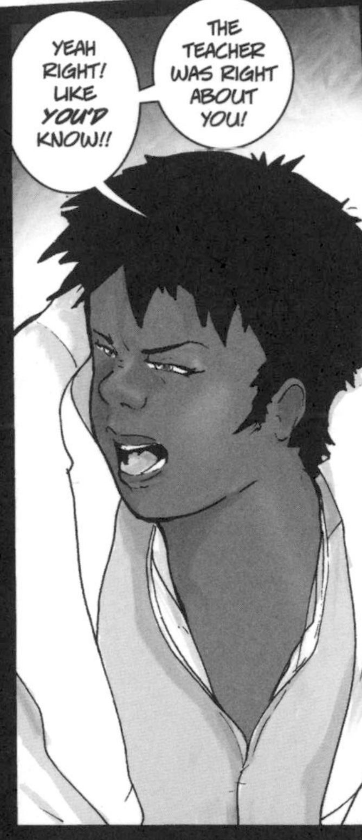

THE TEACHER WAS RIGHT ABOUT YOU!
YEAH RIGHT! LIKE YOU'D KNOW!!

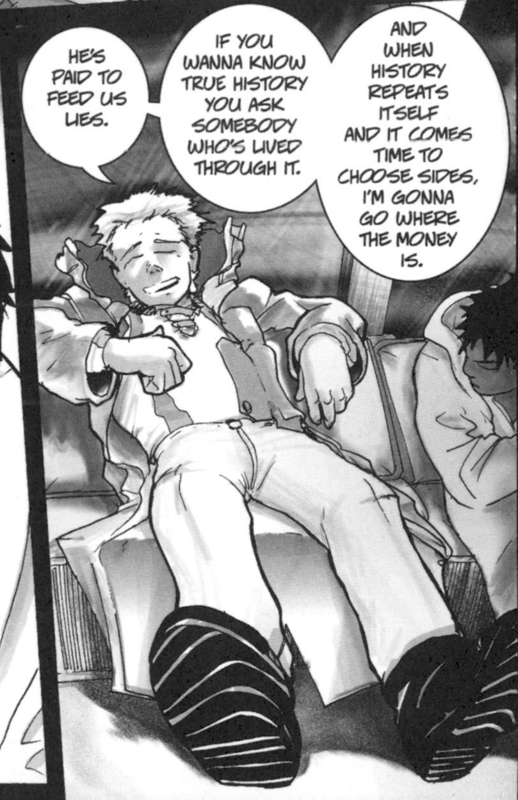

HE'S PAID TO FEED US LIES.
IF YOU WANNA KNOW TRUE HISTORY YOU ASK SOMEBODY WHO'S LIVED THROUGH IT.
AND WHEN HISTORY REPEATS ITSELF AND IT COMES TIME TO CHOOSE SIDES, I'M GONNA GO WHERE THE MONEY IS.

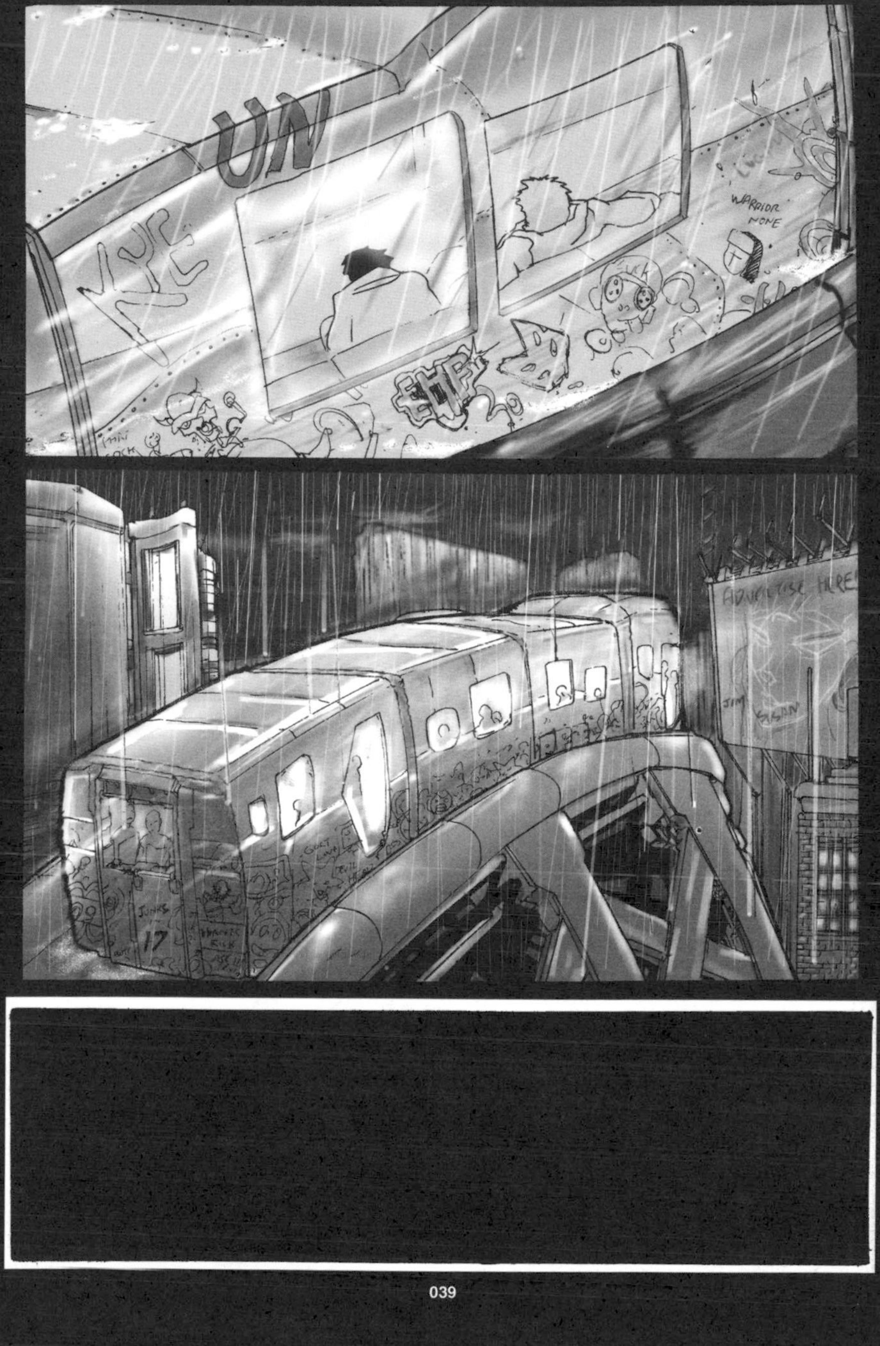
UN
WARRIOR NONE
JIM
JUNKS
17

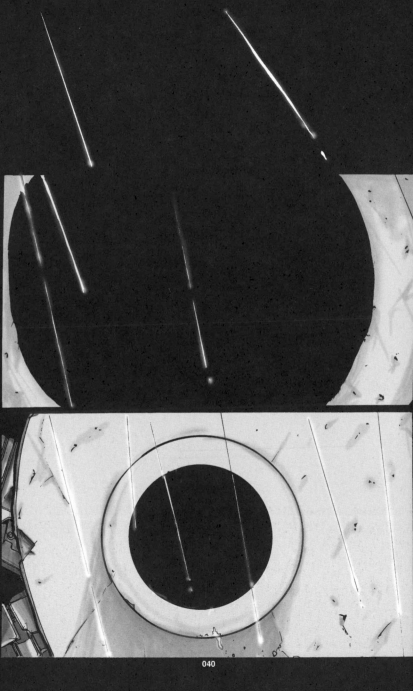

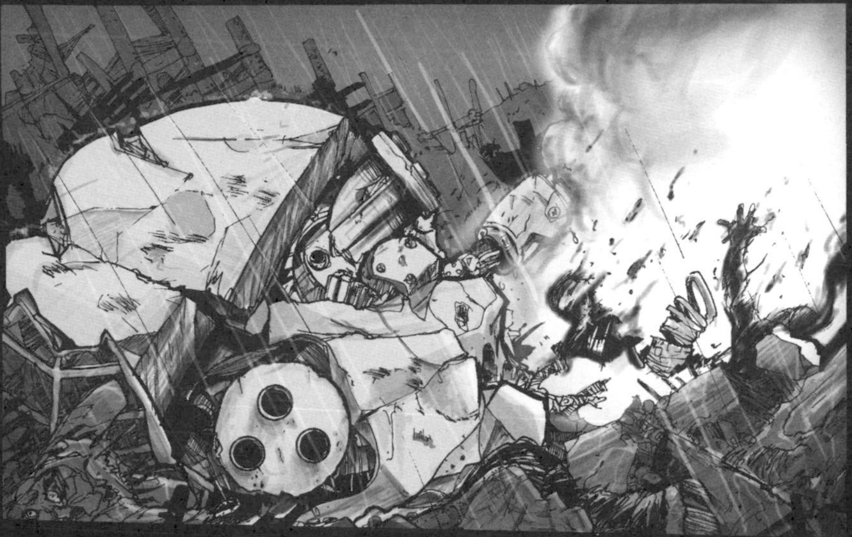

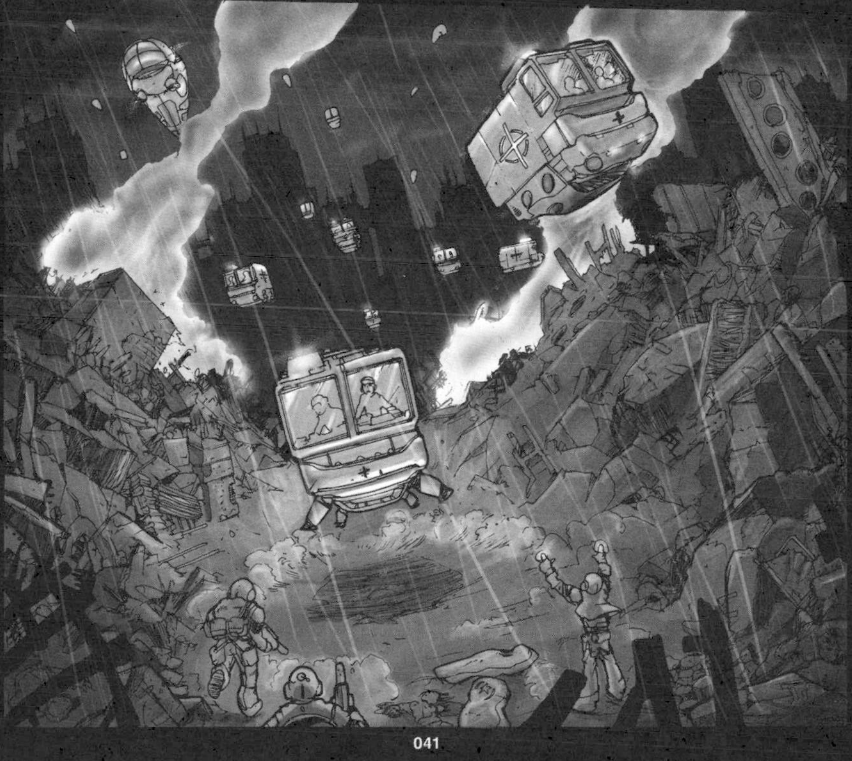

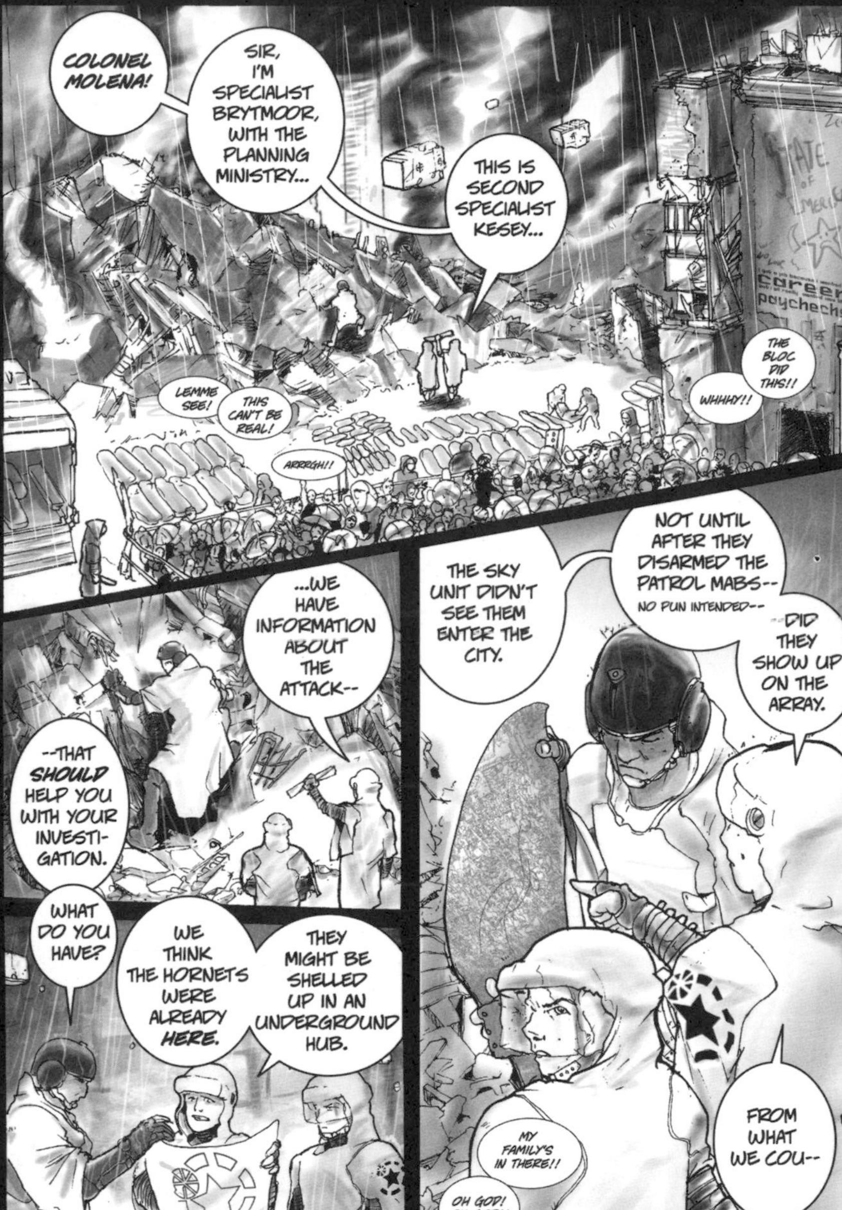
COLONEL MOLENA!
SIR, I'M SPECIALIST BRYTMOOR, WITH THE PLANNING MINISTRY...
THIS IS SECOND SPECIALIST KESEY...
career
paychecks
LEMME SEE!
THIS CAN'T BE REAL!
ARRRGH!!
WHHHY!!
THE BLOC DID THIS!!
...WE HAVE INFORMATION ABOUT THE ATTACK--
--THAT SHOULD HELP YOU WITH YOUR INVESTI-GATION.
WHAT DO YOU HAVE?
WE THINK THE HORNETS WERE ALREADY HERE.
THEY MIGHT BE SHELLED UP IN AN UNDERGROUND HUB.
THE SKY UNIT DIDN'T SEE THEM ENTER THE CITY.
NOT UNTIL AFTER THEY DISARMED THE PATROL MABS-- NO PUN INTENDED--
--DID THEY SHOW UP ON THE ARRAY.
FROM WHAT WE COU--
MY FAMILY'S IN THERE!!
OH GOD! OH GOD!!
WHY WON'T THEY LET ME SEE HIM!?!!
THIS CAN'T BE HAPPENING!!

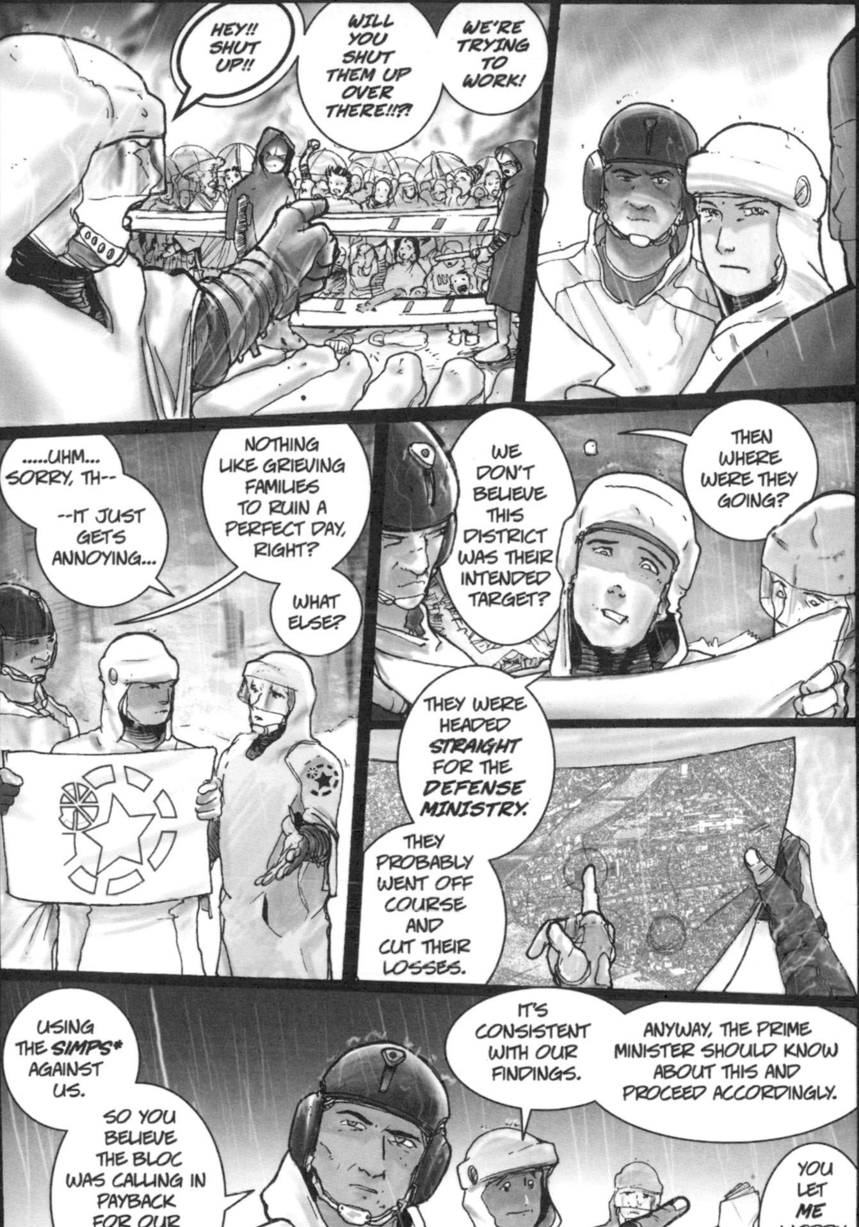
HEY!! SHUT UP!!
WILL YOU SHUT THEM UP OVER THERE!!?!
WE'RE TRYING TO WORK!
.....UHM... SORRY, TH--
--IT JUST GETS ANNOYING...
NOTHING LIKE GRIEVING FAMILIES TO RUIN A PERFECT DAY, RIGHT?
WHAT ELSE?
WE DON'T BELIEVE THIS DISTRICT WAS THEIR INTENDED TARGET?
THEN WHERE WERE THEY GOING?
THEY WERE HEADED STRAIGHT FOR THE DEFENSE MINISTRY.
THEY PROBABLY WENT OFF COURSE AND CUT THEIR LOSSES.
USING THE SIMPS* AGAINST US.
SO YOU BELIEVE THE BLOC WAS CALLING IN PAYBACK FOR OUR RECENT CAMPAIGNS?
IT'S CONSISTENT WITH OUR FINDINGS.
ANYWAY, THE PRIME MINISTER SHOULD KNOW ABOUT THIS AND PROCEED ACCORDINGLY.
YOU LET ME WORRY ABOUT THAT.

*SIMPS: EASTERN BLOC SYMPATHIZERS

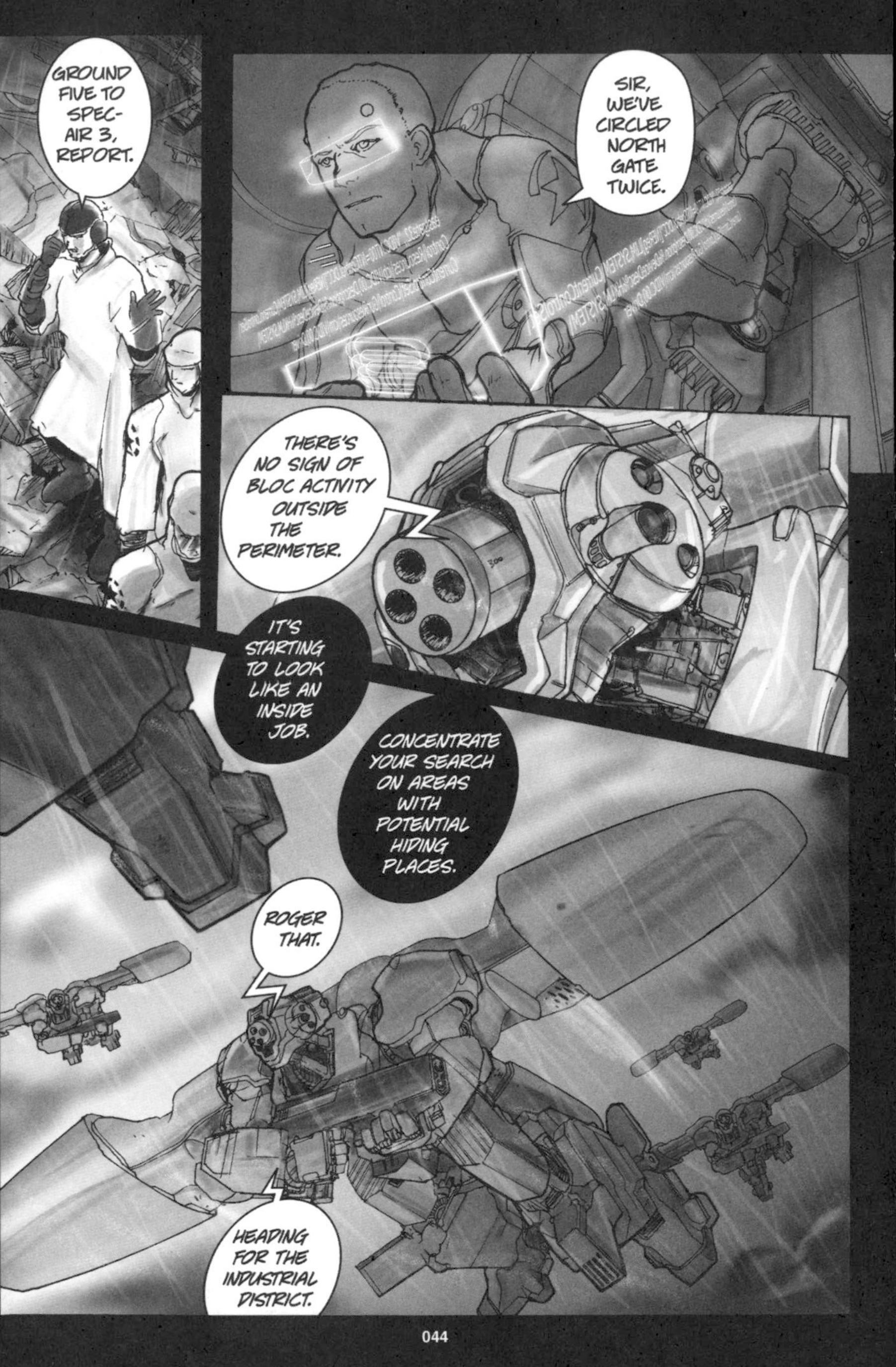
GROUND FIVE TO SPEC-AIR 3, REPORT.
SIR, WE'VE CIRCLED NORTH GATE TWICE.
THERE'S NO SIGN OF BLOC ACTIVITY OUTSIDE THE PERIMETER.
IT'S STARTING TO LOOK LIKE AN INSIDE JOB.
CONCENTRATE YOUR SEARCH ON AREAS WITH POTENTIAL HIDING PLACES.
ROGER THAT.
HEADING FOR THE INDUSTRIAL DISTRICT.

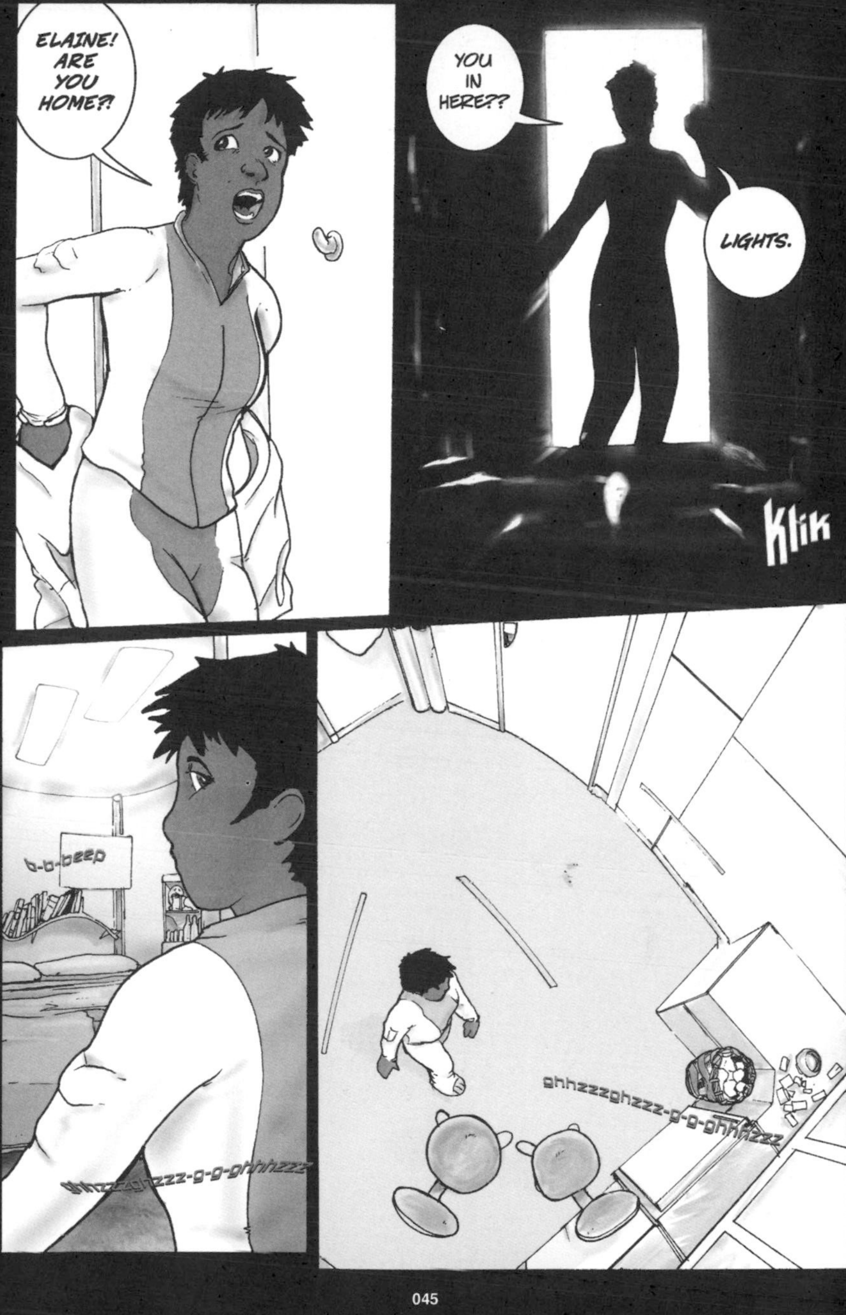
ELAINE! ARE YOU HOME?!
YOU IN HERE??
LIGHTS.
Klik
b-b-beep
ghhzzzghzzz-g-g-ghhhzzz
ghhzzzghzzz-g-g-ghhhzzz

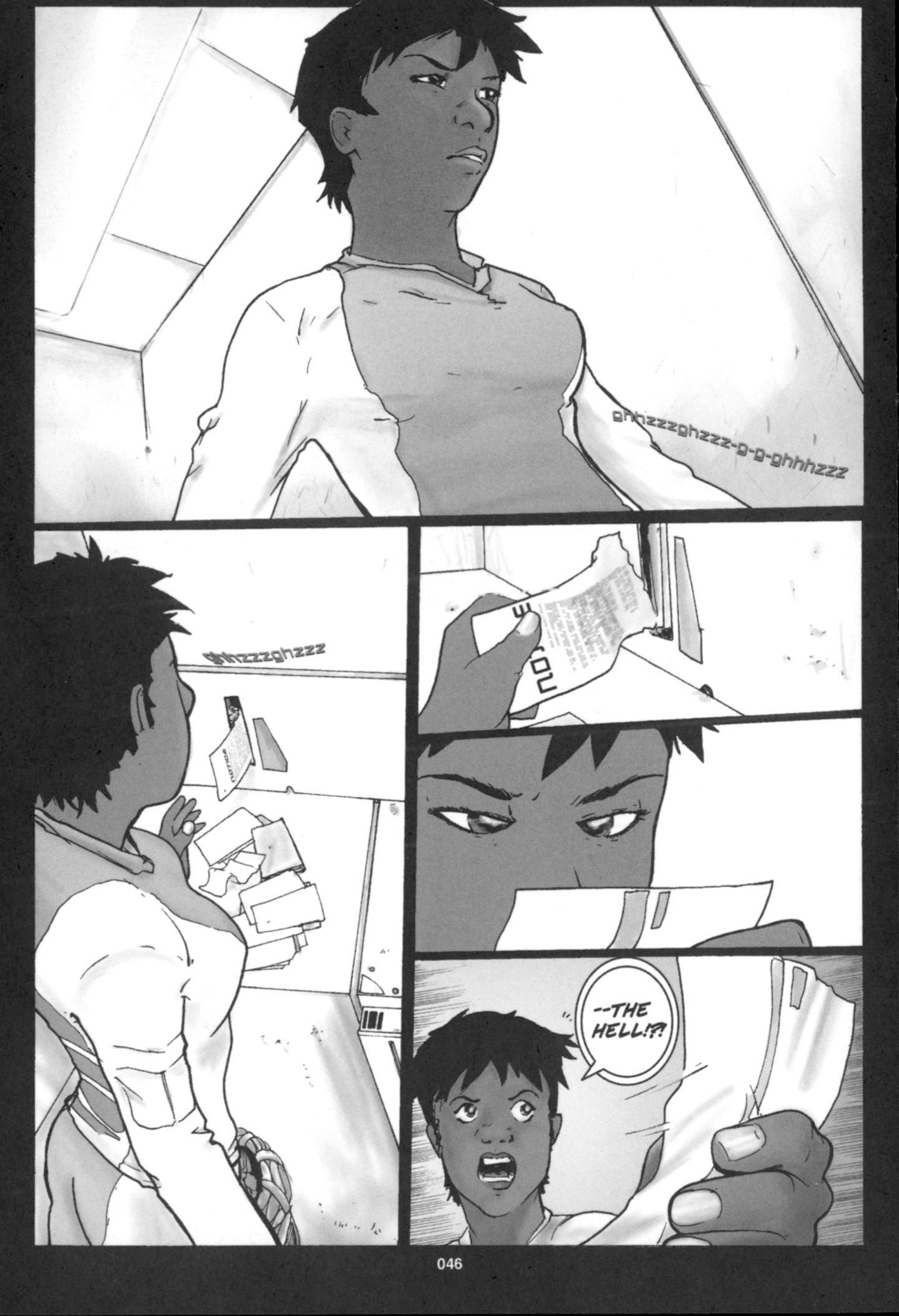
ghhzzzghzzz-g-g-ghhhzzz
ghhzzzghzzz
--THE HELL!?!

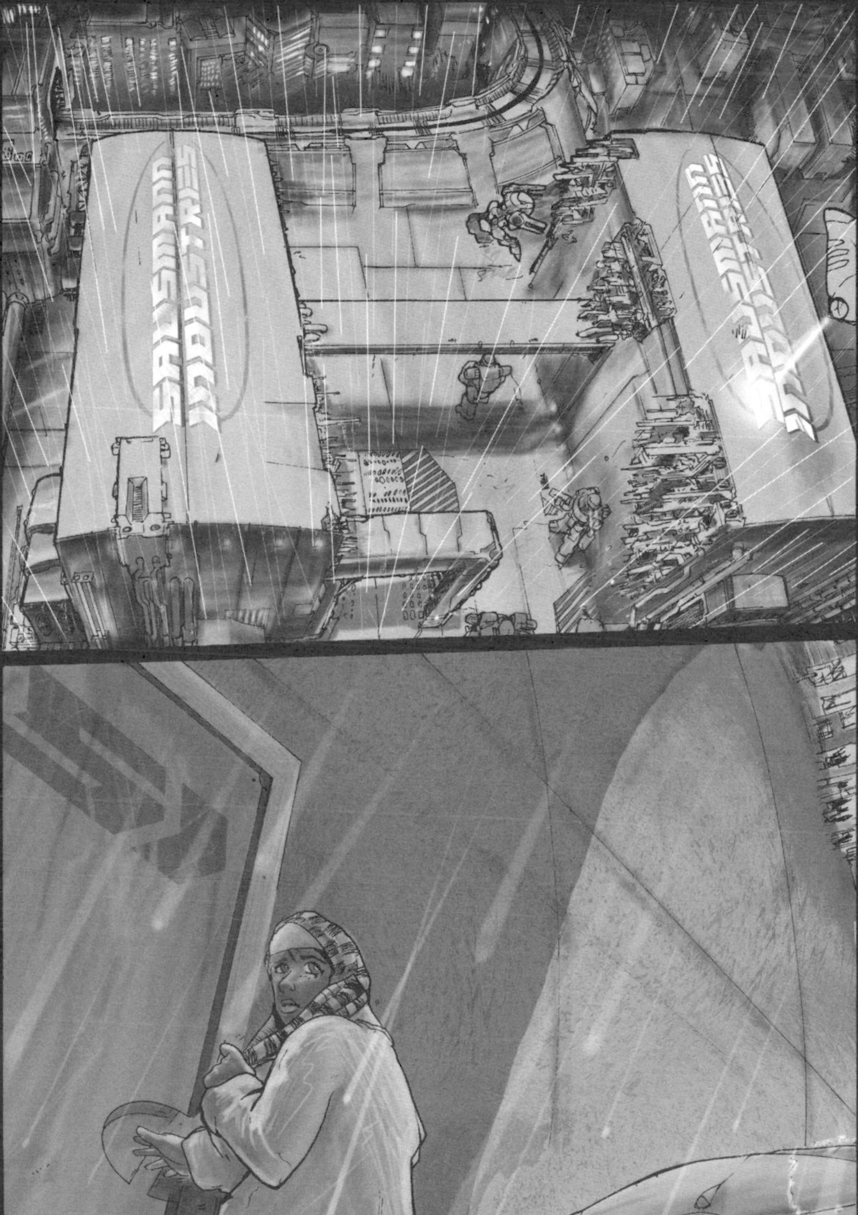

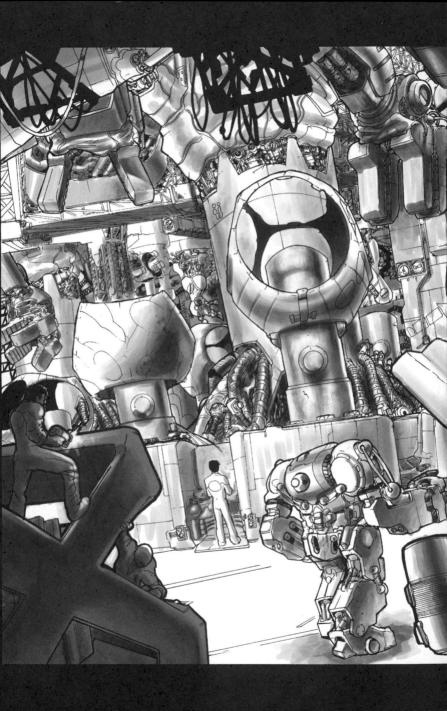

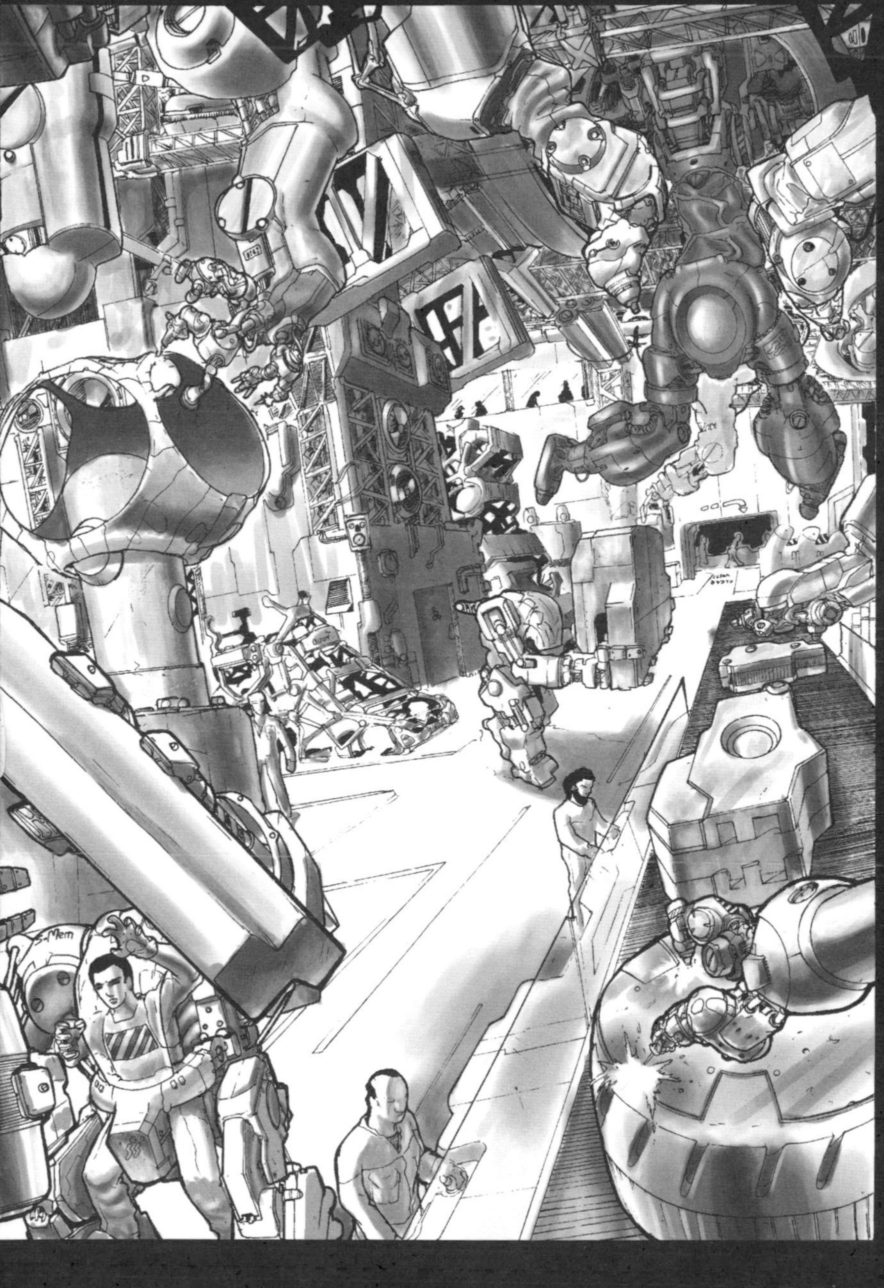
S-Mem

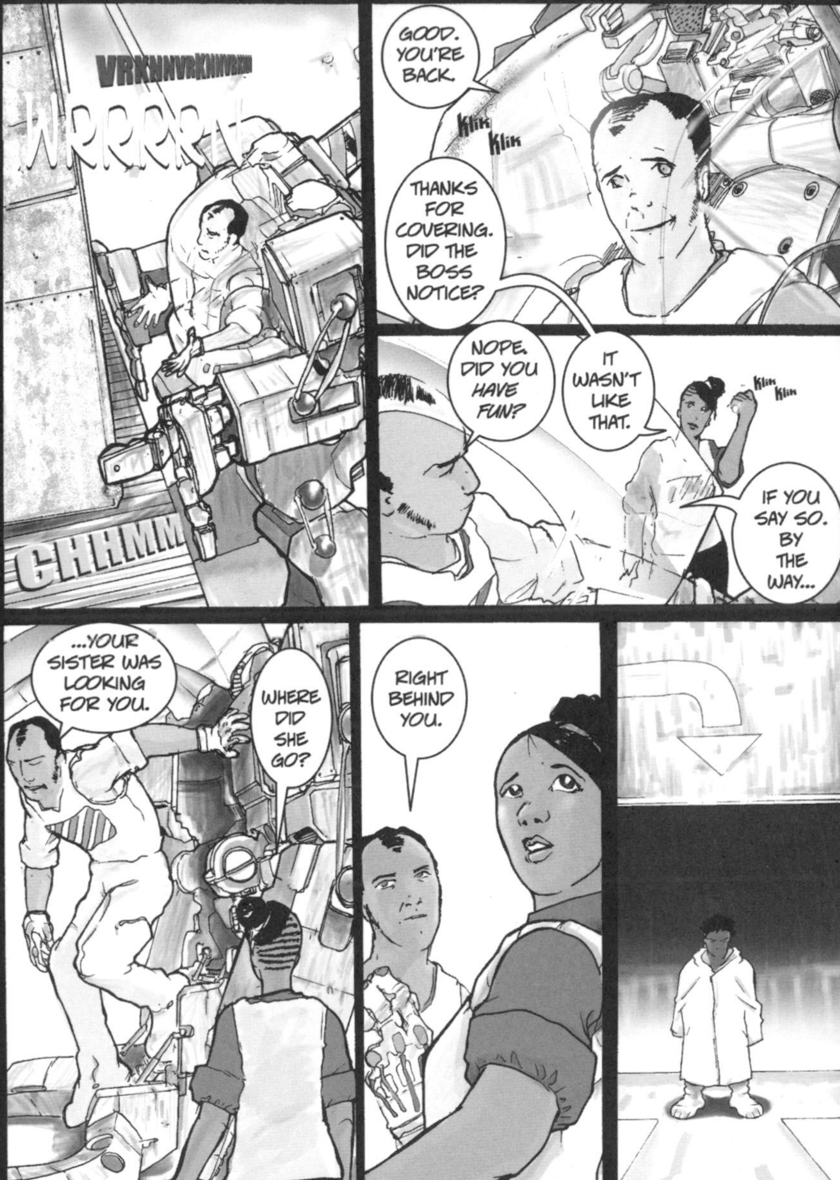
VRKNNVRKNNVRKNN
WRRRRN
CHHMM
GOOD. YOU'RE BACK.
Klik Klik
THANKS FOR COVERING. DID THE BOSS NOTICE?
NOPE. DID YOU HAVE FUN?
IT WASN'T LIKE THAT.
Klik Klik
IF YOU SAY SO. BY THE WAY...
...YOUR SISTER WAS LOOKING FOR YOU.
WHERE DID SHE GO?
RIGHT BEHIND YOU.

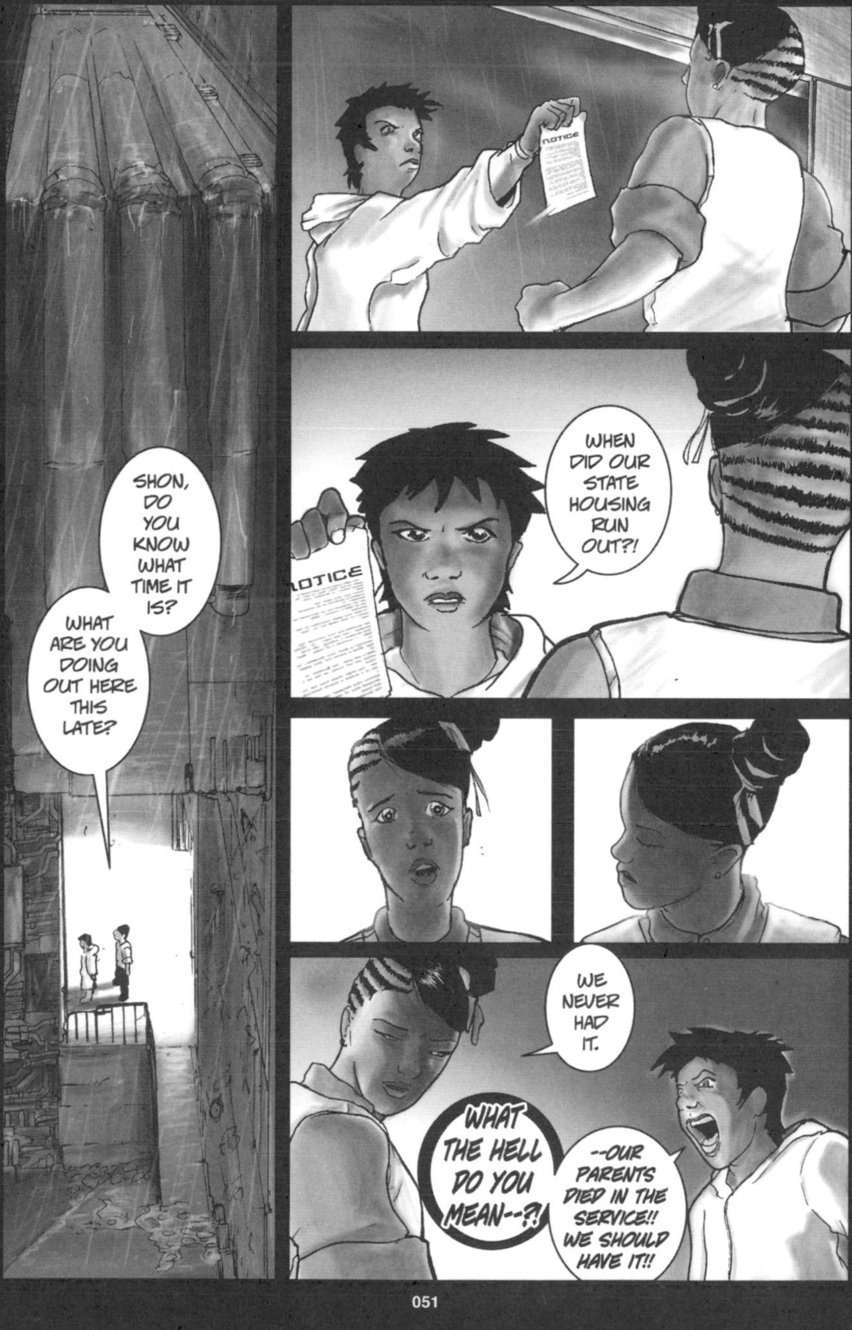
SHON, DO YOU KNOW WHAT TIME IT IS?
WHAT ARE YOU DOING OUT HERE THIS LATE?
NOTICE
WHEN DID OUR STATE HOUSING RUN OUT?!
NOTICE
WE NEVER HAD IT.
WHAT THE HELL DO YOU MEAN--?!
--OUR PARENTS DIED IN THE SERVICE!! WE SHOULD HAVE IT!!

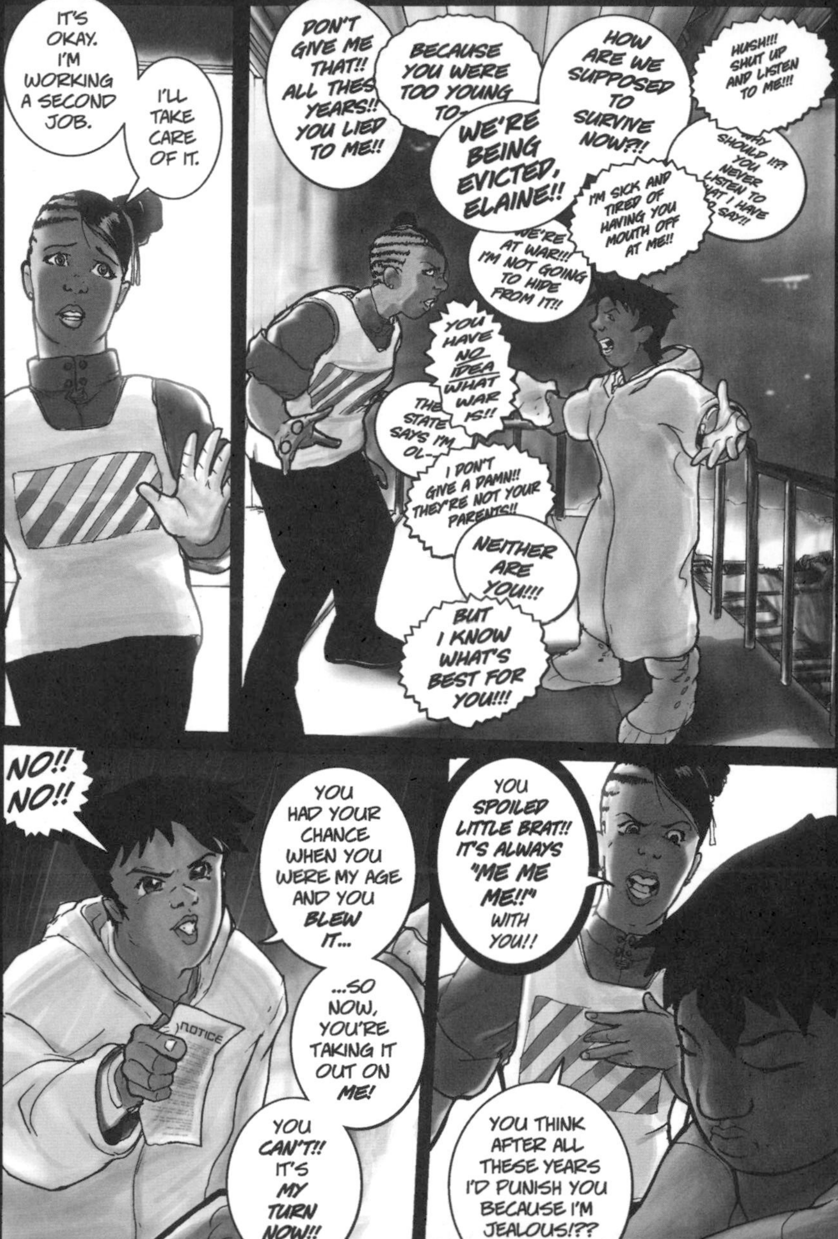
IT'S OKAY. I'M WORKING A SECOND JOB.
I'LL TAKE CARE OF IT.
DON'T GIVE ME THAT!! ALL THES YEARS!! YOU LIED TO ME!!
BECAUSE YOU WERE TOO YOUNG TO-
WE'RE BEING EVICTED, ELAINE!!
HOW ARE WE SUPPOSED TO SURVIVE NOW?!!
HUSH!!! SHUT UP AND LISTEN TO ME!!!
HY SHOULD I!? YOU NEVER LISTEN TO HAT I HAVE O SAY!!
I'M SICK AND TIRED OF HAVING YOU MOUTH OFF AT ME!!
E'RE AT WAR!!! I'M NOT GOING TO HIDE FROM IT!!
YOU HAVE NO IDEA WHAT WAR IS!!
THE STATE SAYS I'M OL-
I DON'T GIVE A DAMN!! THEY'RE NOT YOUR PARENTS!!
NEITHER ARE YOU!!!
BUT I KNOW WHAT'S BEST FOR YOU!!!
NO!! NO!!
YOU HAD YOUR CHANCE WHEN YOU WERE MY AGE AND YOU BLEW IT...
...SO NOW, YOU'RE TAKING IT OUT ON ME!
YOU CAN'T!! IT'S MY TURN NOW!!
NOTICE
YOU SPOILED LITTLE BRAT!! IT'S ALWAYS "ME ME ME!!" WITH YOU!!
YOU THINK AFTER ALL THESE YEARS I'D PUNISH YOU BECAUSE I'M JEALOUS!??

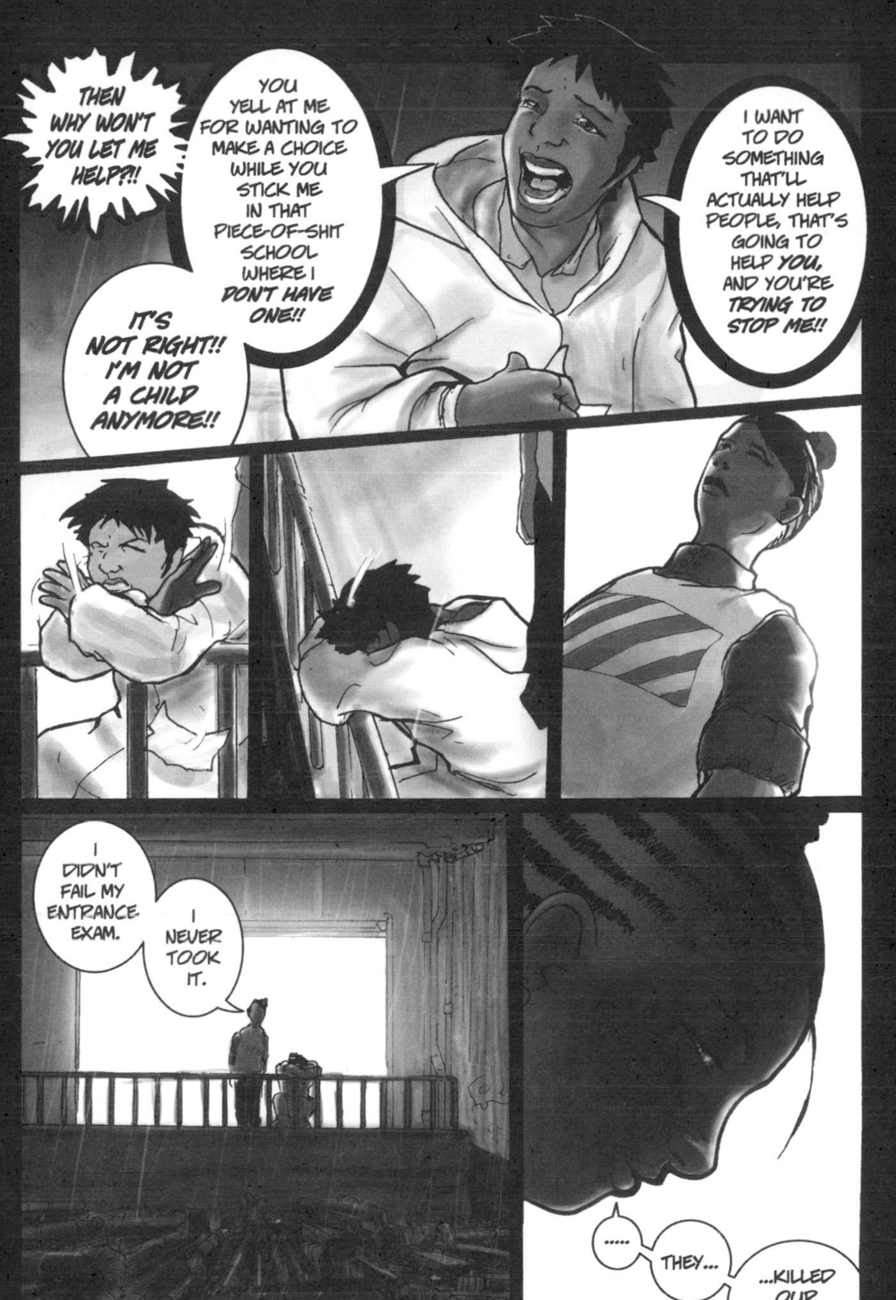
THEN WHY WON'T YOU LET ME HELP?!!
YOU YELL AT ME FOR WANTING TO MAKE A CHOICE WHILE YOU STICK ME IN THAT PIECE-OF-SHIT SCHOOL WHERE I DON'T HAVE ONE!!
IT'S NOT RIGHT!! I'M NOT A CHILD ANYMORE!!
I WANT TO DO SOMETHING THAT'LL ACTUALLY HELP PEOPLE, THAT'S GOING TO HELP YOU, AND YOU'RE TRYING TO STOP ME!!
I DIDN'T FAIL MY ENTRANCE EXAM.
I NEVER TOOK IT.
......
THEY...
...KILLED OUR PARENTS.

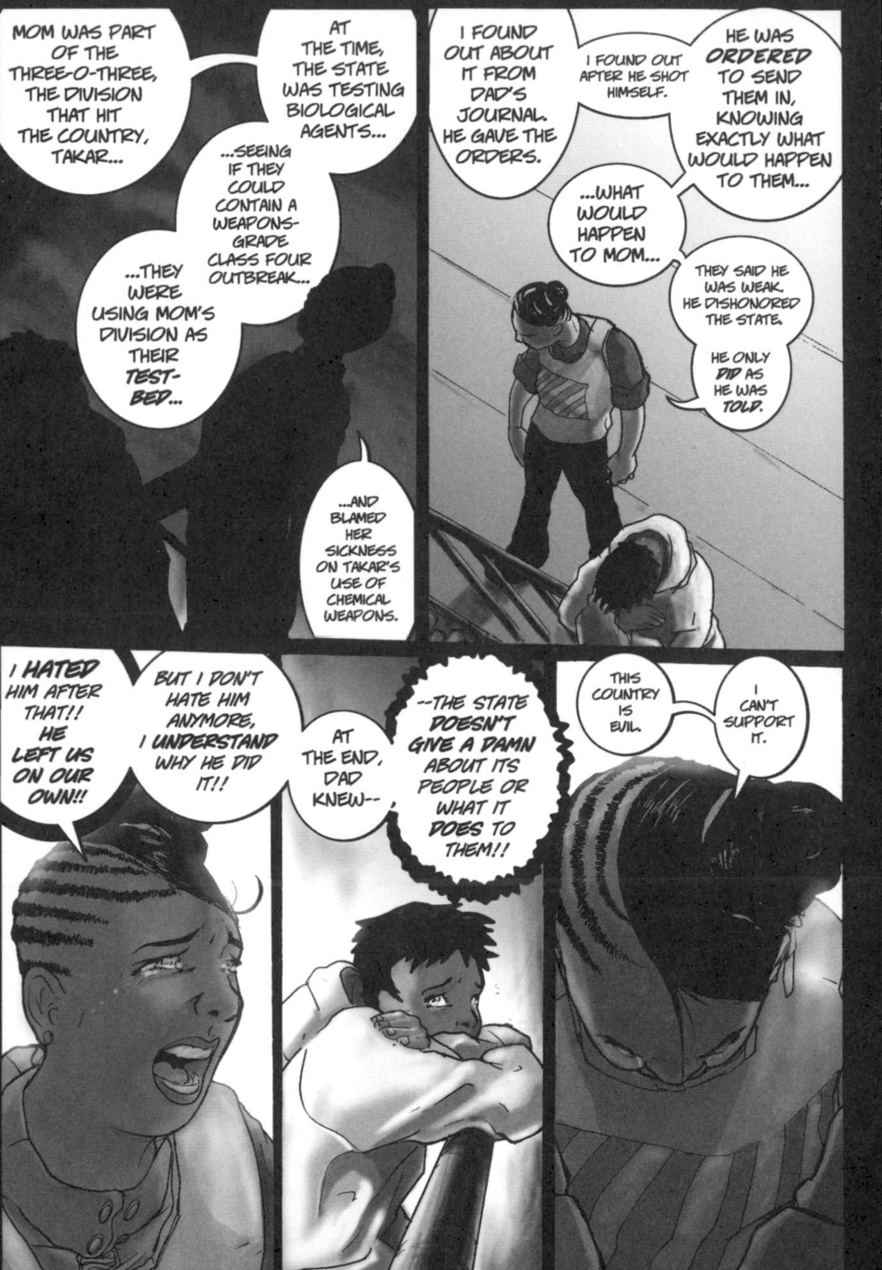
MOM WAS PART OF THE THREE-O-THREE, THE DIVISION THAT HIT THE COUNTRY, TAKAR...
AT THE TIME, THE STATE WAS TESTING BIOLOGICAL AGENTS...
...SEEING IF THEY COULD CONTAIN A WEAPONS-GRADE CLASS FOUR OUTBREAK...
...THEY WERE USING MOM'S DIVISION AS THEIR TEST-BED...
...AND BLAMED HER SICKNESS ON TAKAR'S USE OF CHEMICAL WEAPONS.
I FOUND OUT ABOUT IT FROM DAD'S JOURNAL. HE GAVE THE ORDERS.
I FOUND OUT AFTER HE SHOT HIMSELF.
HE WAS ORDERED TO SEND THEM IN, KNOWING EXACTLY WHAT WOULD HAPPEN TO THEM...
...WHAT WOULD HAPPEN TO MOM...
THEY SAID HE WAS WEAK. HE DISHONORED THE STATE.
HE ONLY DID AS HE WAS TOLD.
I HATED HIM AFTER THAT!! HE LEFT US ON OUR OWN!!
BUT I DON'T HATE HIM ANYMORE, I UNDERSTAND WHY HE DID IT!!
AT THE END, DAD KNEW--
--THE STATE DOESN'T GIVE A DAMN ABOUT ITS PEOPLE OR WHAT IT DOES TO THEM!!
THIS COUNTRY IS EVIL.
I CAN'T SUPPORT IT.

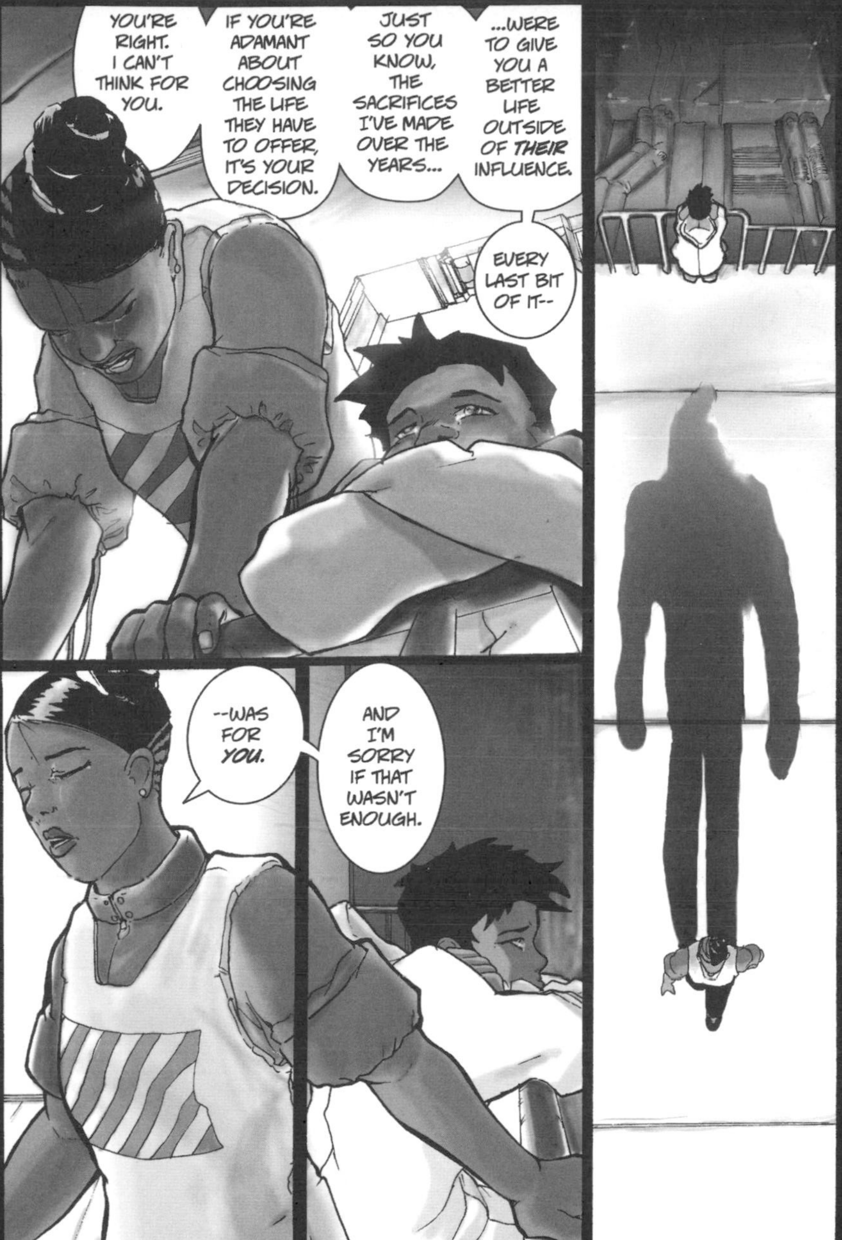
YOU'RE RIGHT. I CAN'T THINK FOR YOU.
IF YOU'RE ADAMANT ABOUT CHOOSING THE LIFE THEY HAVE TO OFFER, IT'S YOUR DECISION.
JUST SO YOU KNOW, THE SACRIFICES I'VE MADE OVER THE YEARS...
...WERE TO GIVE YOU A BETTER LIFE OUTSIDE OF ***THEIR*** INFLUENCE.
EVERY LAST BIT OF IT--
--WAS FOR ***YOU.***
AND I'M SORRY IF THAT WASN'T ENOUGH.

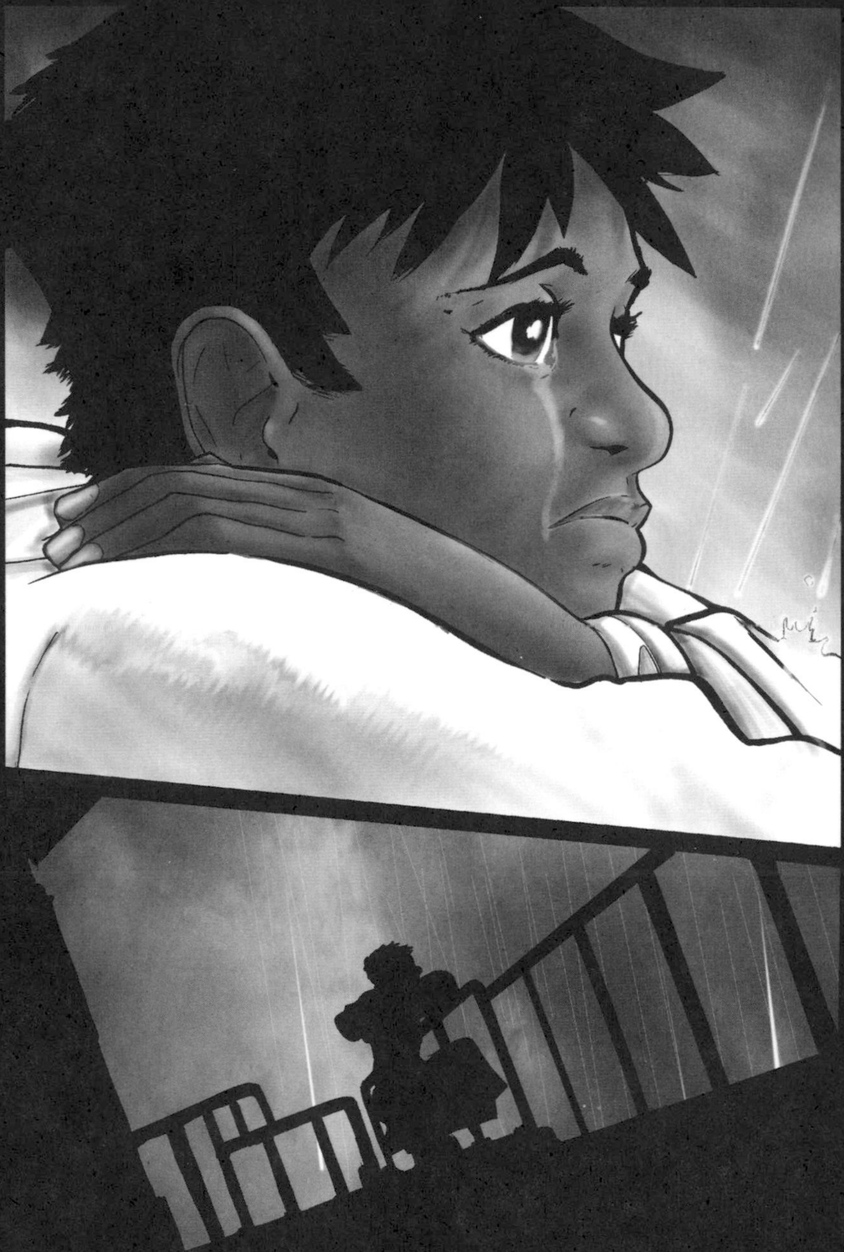

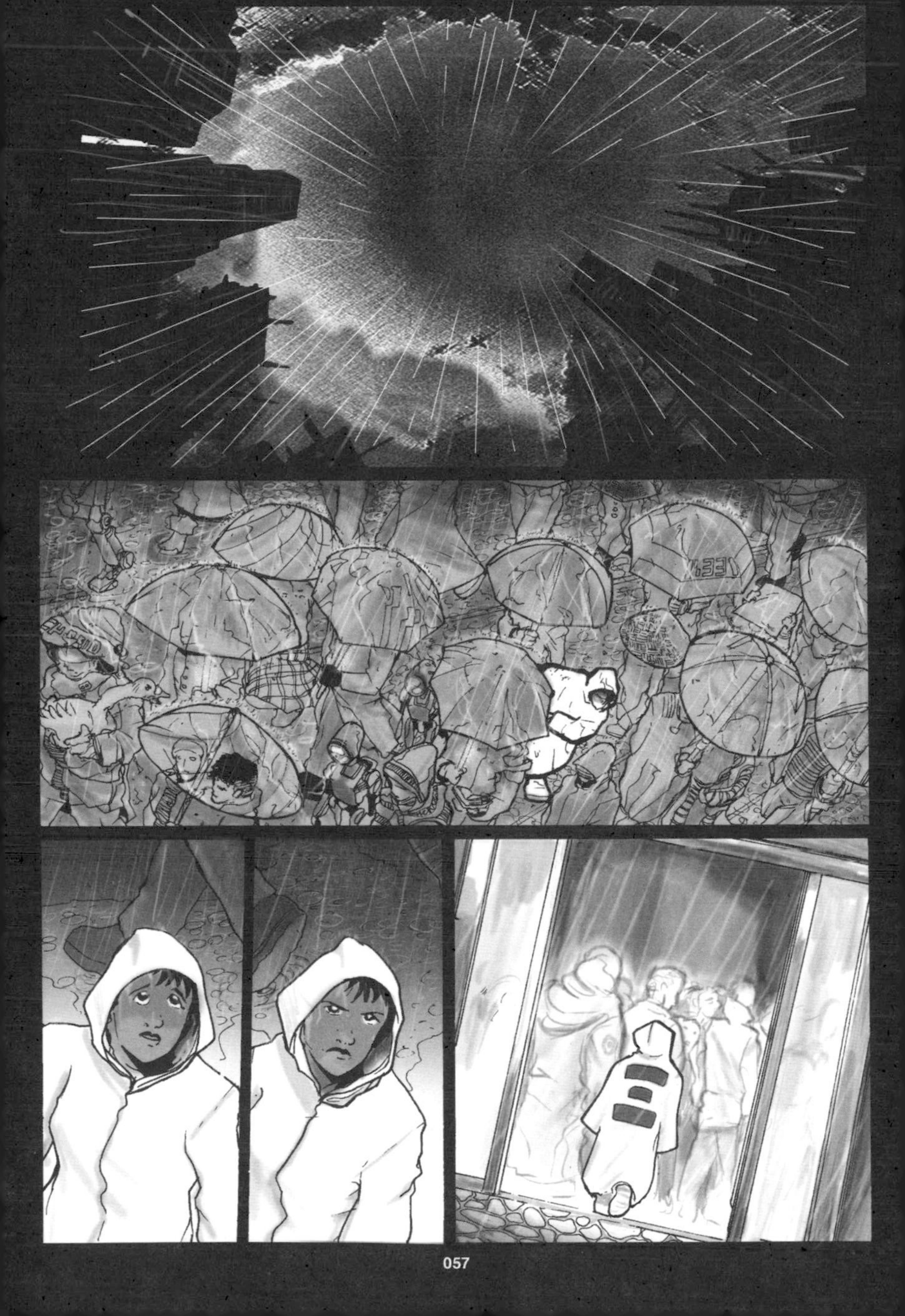

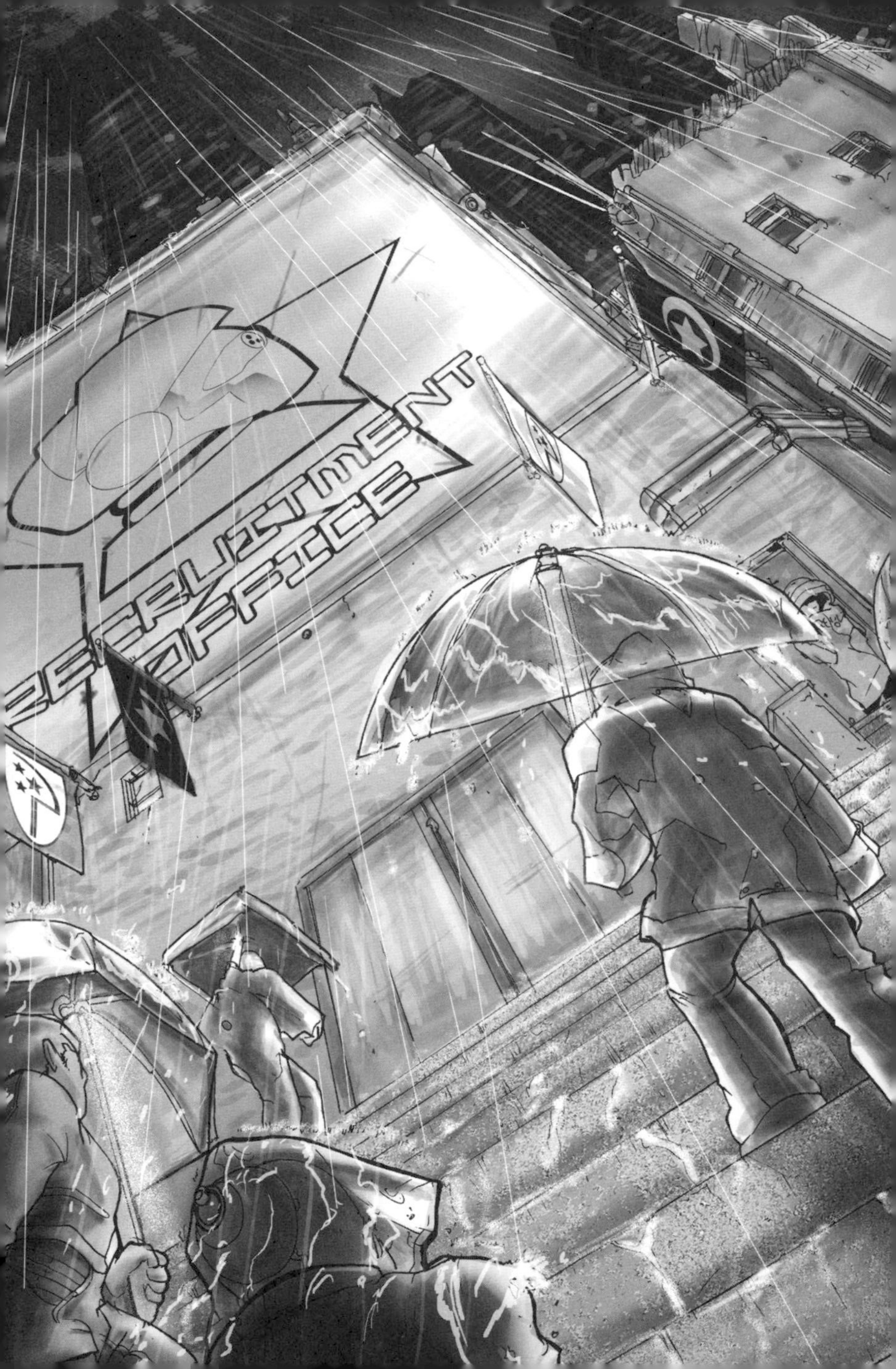
RECRUITMENT
OFFICE

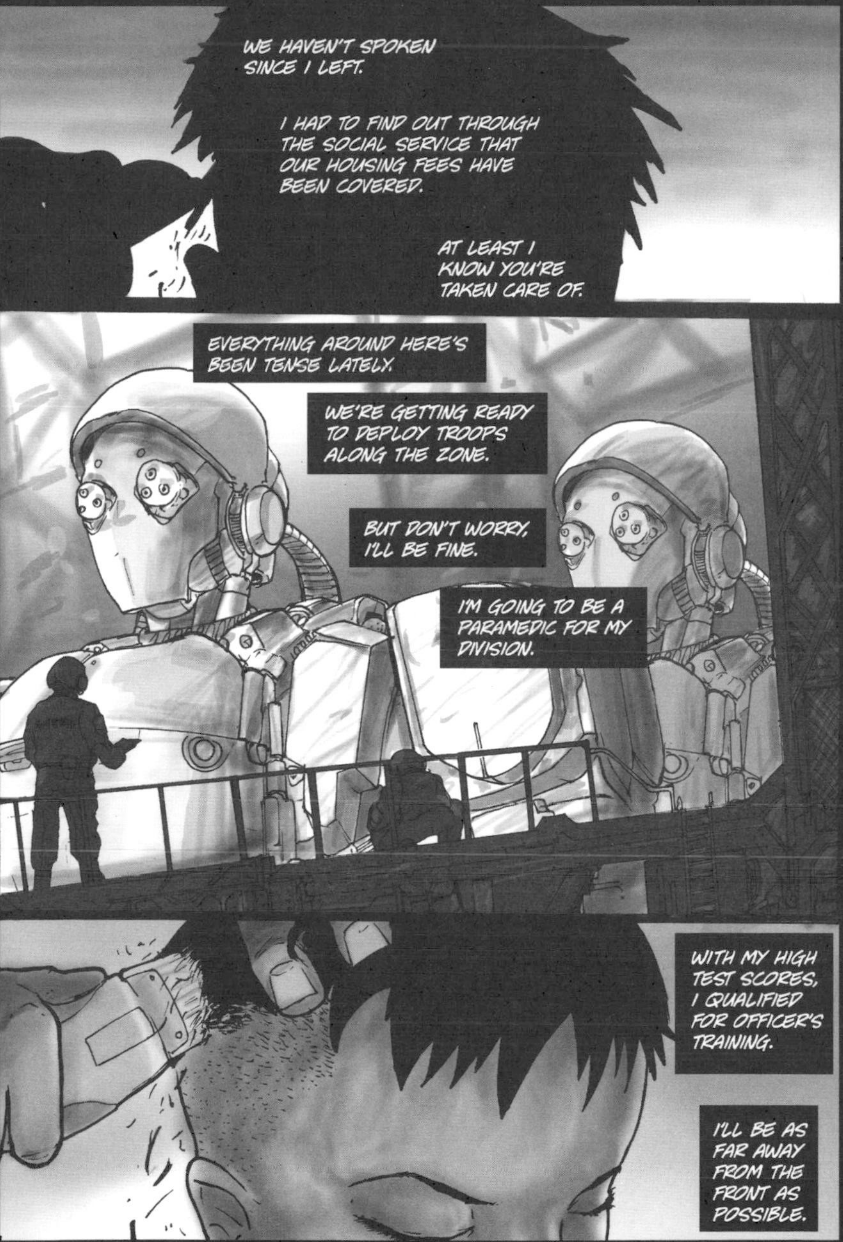
WE HAVEN'T SPOKEN SINCE I LEFT.
I HAD TO FIND OUT THROUGH THE SOCIAL SERVICE THAT OUR HOUSING FEES HAVE BEEN COVERED.
AT LEAST I KNOW YOU'RE TAKEN CARE OF.
EVERYTHING AROUND HERE'S BEEN TENSE LATELY.
WE'RE GETTING READY TO DEPLOY TROOPS ALONG THE ZONE.
BUT DON'T WORRY, I'LL BE FINE.
I'M GOING TO BE A PARAMEDIC FOR MY DIVISION.
WITH MY HIGH TEST SCORES, I QUALIFIED FOR OFFICER'S TRAINING.
I'LL BE AS FAR AWAY FROM THE FRONT AS POSSIBLE.

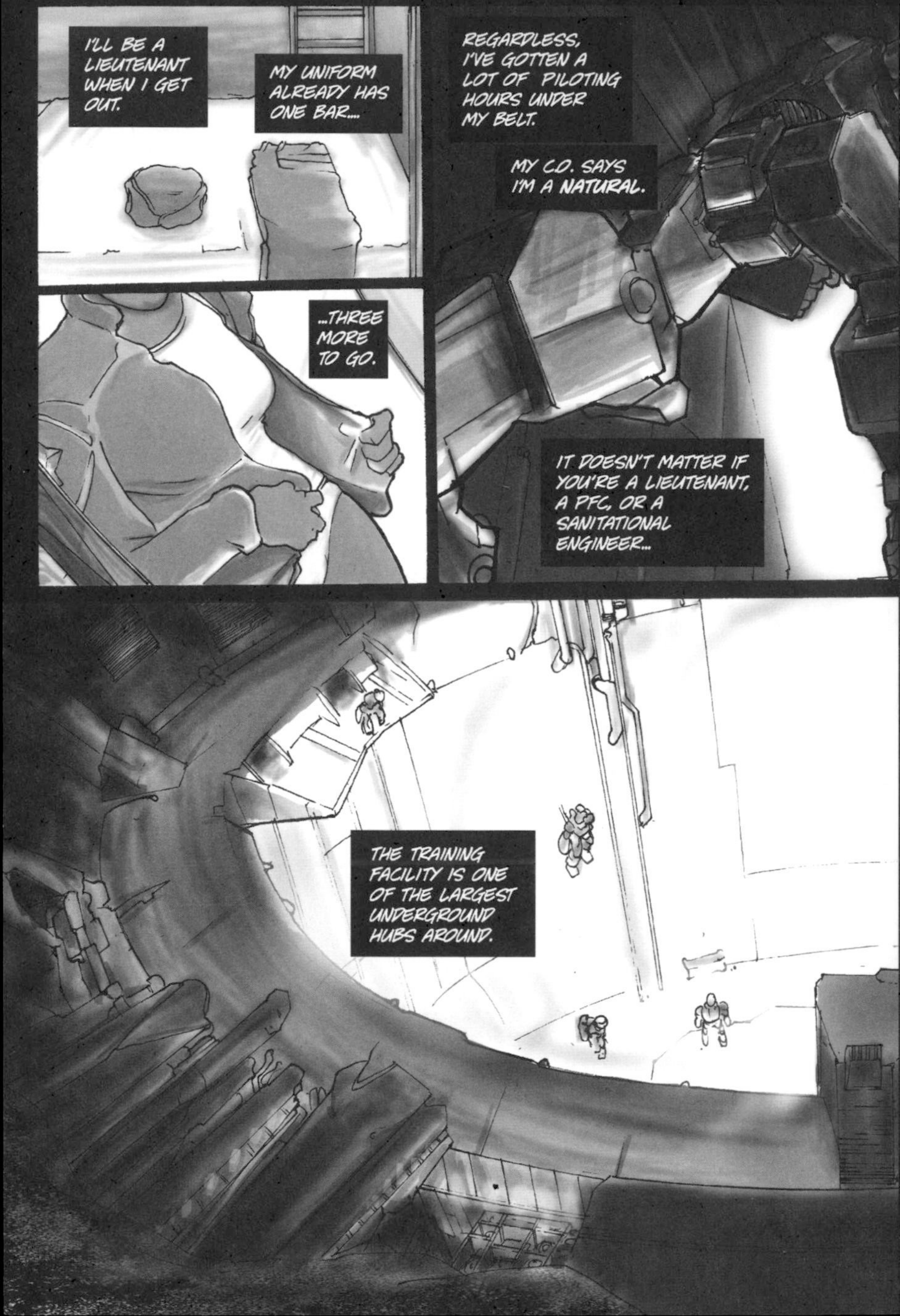
I'LL BE A LIEUTENANT WHEN I GET OUT.
MY UNIFORM ALREADY HAS ONE BAR...
...THREE MORE TO GO.
REGARDLESS, I'VE GOTTEN A LOT OF PILOTING HOURS UNDER MY BELT.
MY C.O. SAYS I'M A NATURAL.
IT DOESN'T MATTER IF YOU'RE A LIEUTENANT, A PFC, OR A SANITATIONAL ENGINEER...
THE TRAINING FACILITY IS ONE OF THE LARGEST UNDERGROUND HUBS AROUND.

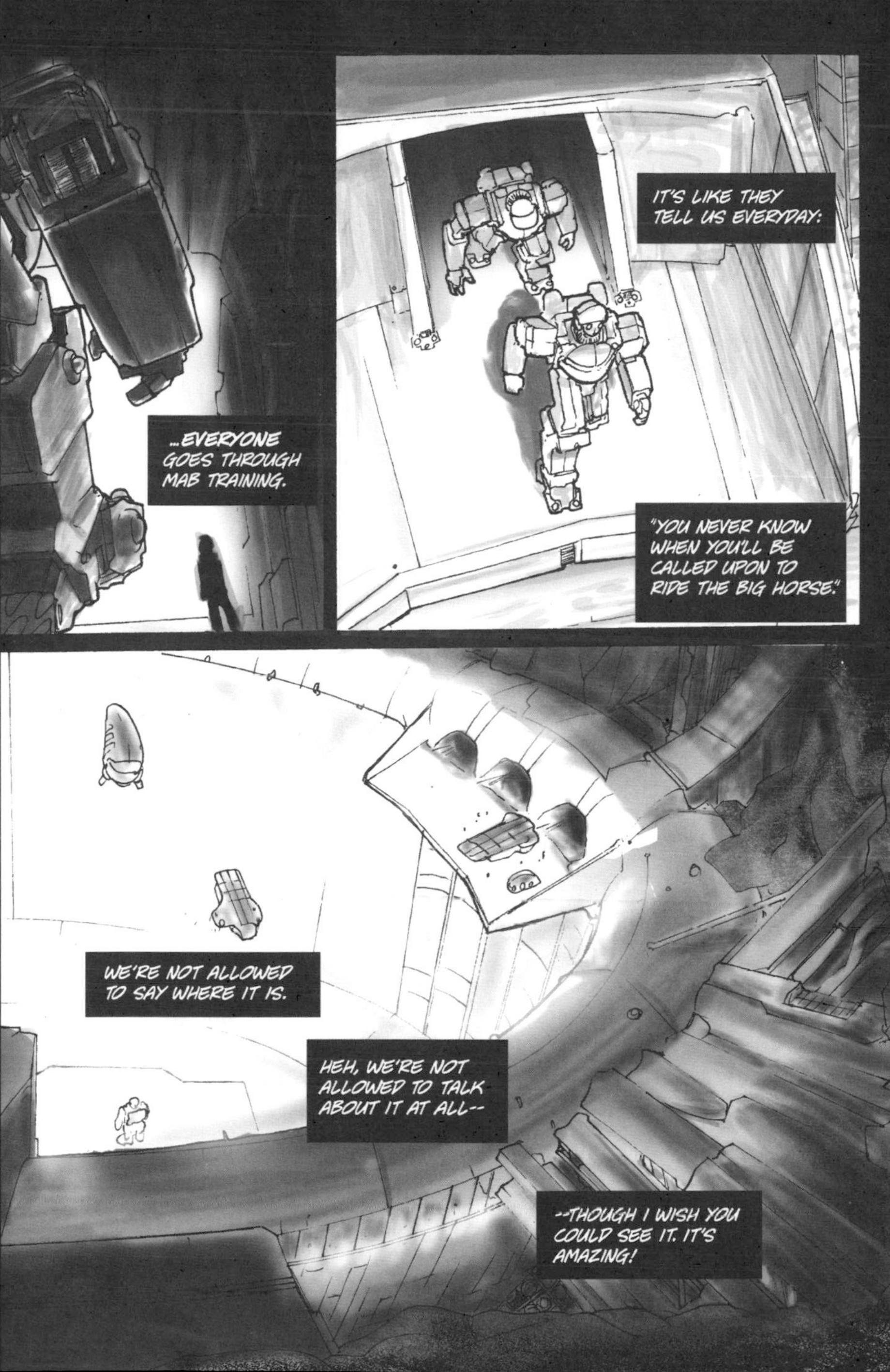
...EVERYONE GOES THROUGH MAB TRAINING.
IT'S LIKE THEY TELL US EVERYDAY:
"YOU NEVER KNOW WHEN YOU'LL BE CALLED UPON TO RIDE THE BIG HORSE."
WE'RE NOT ALLOWED TO SAY WHERE IT IS.
HEH, WE'RE NOT ALLOWED TO TALK ABOUT IT AT ALL--
--THOUGH I WISH YOU COULD SEE IT. IT'S AMAZING!

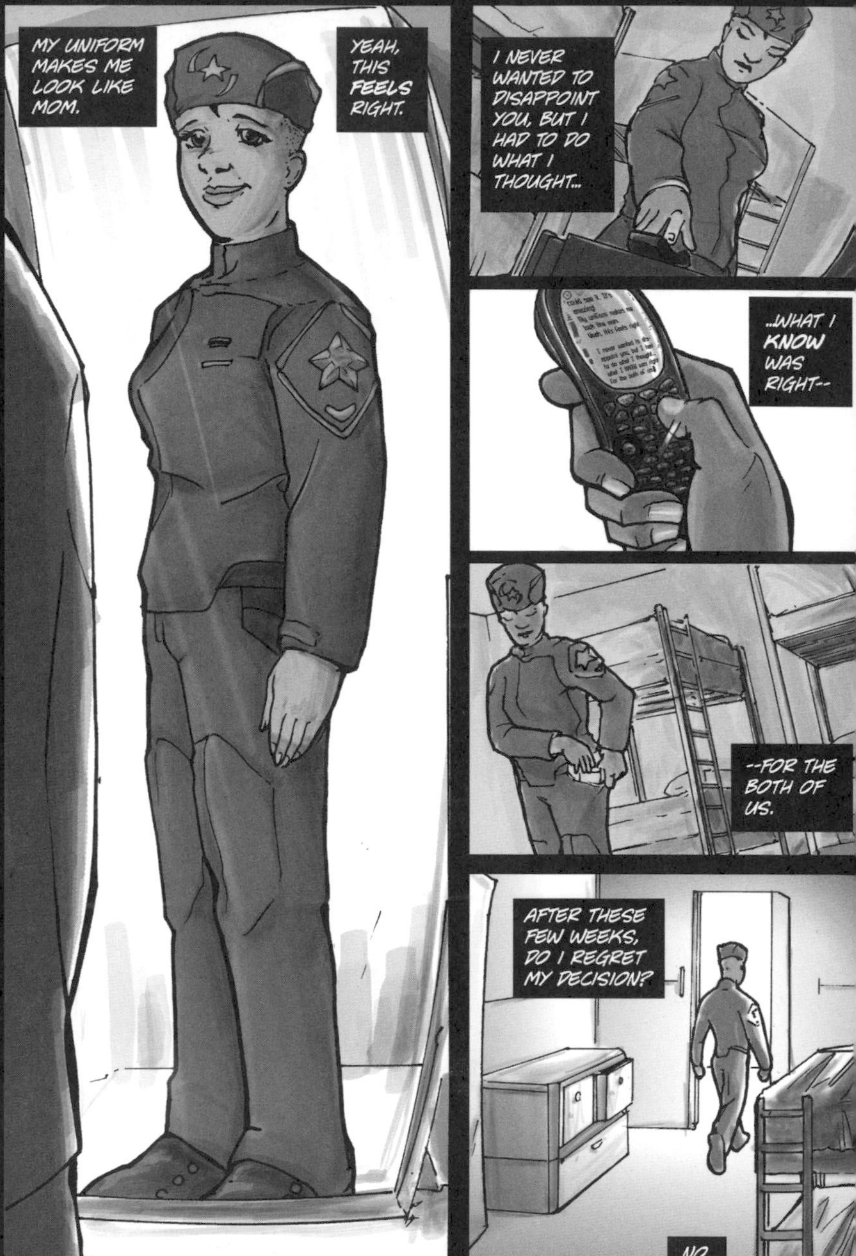
MY UNIFORM MAKES ME LOOK LIKE MOM.
YEAH, THIS FEELS RIGHT.
I NEVER WANTED TO DISAPPOINT YOU, BUT I HAD TO DO WHAT I THOUGHT...
...WHAT I KNOW WAS RIGHT--
--FOR THE BOTH OF US.
AFTER THESE FEW WEEKS, DO I REGRET MY DECISION?
NO.

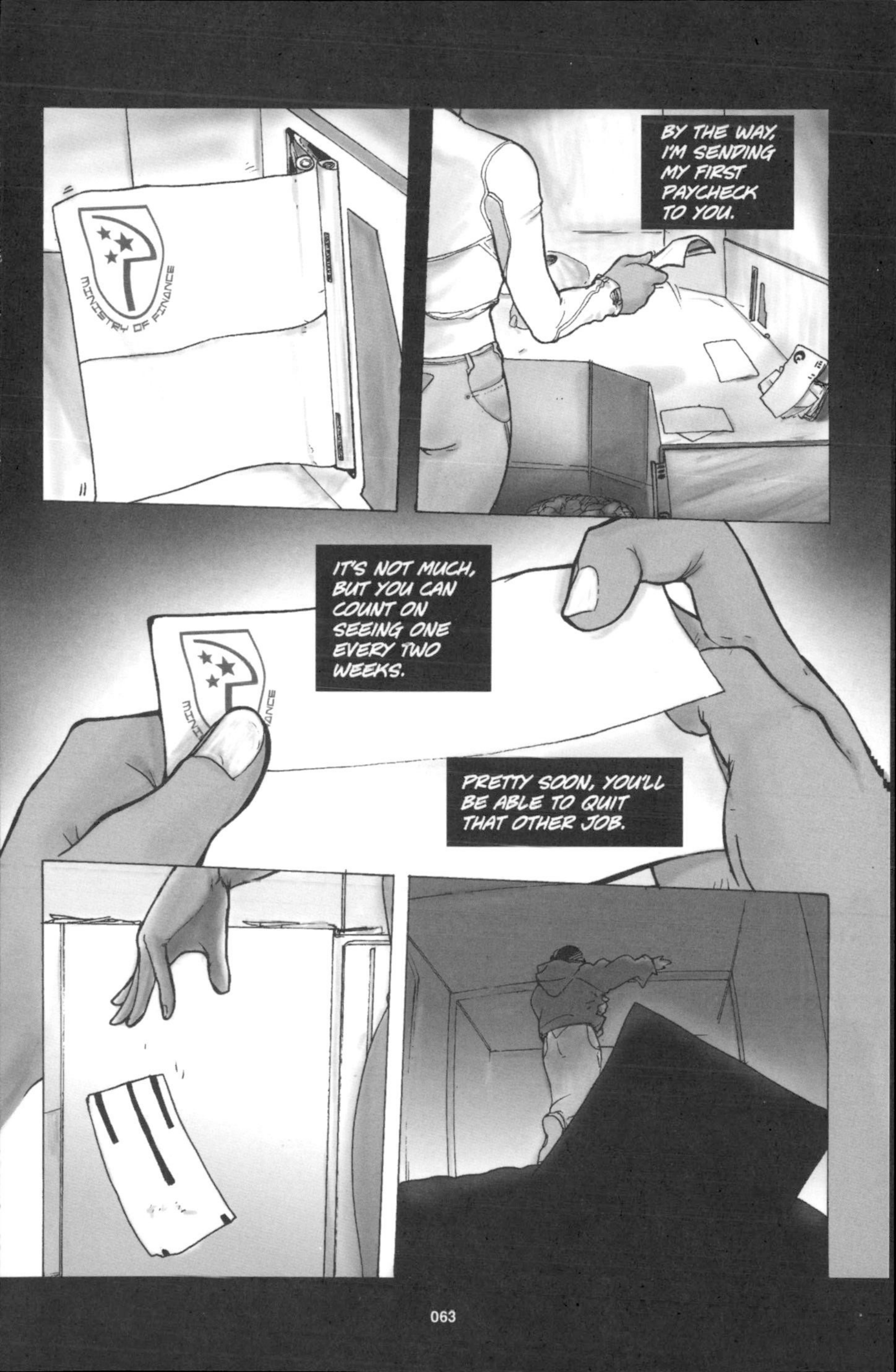
MINISTRY OF FINANCE
BY THE WAY, I'M SENDING MY FIRST PAYCHECK TO YOU.
IT'S NOT MUCH, BUT YOU CAN COUNT ON SEEING ONE EVERY TWO WEEKS.
PRETTY SOON, YOU'LL BE ABLE TO QUIT THAT OTHER JOB.

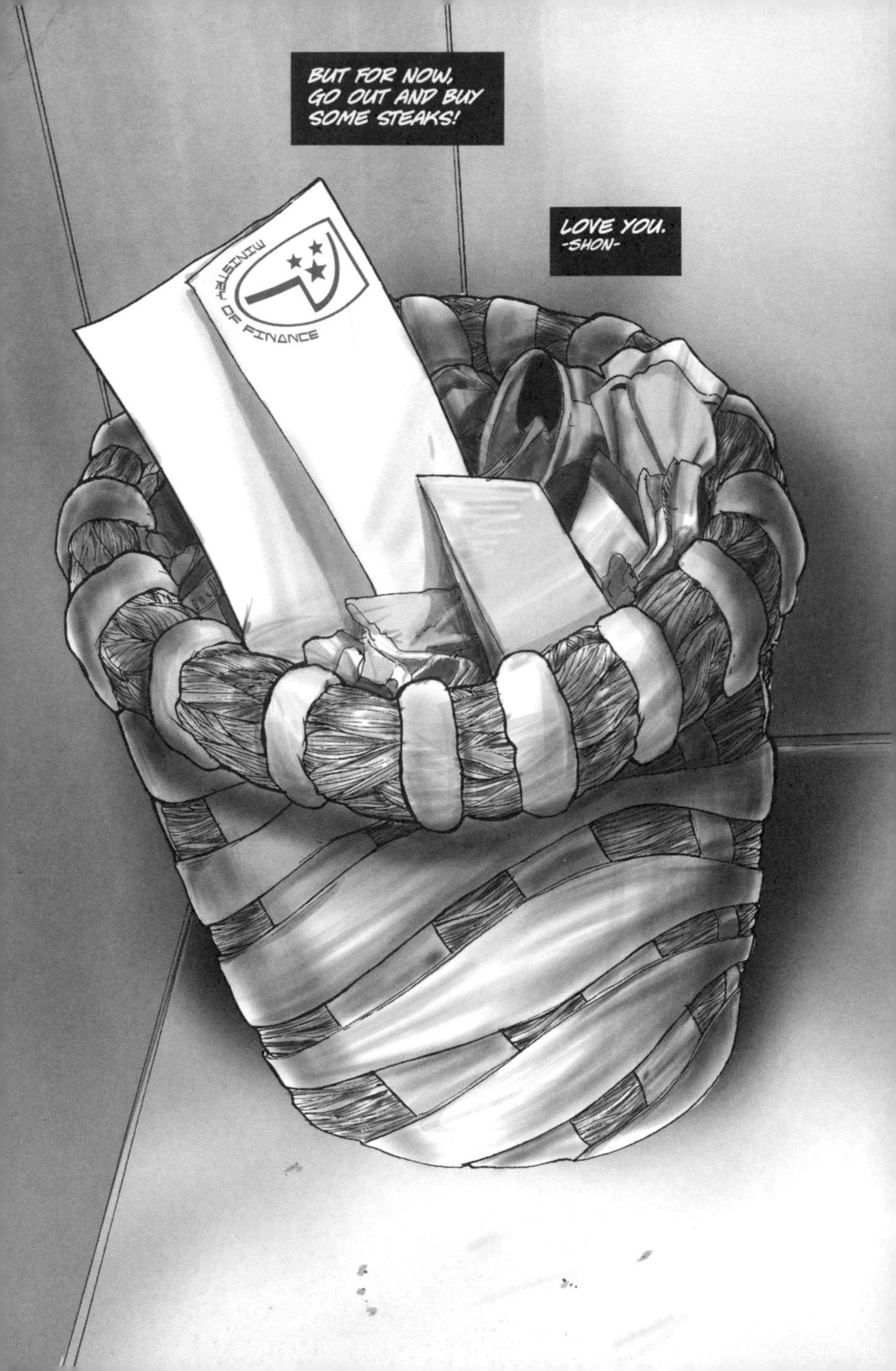
BUT FOR NOW, GO OUT AND BUY SOME STEAKS!
LOVE YOU. -SHON-
MINISTRY OF FINANCE

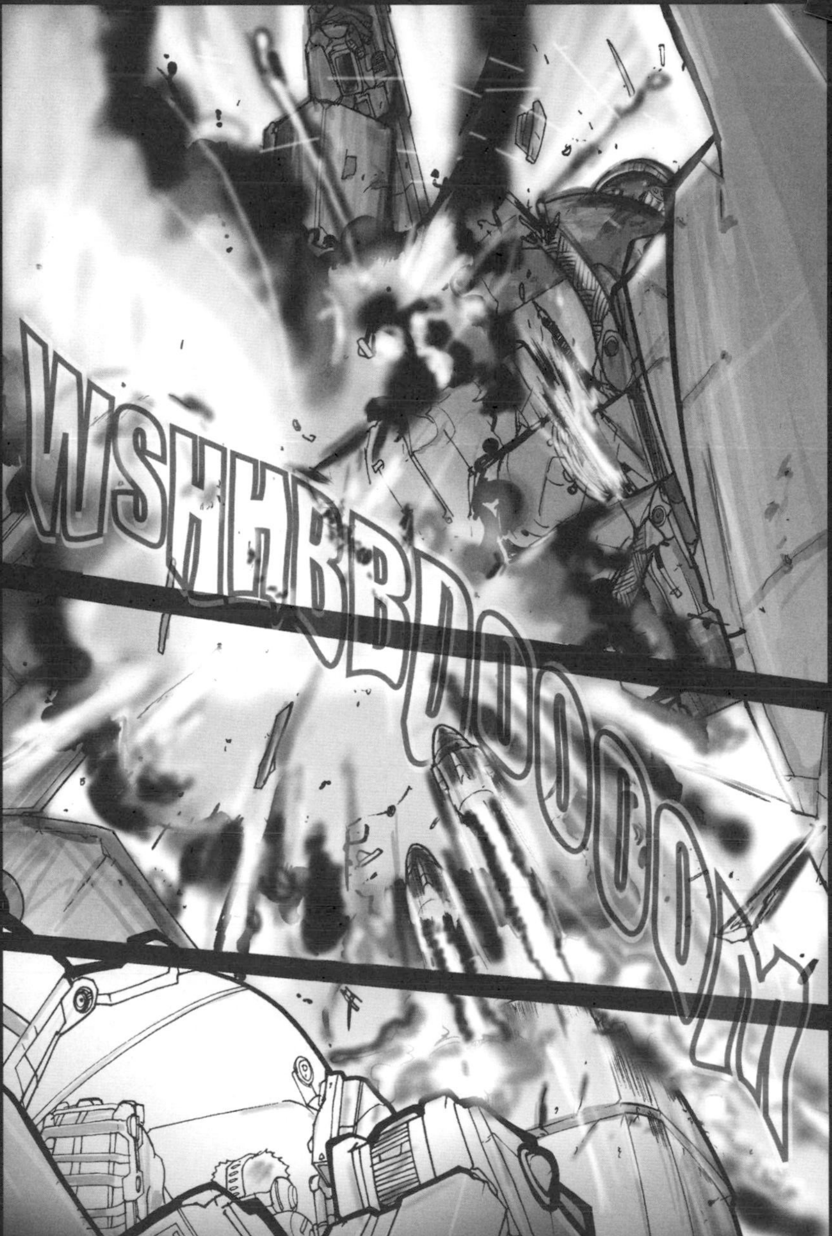
WSHBBOOOOOM

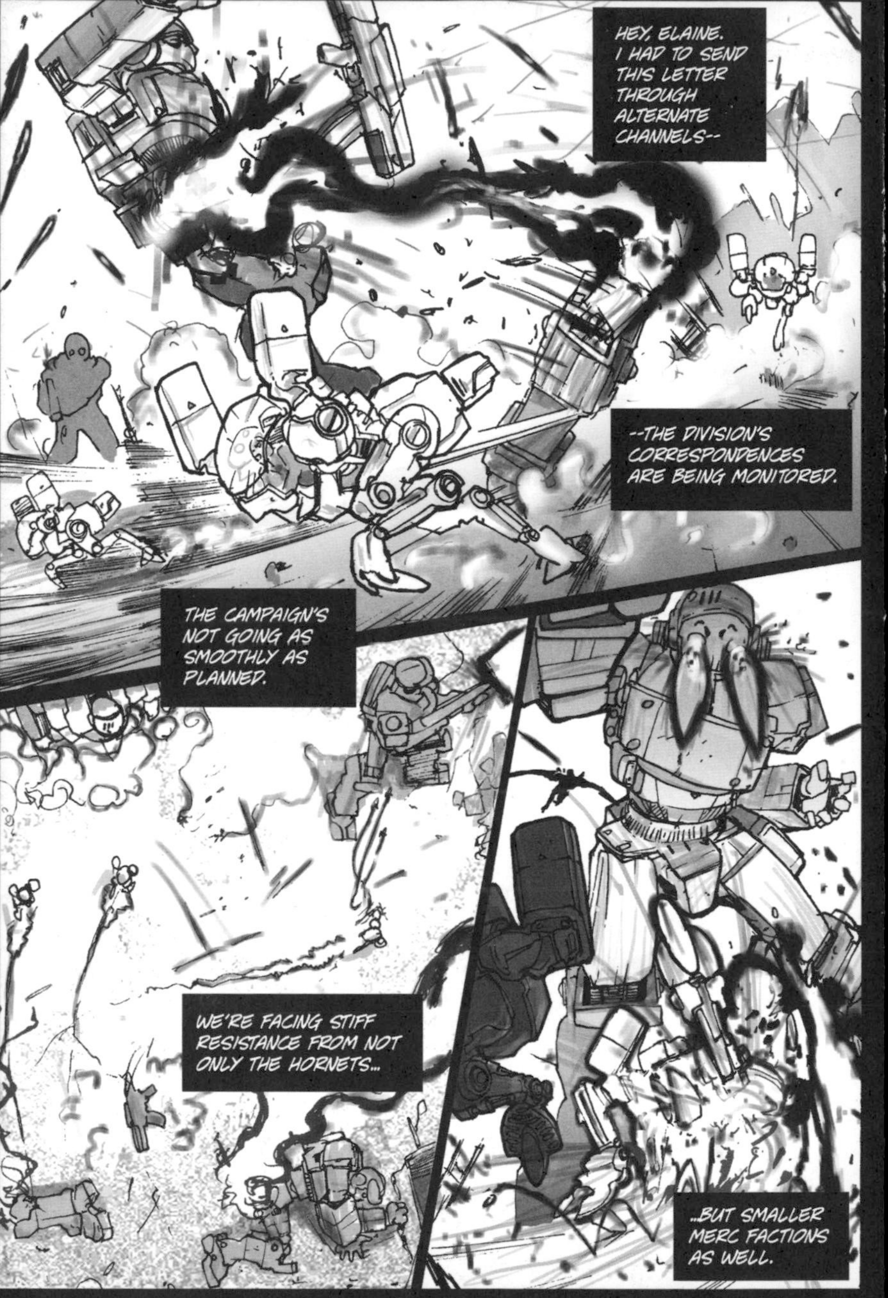
HEY, ELAINE. I HAD TO SEND THIS LETTER THROUGH ALTERNATE CHANNELS--
--THE DIVISION'S CORRESPONDENCES ARE BEING MONITORED.
THE CAMPAIGN'S NOT GOING AS SMOOTHLY AS PLANNED.
WE'RE FACING STIFF RESISTANCE FROM NOT ONLY THE HORNETS...
...BUT SMALLER MERC FACTIONS AS WELL.

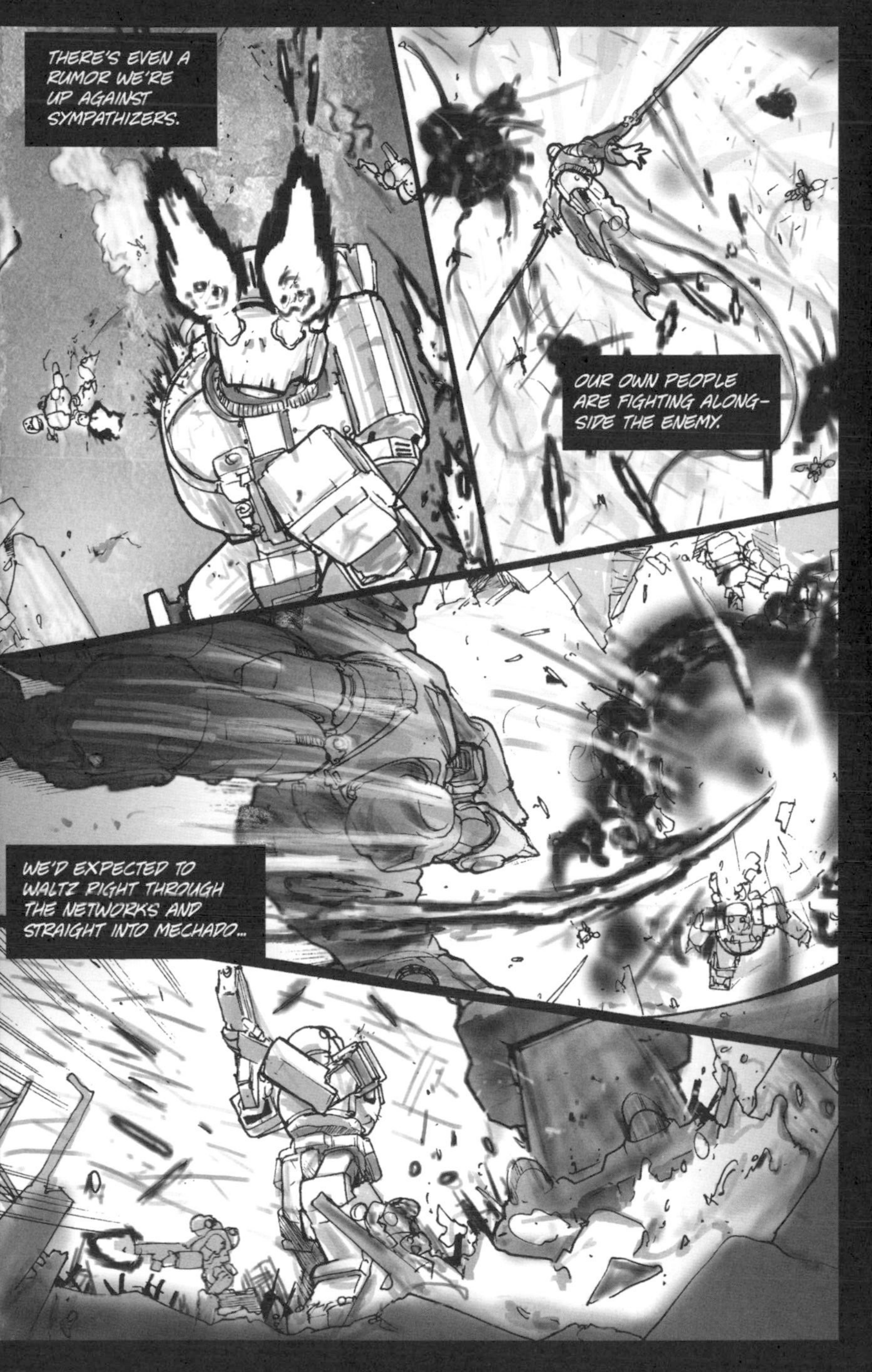
THERE'S EVEN A RUMOR WE'RE UP AGAINST SYMPATHIZERS.
OUR OWN PEOPLE ARE FIGHTING ALONG-SIDE THE ENEMY.
WE'D EXPECTED TO WALTZ RIGHT THROUGH THE NETWORKS AND STRAIGHT INTO MECHADO...

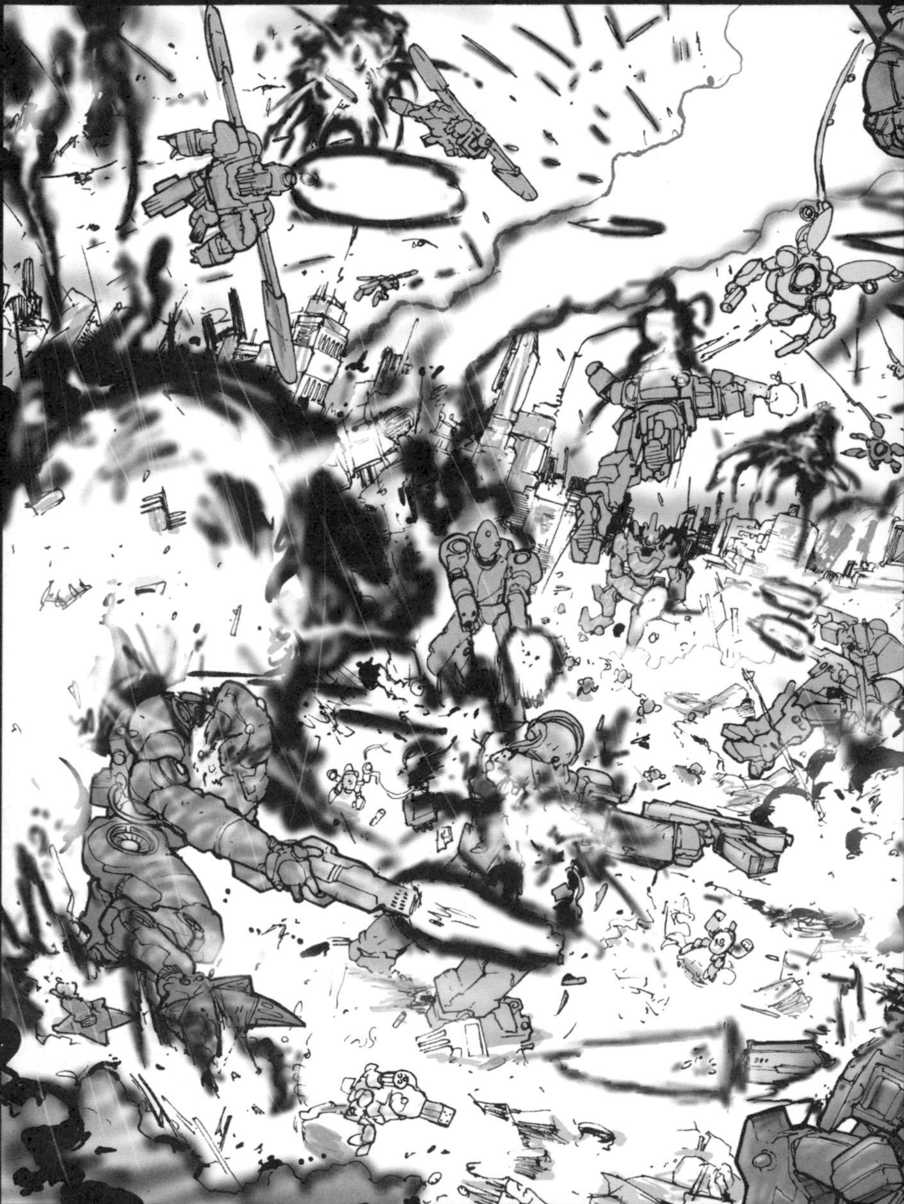

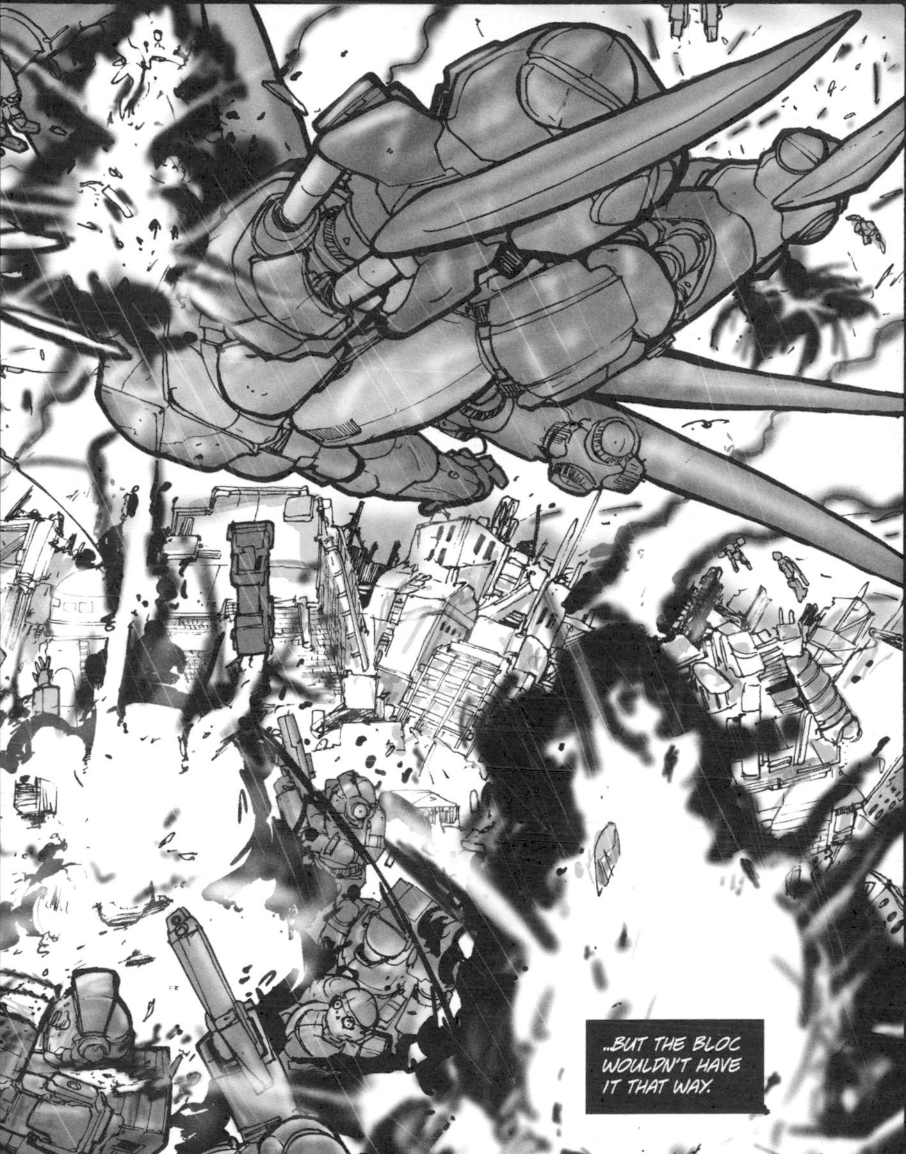
..BUT THE BLOC
WOULDN'T HAVE
IT THAT WAY.

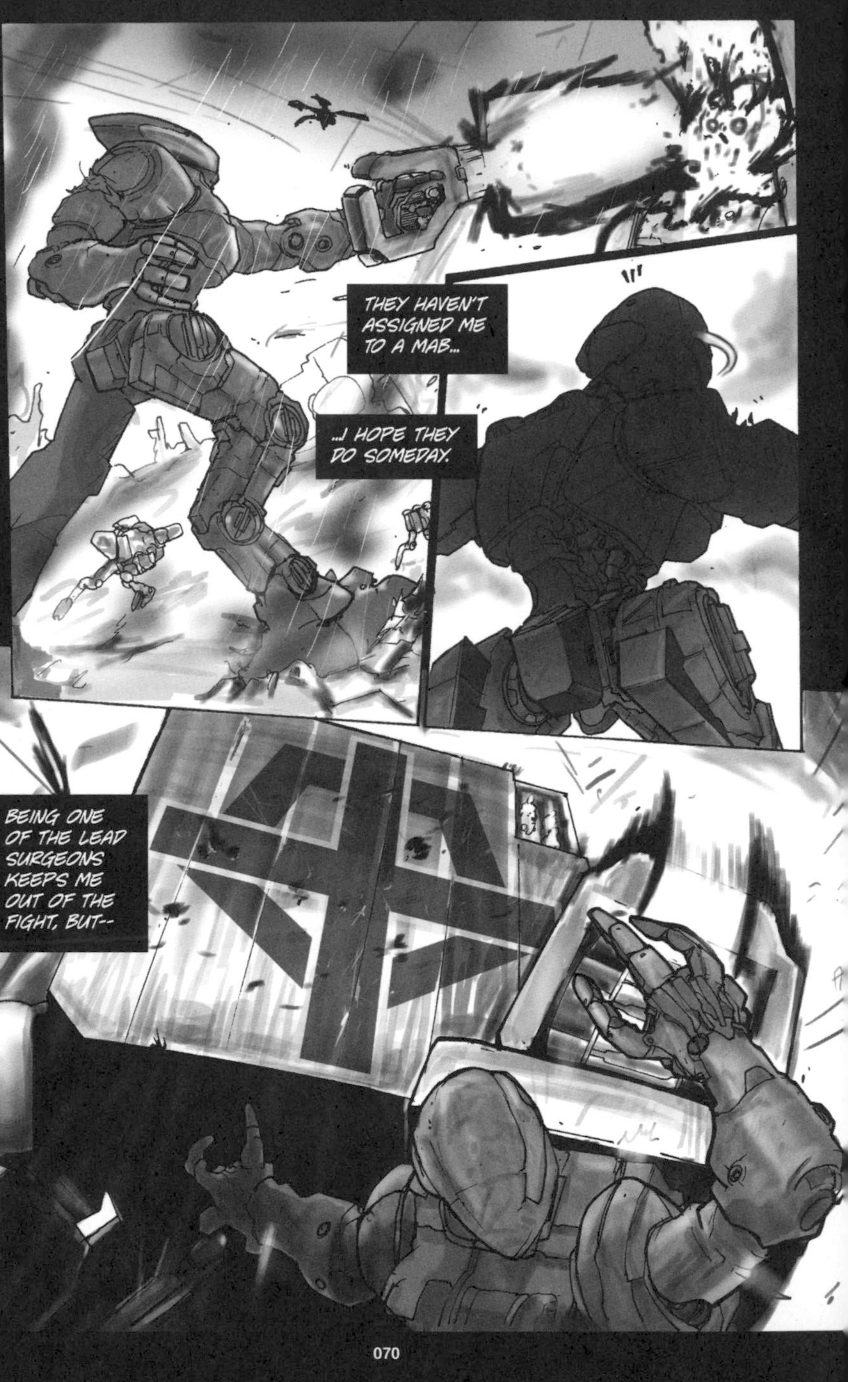
THEY HAVEN'T ASSIGNED ME TO A MAB...
...I HOPE THEY DO SOMEDAY.
BEING ONE OF THE LEAD SURGEONS KEEPS ME OUT OF THE FIGHT, BUT--

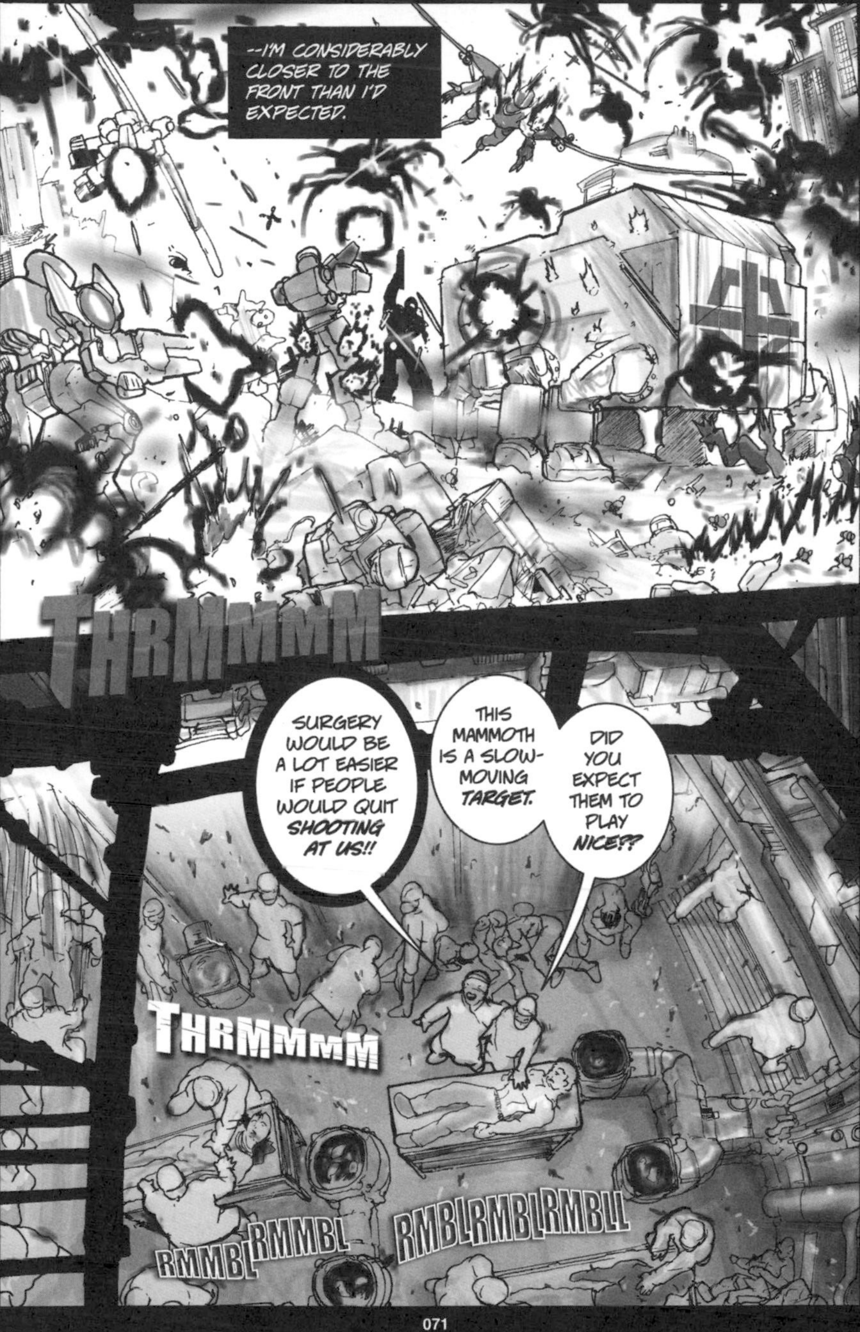
--I'M CONSIDERABLY CLOSER TO THE FRONT THAN I'D EXPECTED.
THRMMMM
SURGERY WOULD BE A LOT EASIER IF PEOPLE WOULD QUIT SHOOTING AT US!!
THIS MAMMOTH IS A SLOW-MOVING TARGET.
DID YOU EXPECT THEM TO PLAY NICE??
THRMMMM
RMMBLRMMBL
RMBLRMBLRMBLL

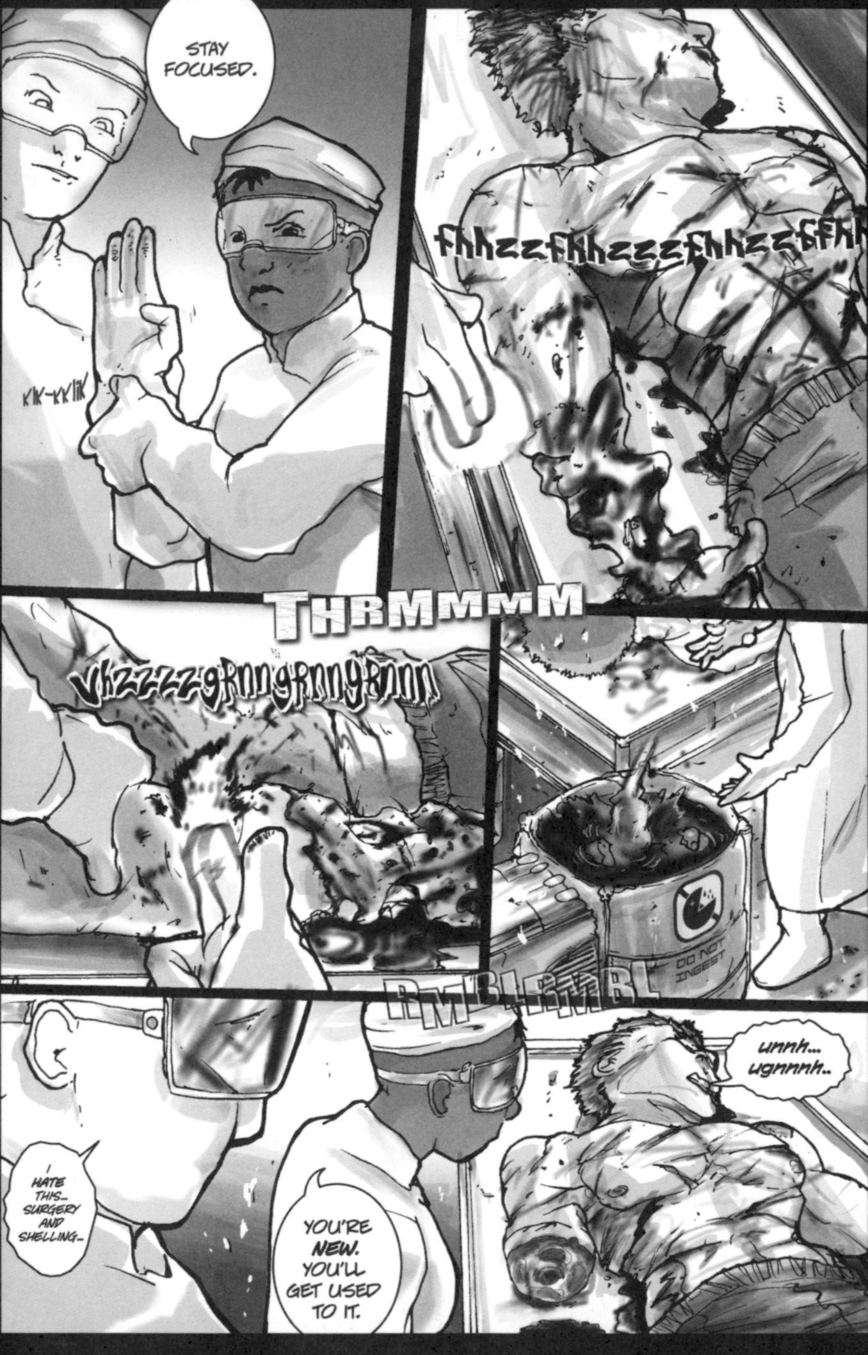
STAY FOCUSED.
KIK-KKLIK
fhhzzfhhzzzfhhzzffhh
THRMMMMM
vhzzzzzgRnngRnngRnnn
DO NOT INGEST
RMBLRMBL
unnh... ugnnnh..
I HATE THIS... SURGERY AND SHELLING...
YOU'RE NEW. YOU'LL GET USED TO IT.

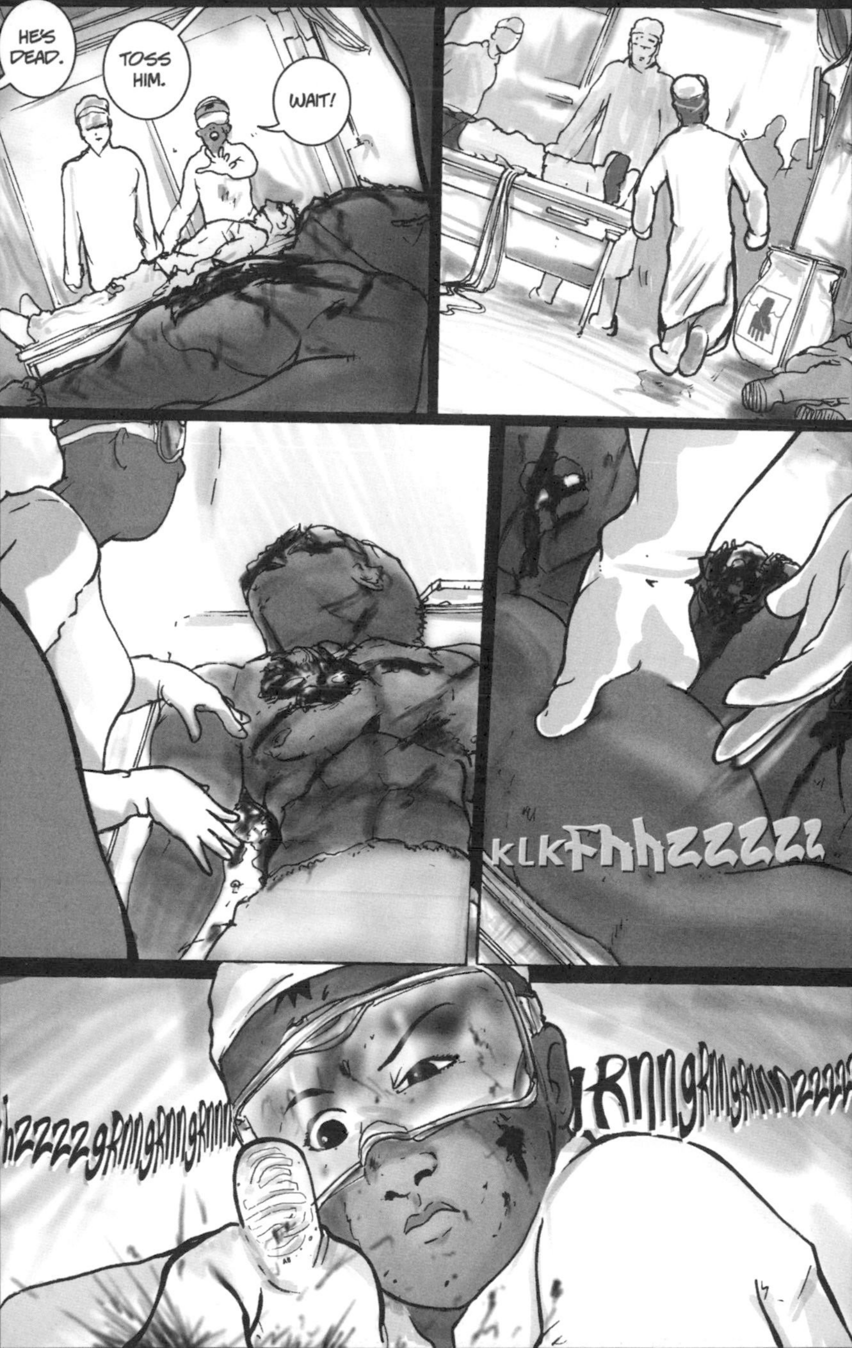
HE'S DEAD.
TOSS HIM.
WAIT!
klkFhhzzzzz

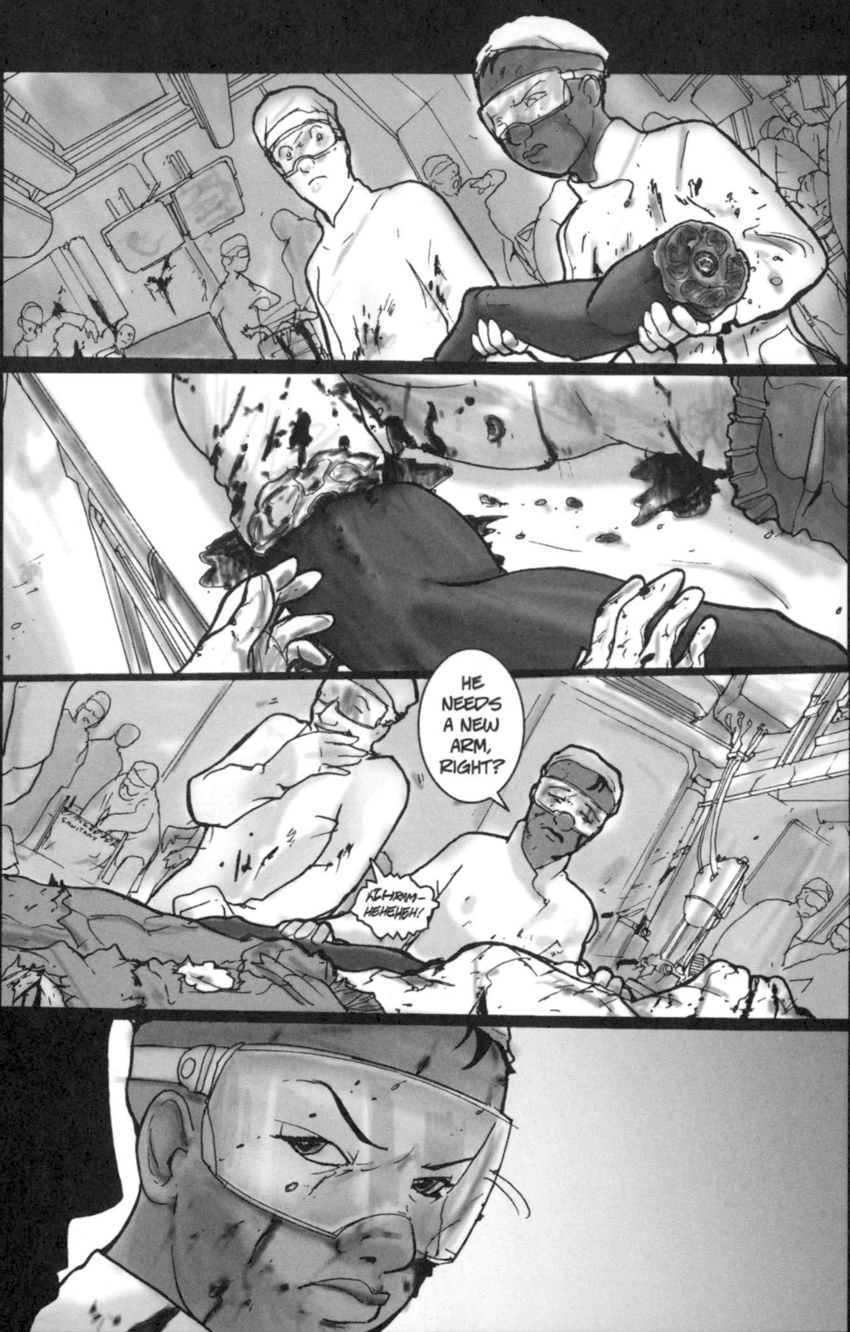
HE NEEDS A NEW ARM, RIGHT?
KCHRMM-HEHEHEH!
SANITARY

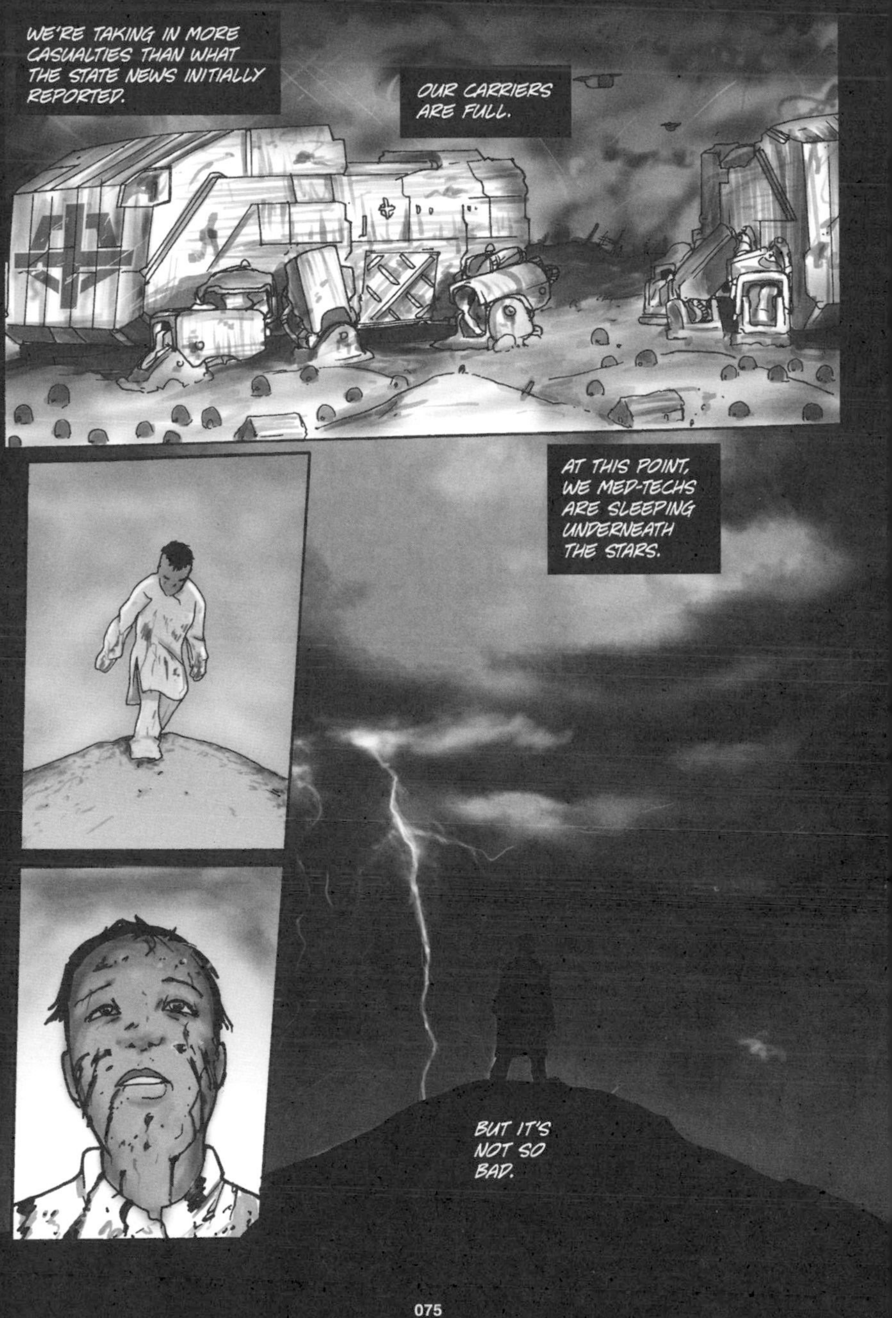
WE'RE TAKING IN MORE CASUALTIES THAN WHAT THE STATE NEWS INITIALLY REPORTED.
OUR CARRIERS ARE FULL.
AT THIS POINT, WE MED-TECHS ARE SLEEPING UNDERNEATH THE STARS.
BUT IT'S NOT SO BAD.

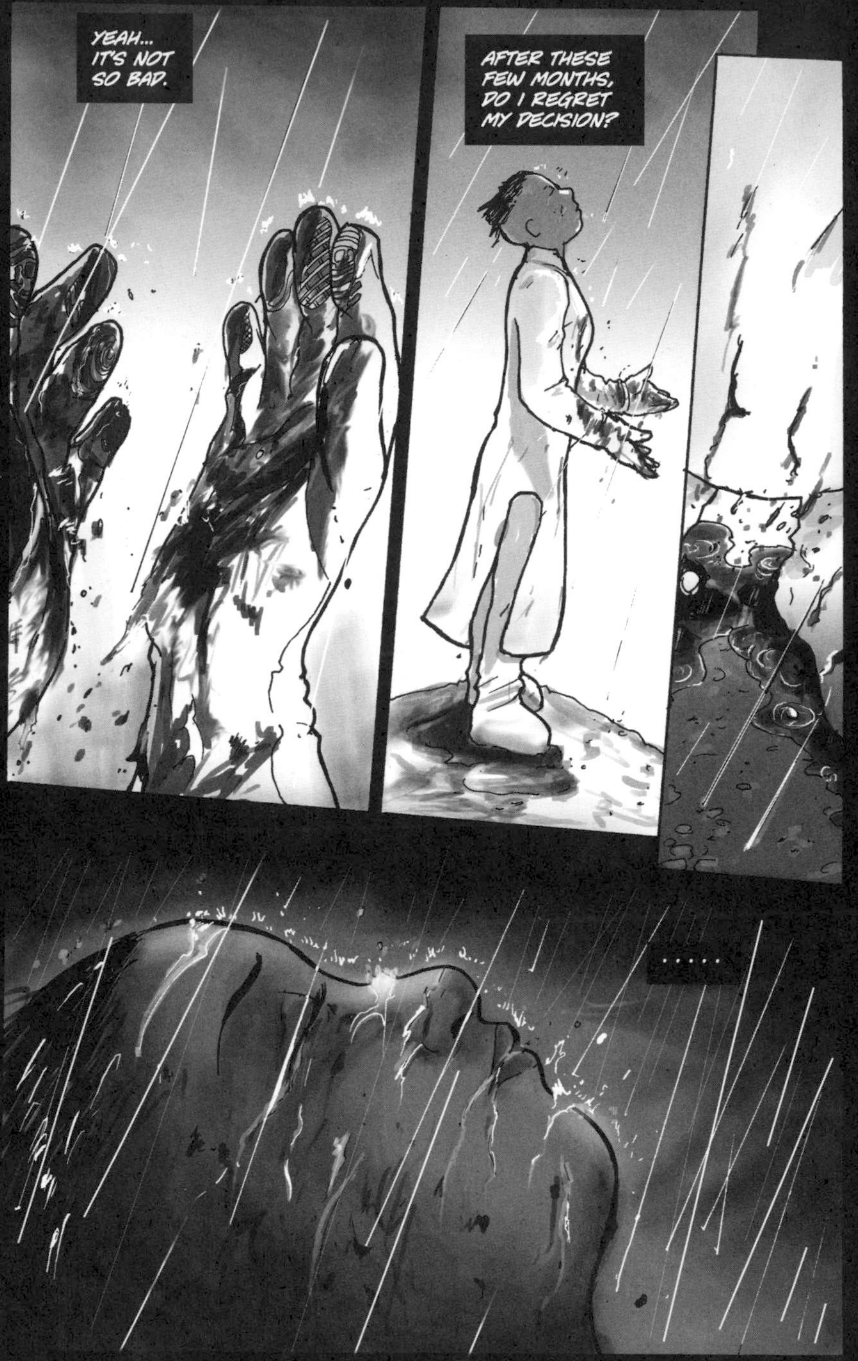
YEAH... IT'S NOT SO BAD.
AFTER THESE FEW MONTHS, DO I REGRET MY DECISION?
.....

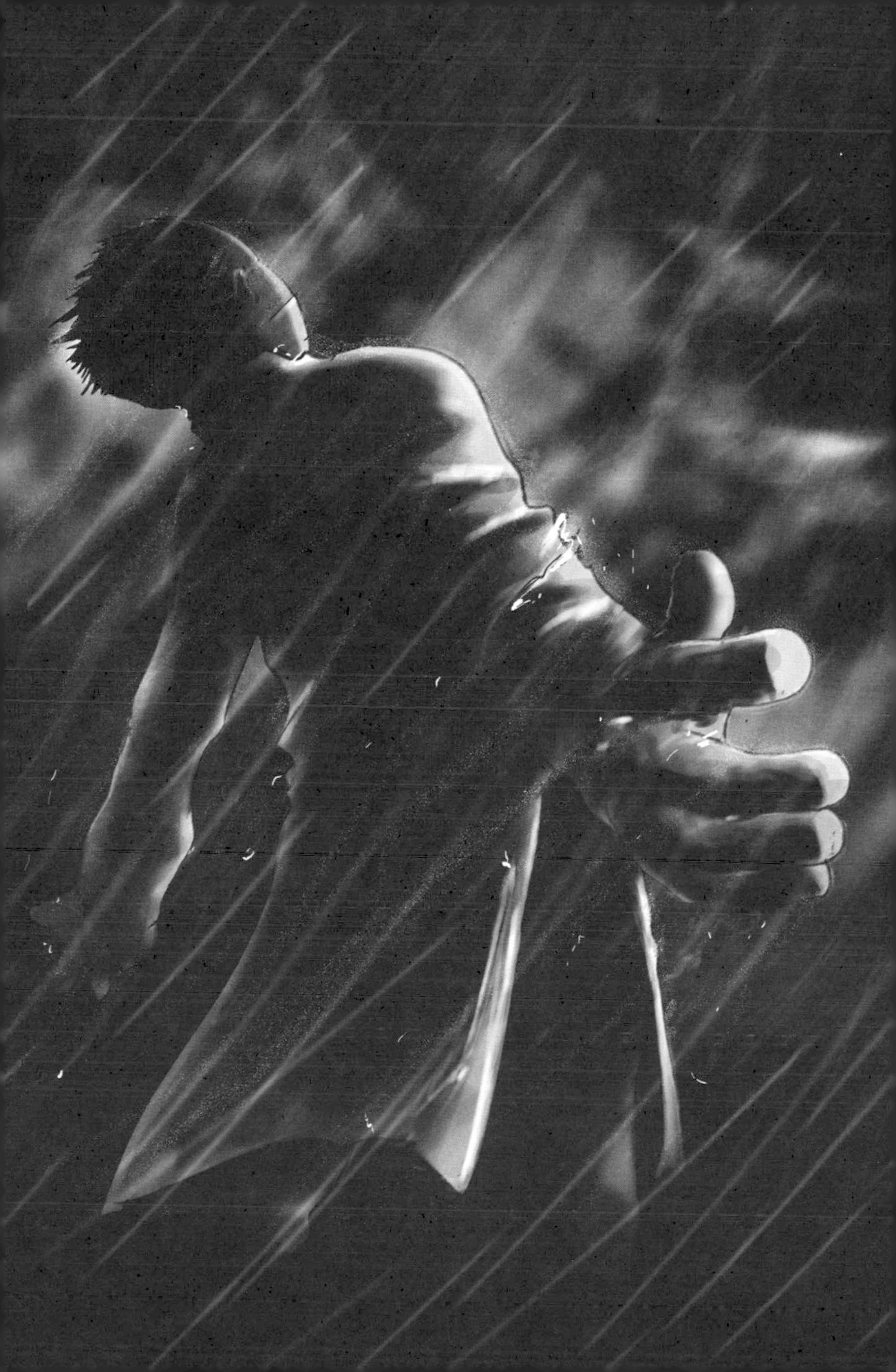

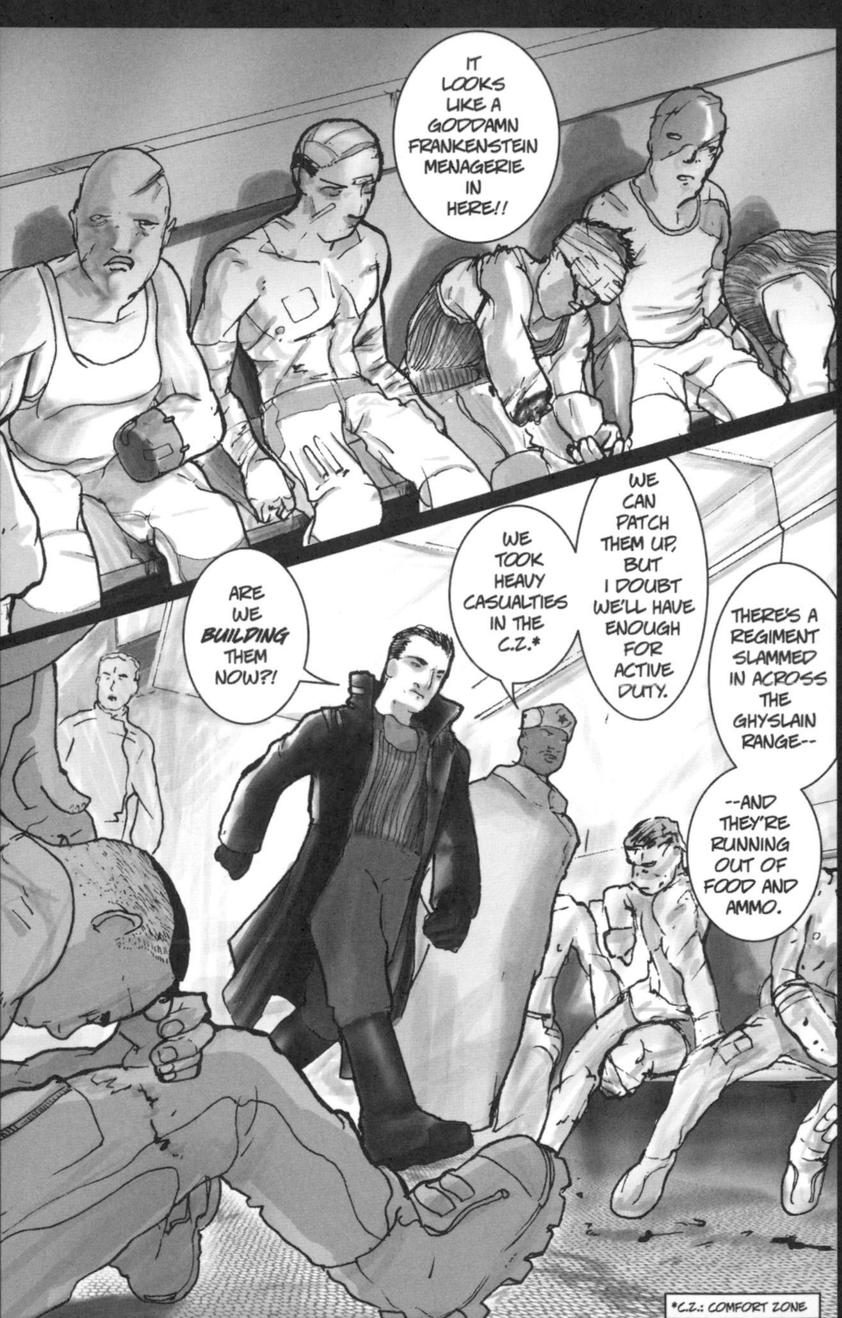
IT LOOKS LIKE A GODDAMN FRANKENSTEIN MENAGERIE IN HERE!!
ARE WE BUILDING THEM NOW?!
WE TOOK HEAVY CASUALTIES IN THE C.Z.*
WE CAN PATCH THEM UP, BUT I DOUBT WE'LL HAVE ENOUGH FOR ACTIVE DUTY.
THERE'S A REGIMENT SLAMMED IN ACROSS THE GHYSLAIN RANGE--
--AND THEY'RE RUNNING OUT OF FOOD AND AMMO.
*C.Z.: COMFORT ZONE

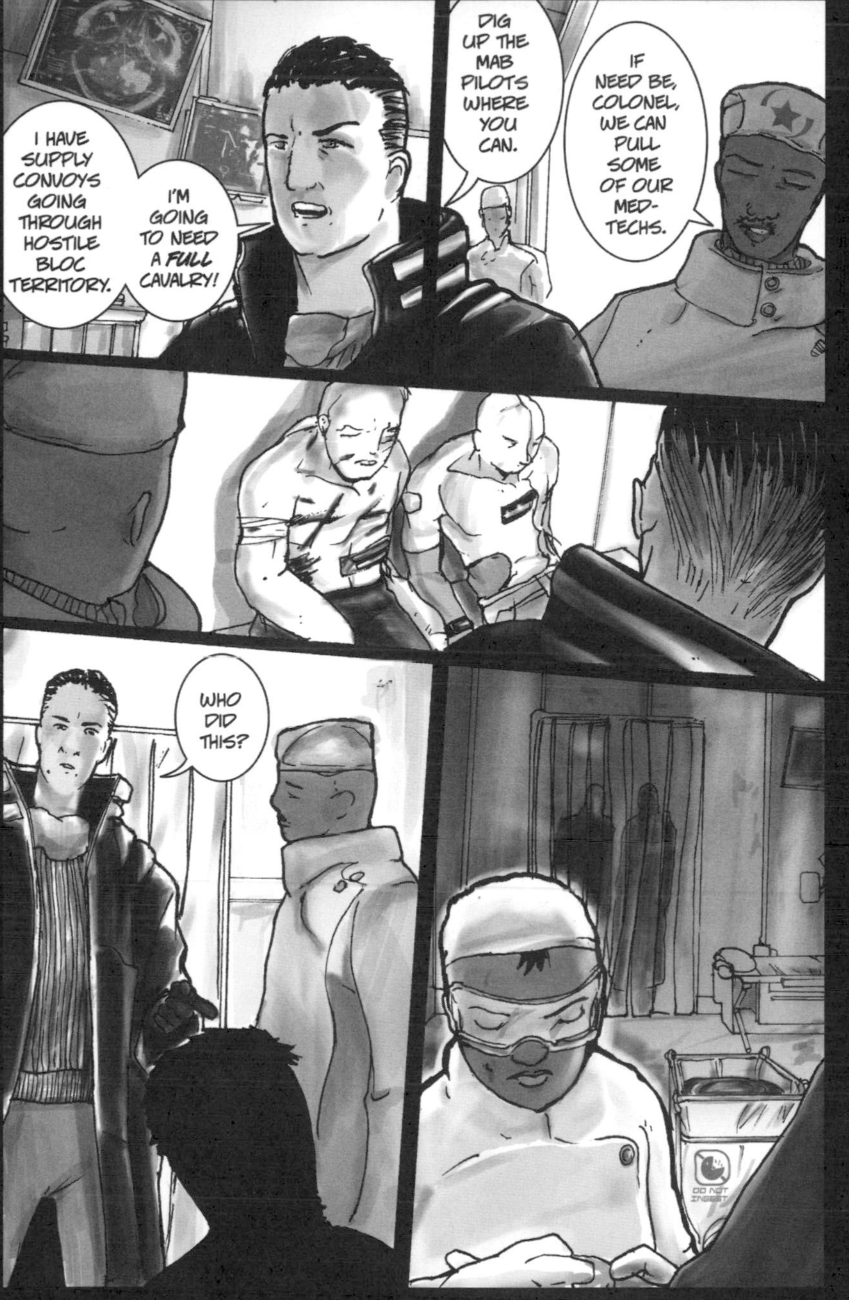
I HAVE SUPPLY CONVOYS GOING THROUGH HOSTILE BLOC TERRITORY.
I'M GOING TO NEED A *FULL* CAVALRY!
DIG UP THE MAB PILOTS WHERE YOU CAN.
IF NEED BE, COLONEL, WE CAN PULL SOME OF OUR MED-TECHS.
WHO DID THIS?
DO NOT INGEST

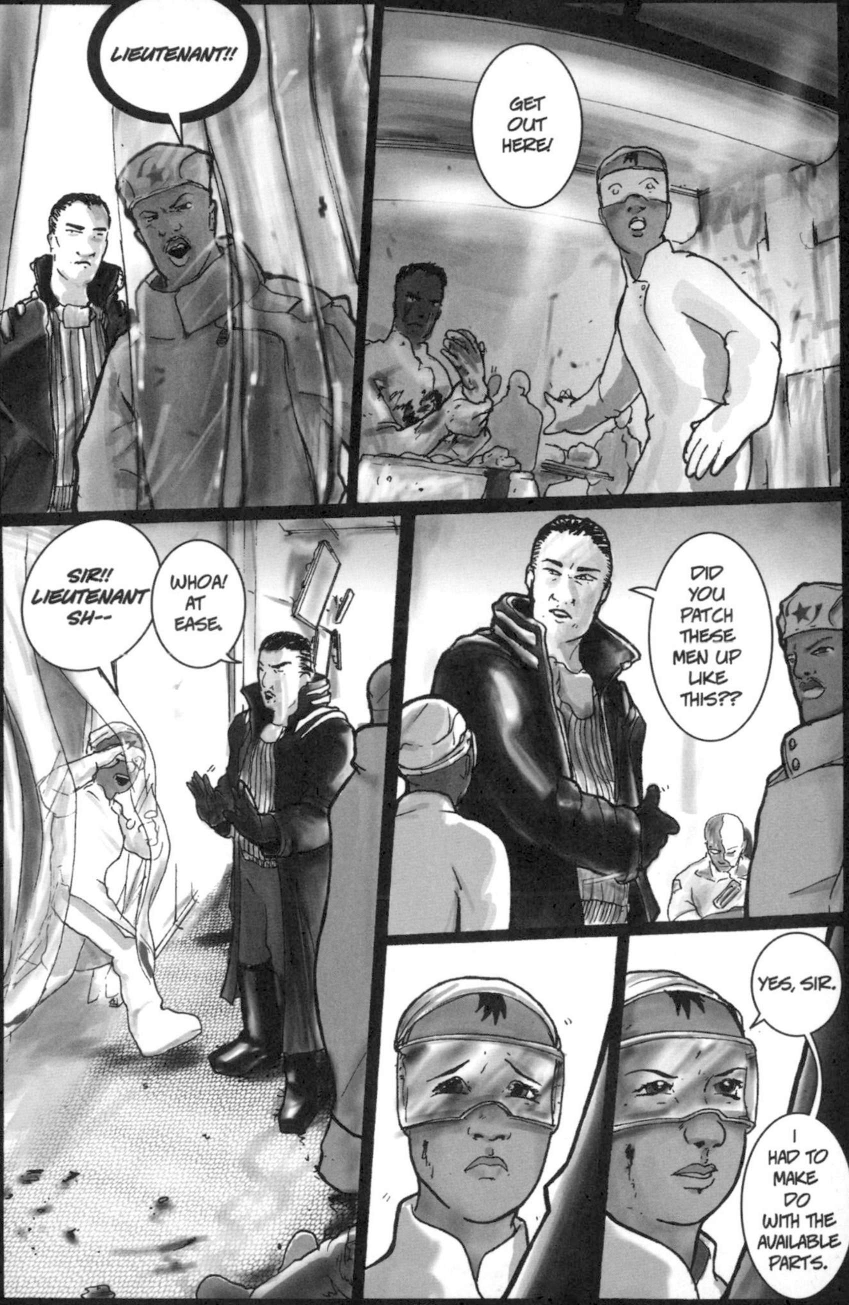
LIEUTENANT!!
GET OUT HERE!
SIR!! LIEUTENANT SH--
WHOA! AT EASE.
DID YOU PATCH THESE MEN UP LIKE THIS??
YES, SIR.
I HAD TO MAKE DO WITH THE AVAILABLE PARTS.

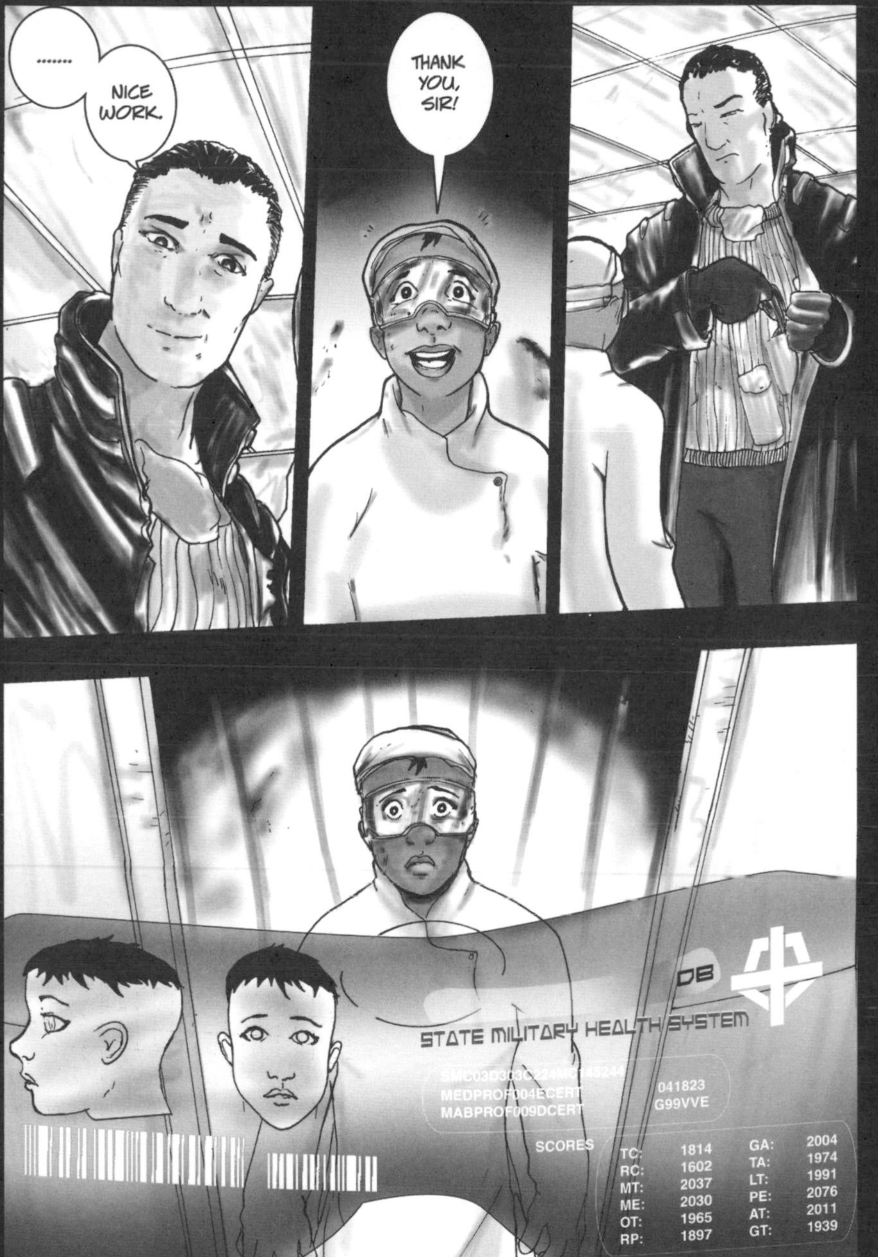
....
NICE WORK.
THANK YOU, SIR!
DB
STATE MILITARY HEALTH SYSTEM
SMC03D303C224MC145244
MEDPROF004ECERT
MABPROF009DCERT
041823
G99VVE
SCORES
TC: 1814
RC: 1602
MT: 2037
ME: 2030
OT: 1965
RP: 1897
GA: 2004
TA: 1974
LT: 1991
PE: 2076
AT: 2011
GT: 1939

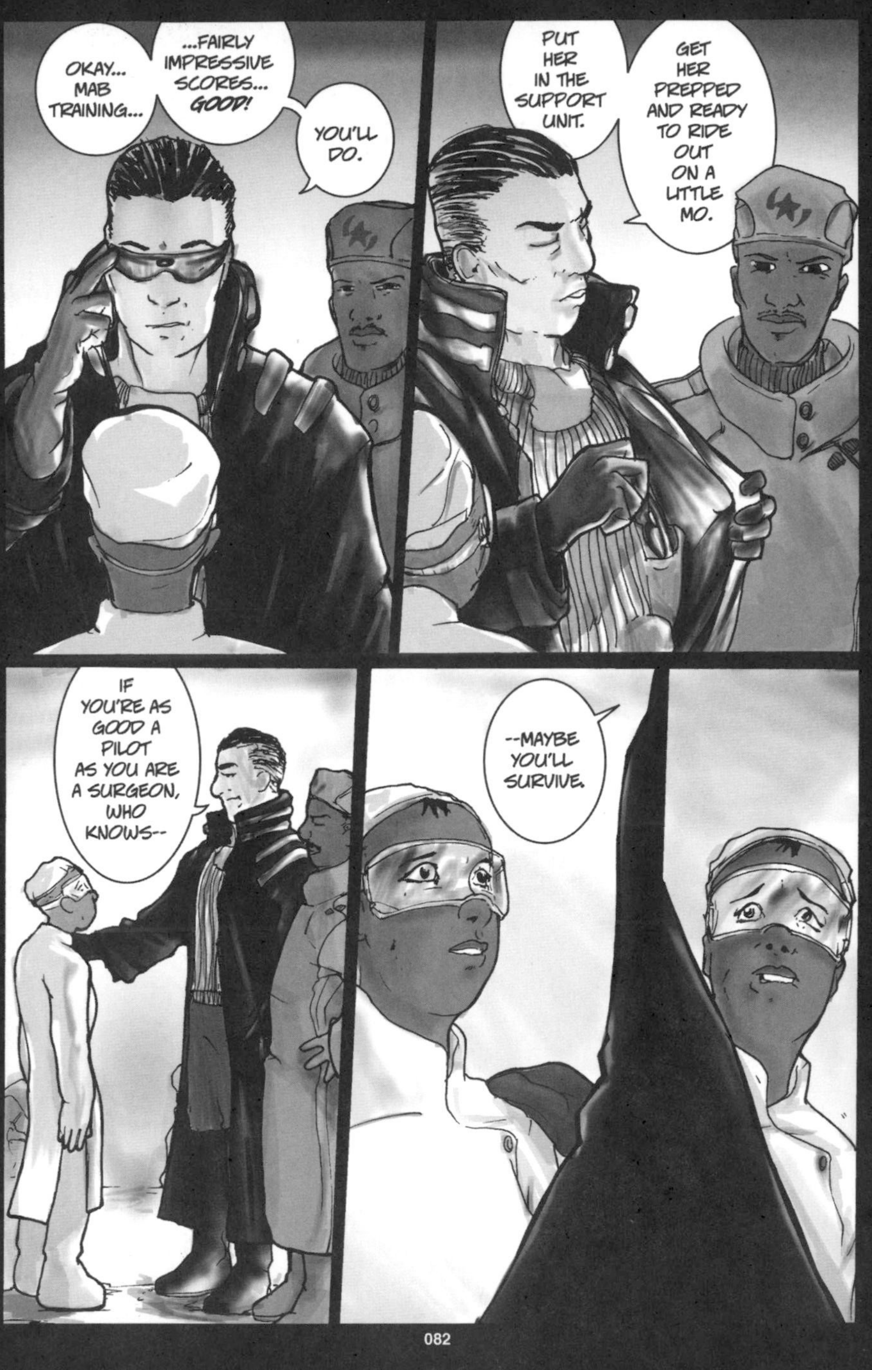
OKAY... MAB TRAINING...
...FAIRLY IMPRESSIVE SCORES... GOOD!
YOU'LL DO.
PUT HER IN THE SUPPORT UNIT.
GET HER PREPPED AND READY TO RIDE OUT ON A LITTLE MO.
IF YOU'RE AS GOOD A PILOT AS YOU ARE A SURGEON, WHO KNOWS--
--MAYBE YOU'LL SURVIVE.

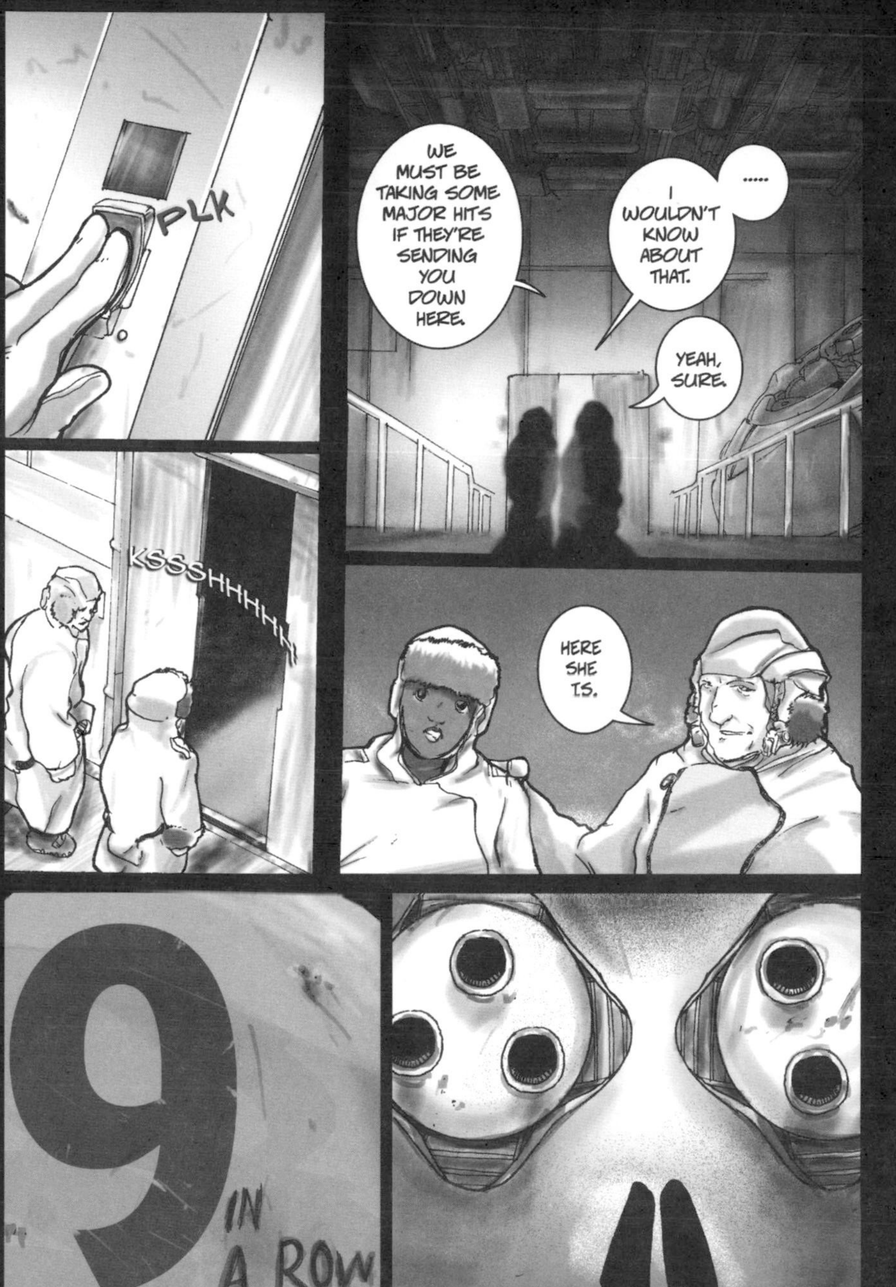
PLK
WE MUST BE TAKING SOME MAJOR HITS IF THEY'RE SENDING YOU DOWN HERE.
.....
I WOULDN'T KNOW ABOUT THAT.
YEAH, SURE.
KSSSHHHHHH
HERE SHE IS.
9 IN A ROW

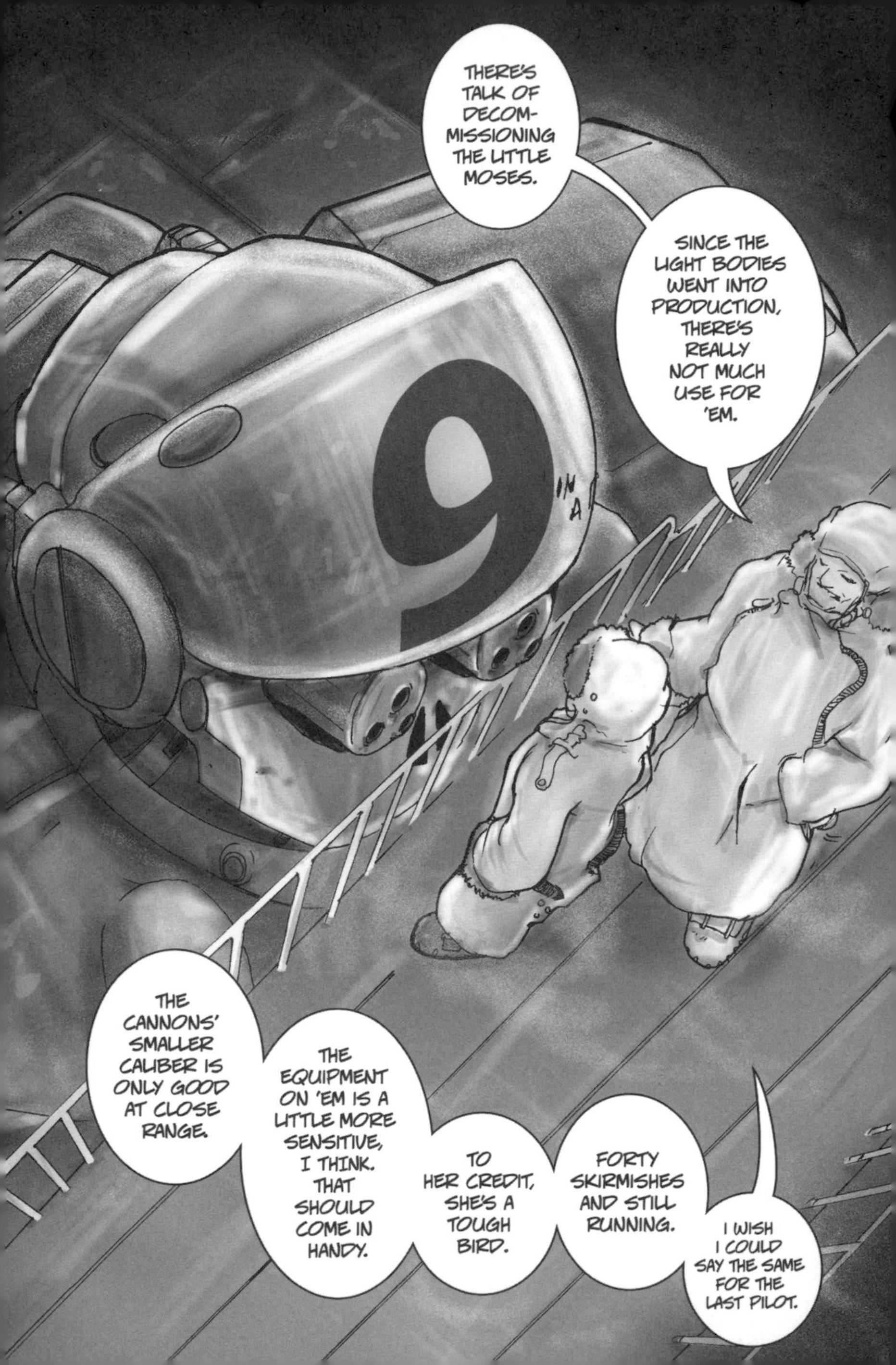
THERE'S TALK OF DECOM-MISSIONING THE LITTLE MOSES.
SINCE THE LIGHT BODIES WENT INTO PRODUCTION, THERE'S REALLY NOT MUCH USE FOR 'EM.
THE CANNONS' SMALLER CALIBER IS ONLY GOOD AT CLOSE RANGE.
THE EQUIPMENT ON 'EM IS A LITTLE MORE SENSITIVE, I THINK. THAT SHOULD COME IN HANDY.
TO HER CREDIT, SHE'S A TOUGH BIRD.
FORTY SKIRMISHES AND STILL RUNNING.
I WISH I COULD SAY THE SAME FOR THE LAST PILOT.

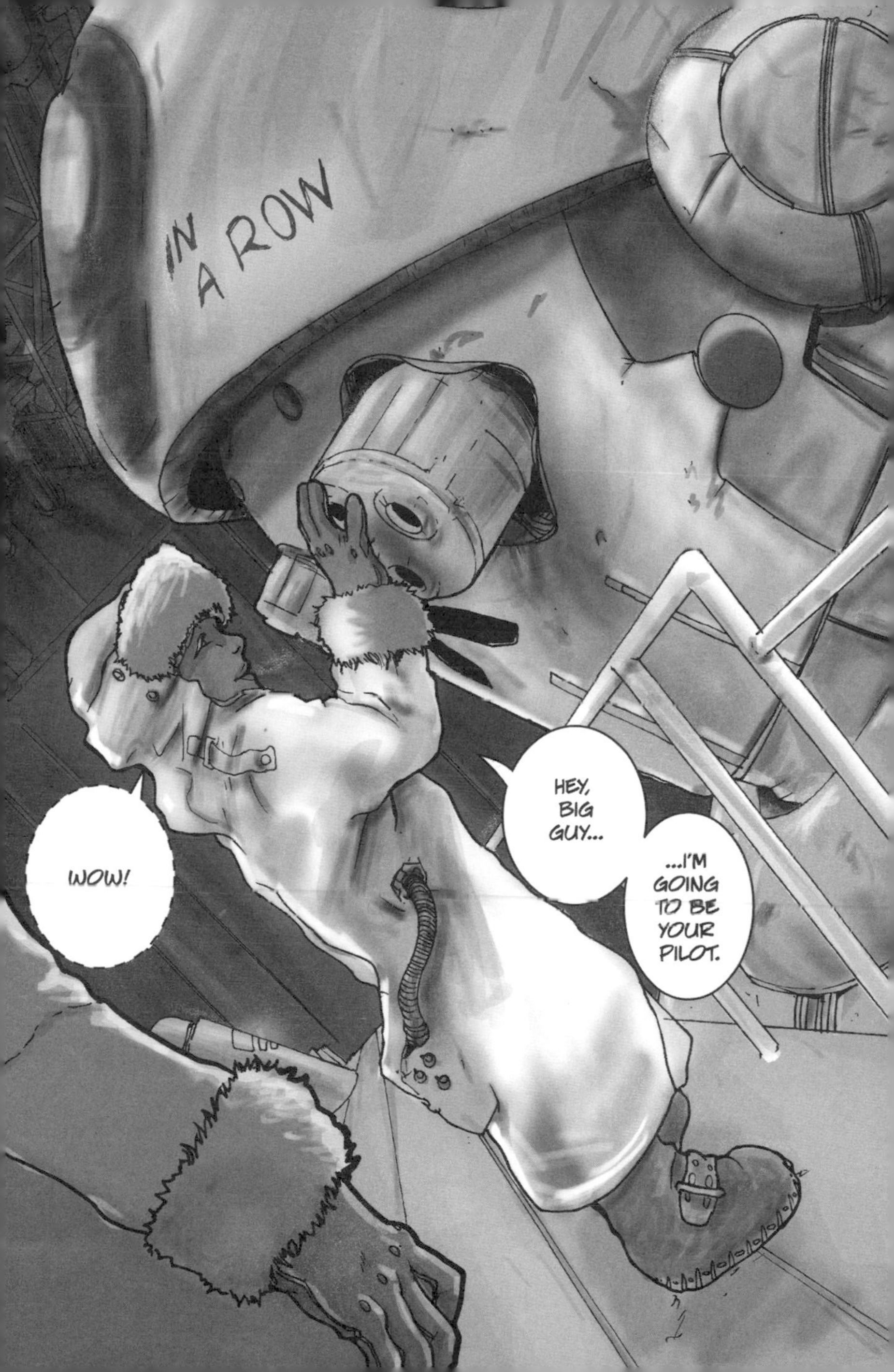
IN A ROW
HEY, BIG GUY...
...I'M GOING TO BE YOUR PILOT.
WOW!

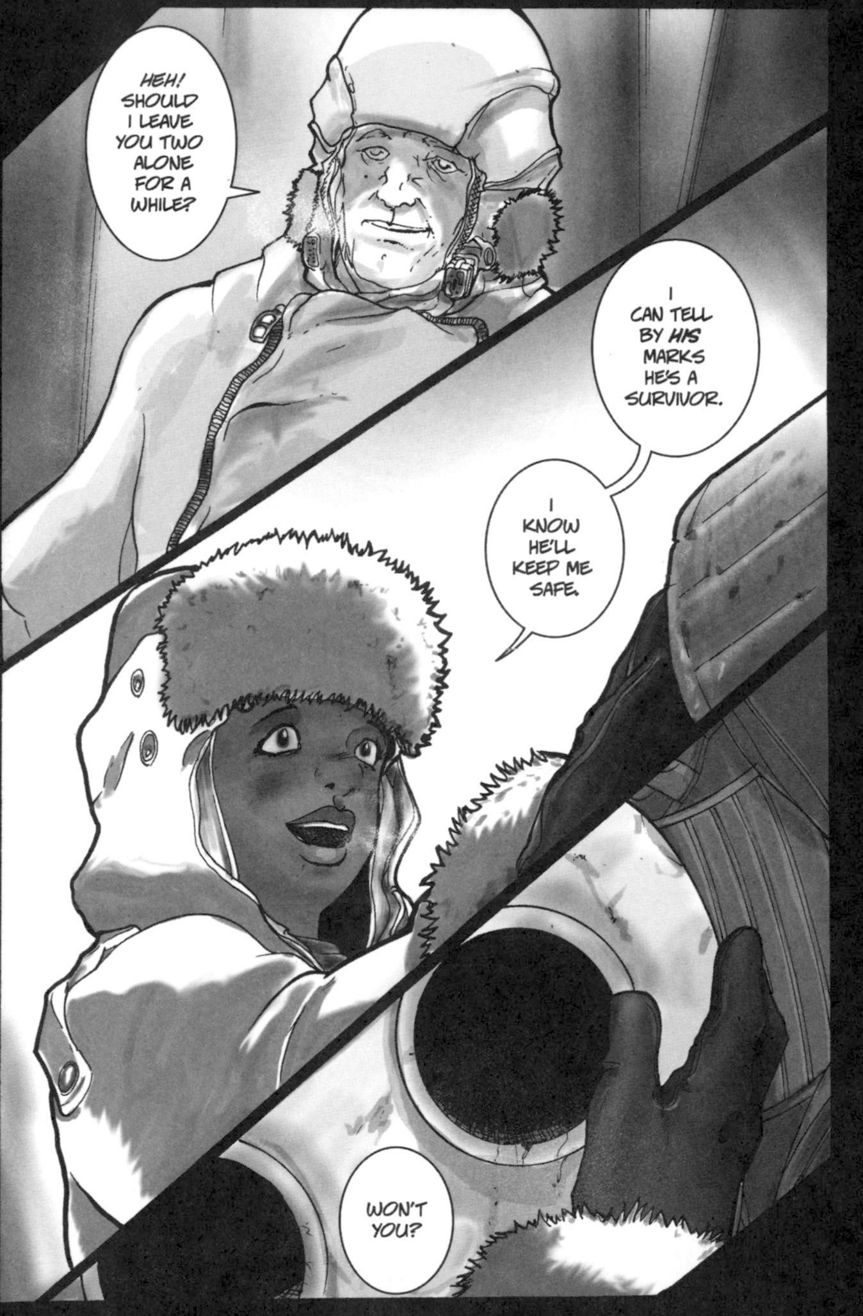
HEH! SHOULD I LEAVE YOU TWO ALONE FOR A WHILE?
I CAN TELL BY HIS MARKS HE'S A SURVIVOR.
I KNOW HE'LL KEEP ME SAFE.
WON'T YOU?

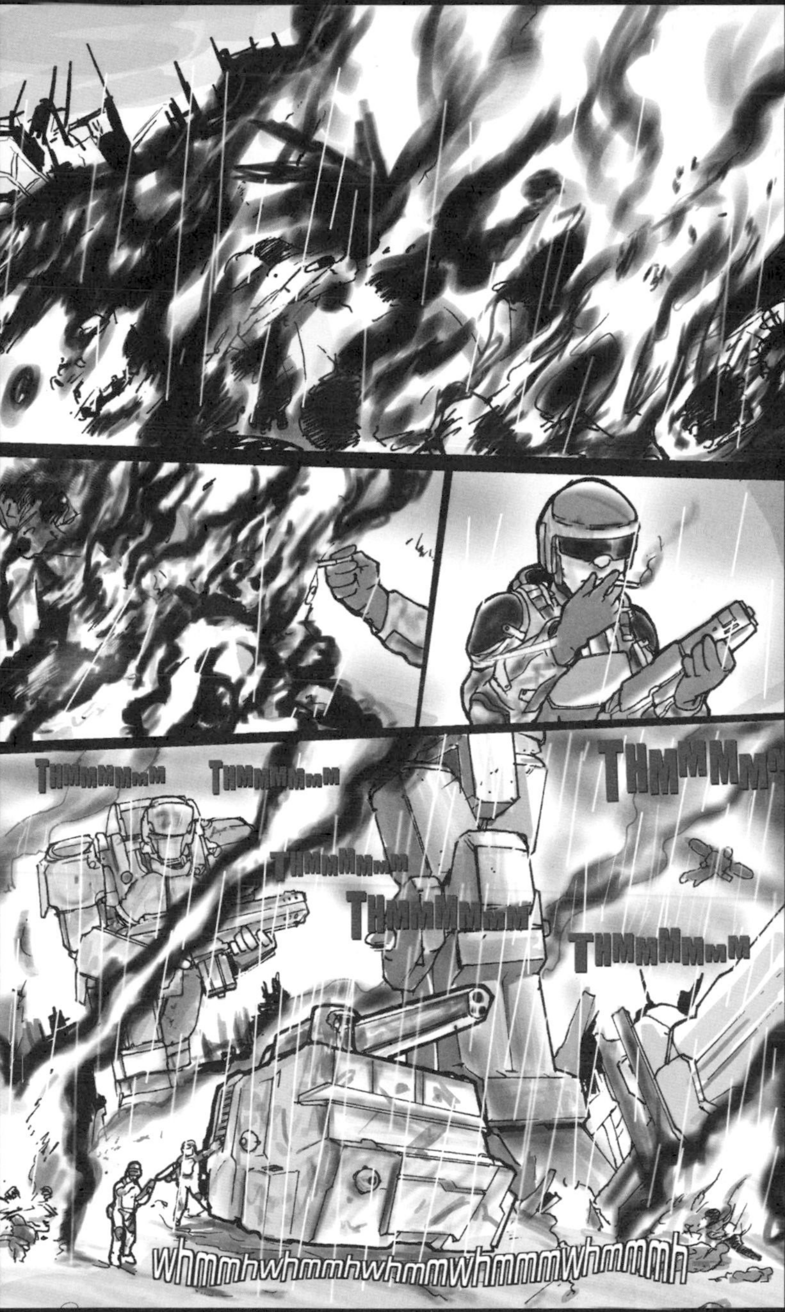
THMMMMMMM
THMMMMMMM
THMMMM
THMMMMMMM
THMMMMMMM
THMMMMMMM
whmmhwhmmmhwhmmmWhmmmmWhmmmmh

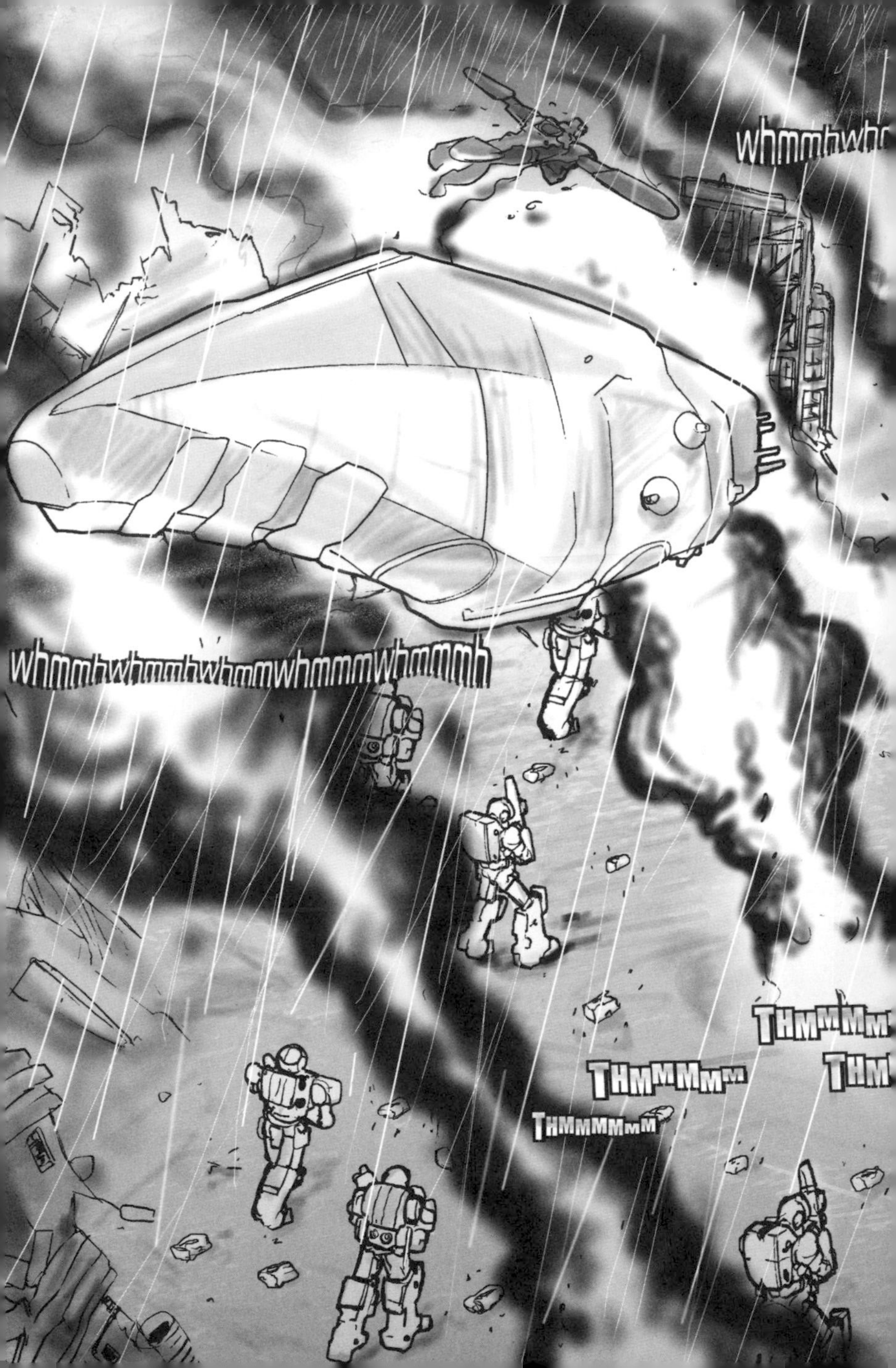
whmmhwhm
whmmhwhmmhwhmmwhmmmwhmmmh
THMMMM
THMMMMM
THM
THMMMMMM

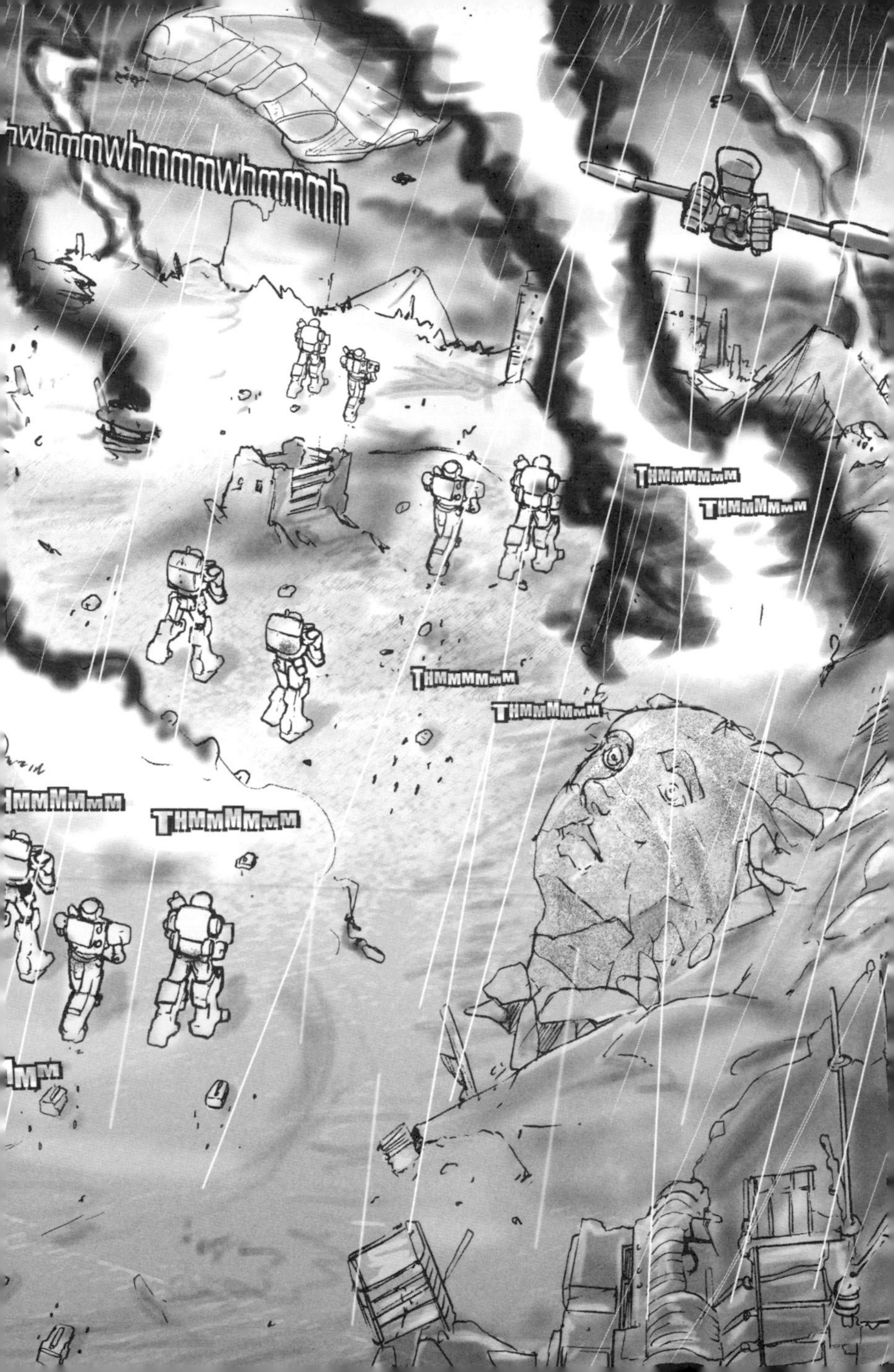

hwhmmwhmmmwhmmmh
THMMMMMM
THMMMMMM
THMMMMMM
THMMMMMM
IMMMMMM
THMMMMMM
IMM

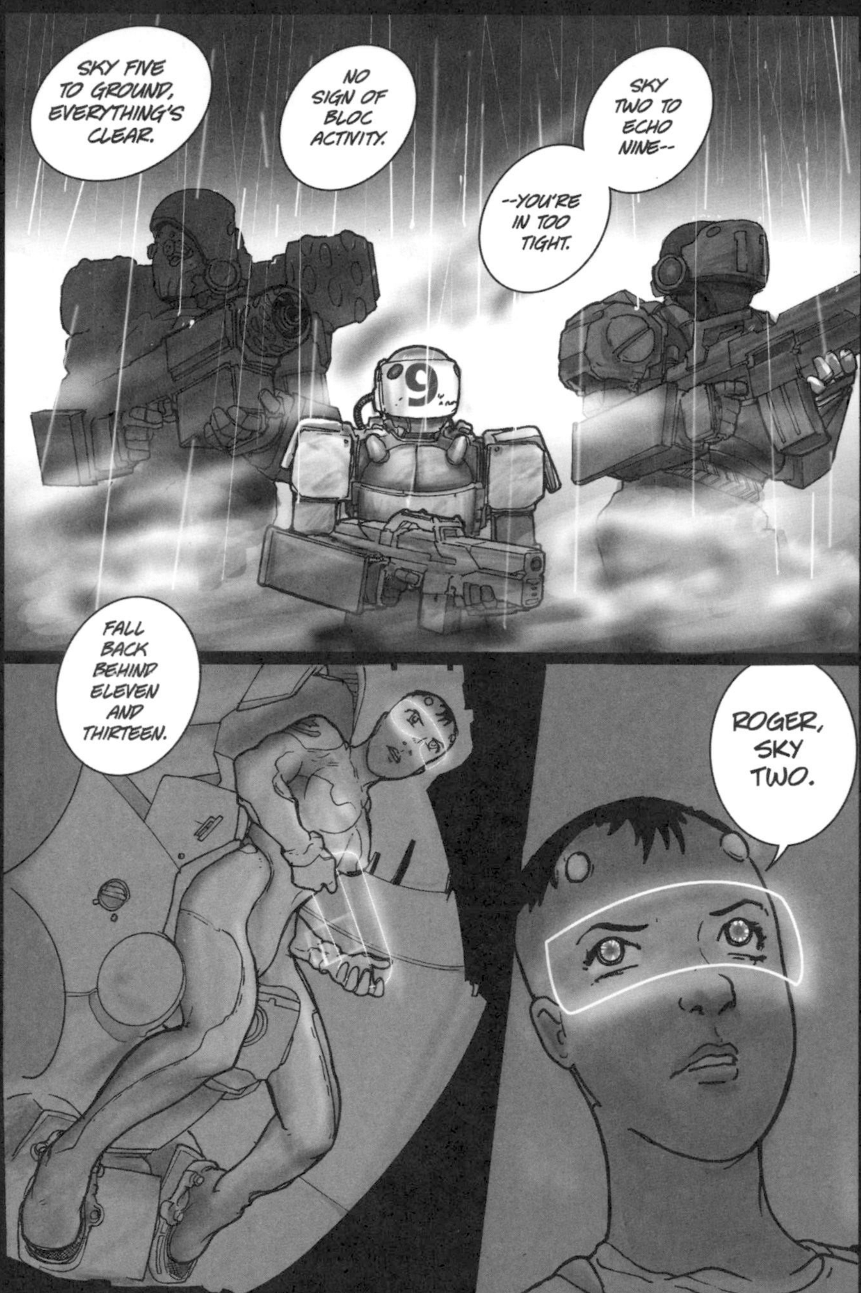
SKY FIVE TO GROUND, EVERYTHING'S CLEAR.
NO SIGN OF BLOC ACTIVITY.
SKY TWO TO ECHO NINE--
--YOU'RE IN TOO TIGHT.
FALL BACK BEHIND ELEVEN AND THIRTEEN.
ROGER, SKY TWO.

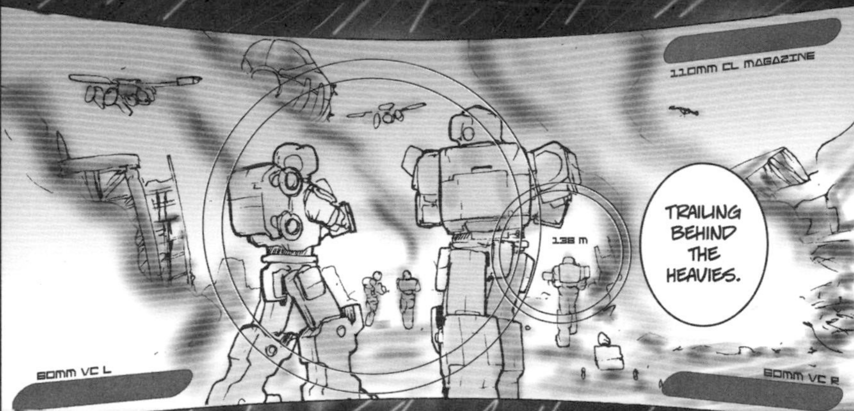
110MM CL MAGAZINE
138 M
TRAILING BEHIND THE HEAVIES.
60MM VC L
60MM VC R

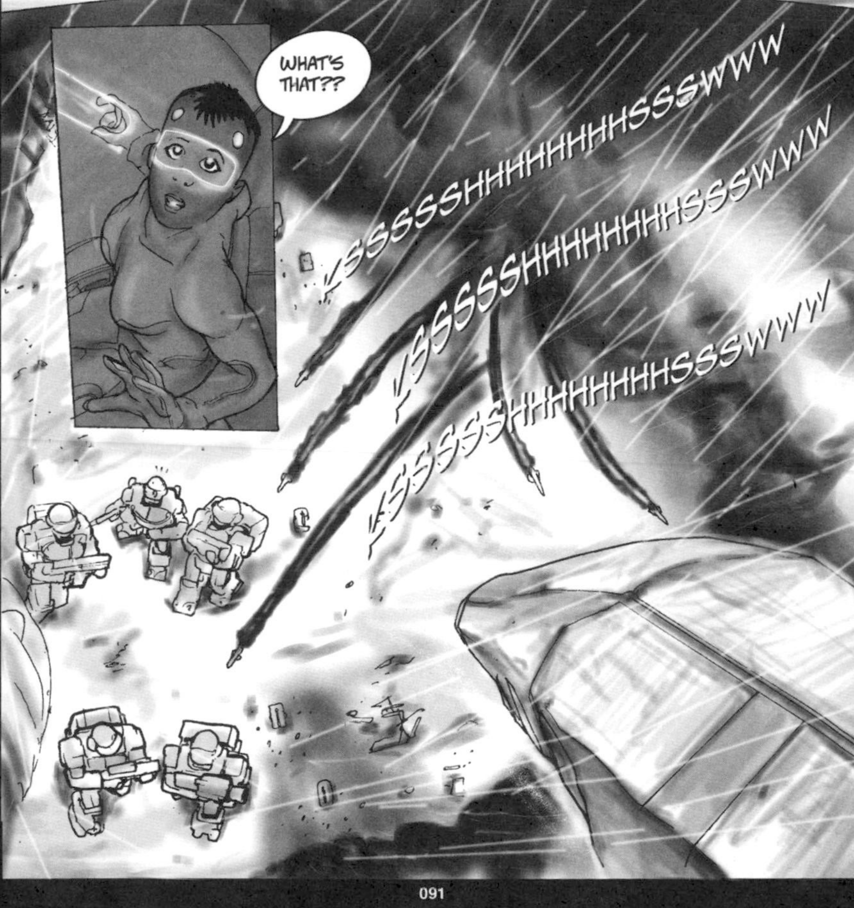
WHAT'S THAT??
KSSSSSHHHHHHHHHSSSWWW
KSSSSSHHHHHHHHHHSSSWWW
KSSSSSHHHHHHHHHHSSSWWW

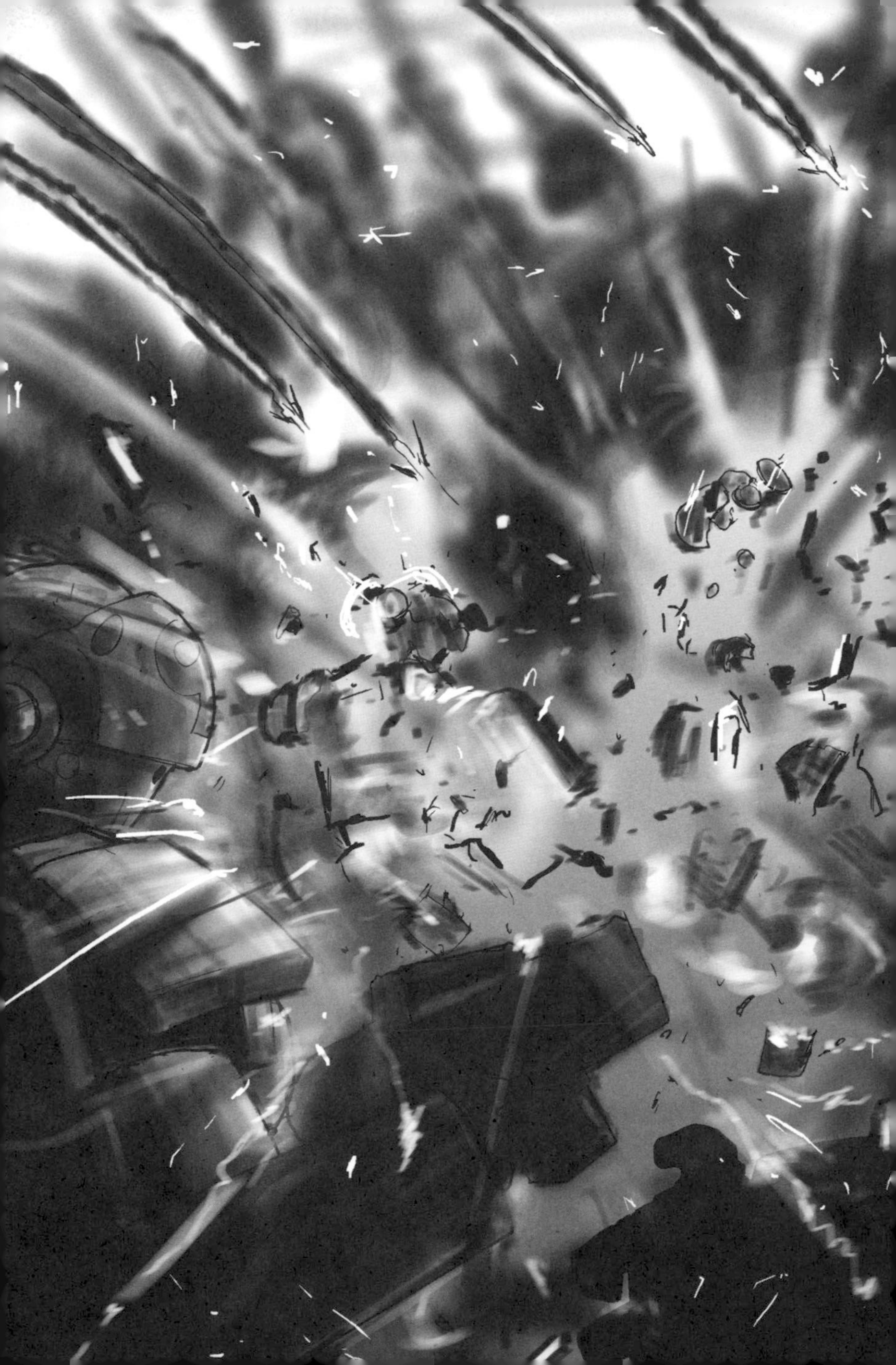

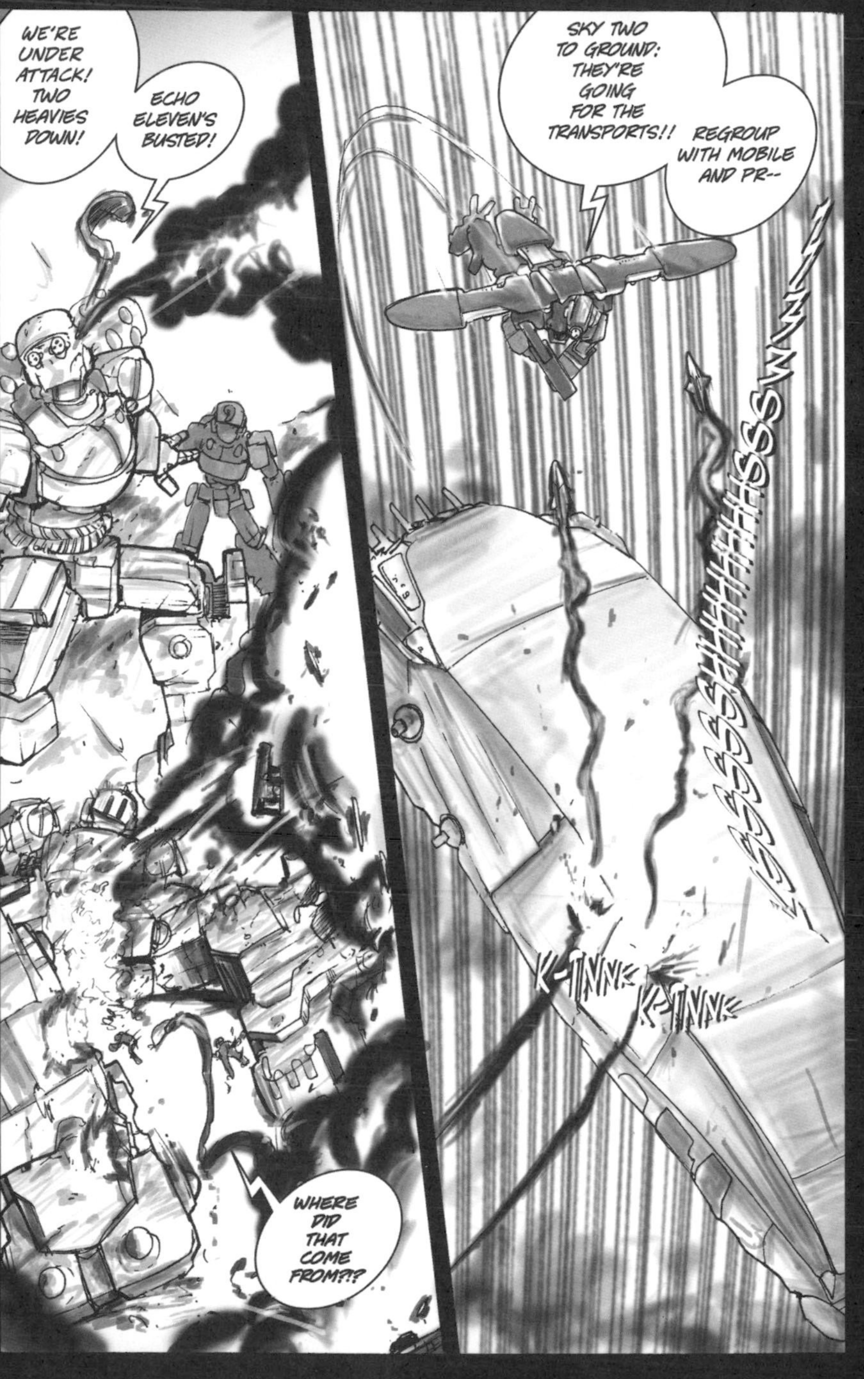
WE'RE UNDER ATTACK! TWO HEAVIES DOWN!
ECHO ELEVEN'S BUSTED!
SKY TWO TO GROUND: THEY'RE GOING FOR THE TRANSPORTS!!
REGROUP WITH MOBILE AND PR--
K-TINNK
K-TINNK
WHERE DID THAT COME FROM?!?

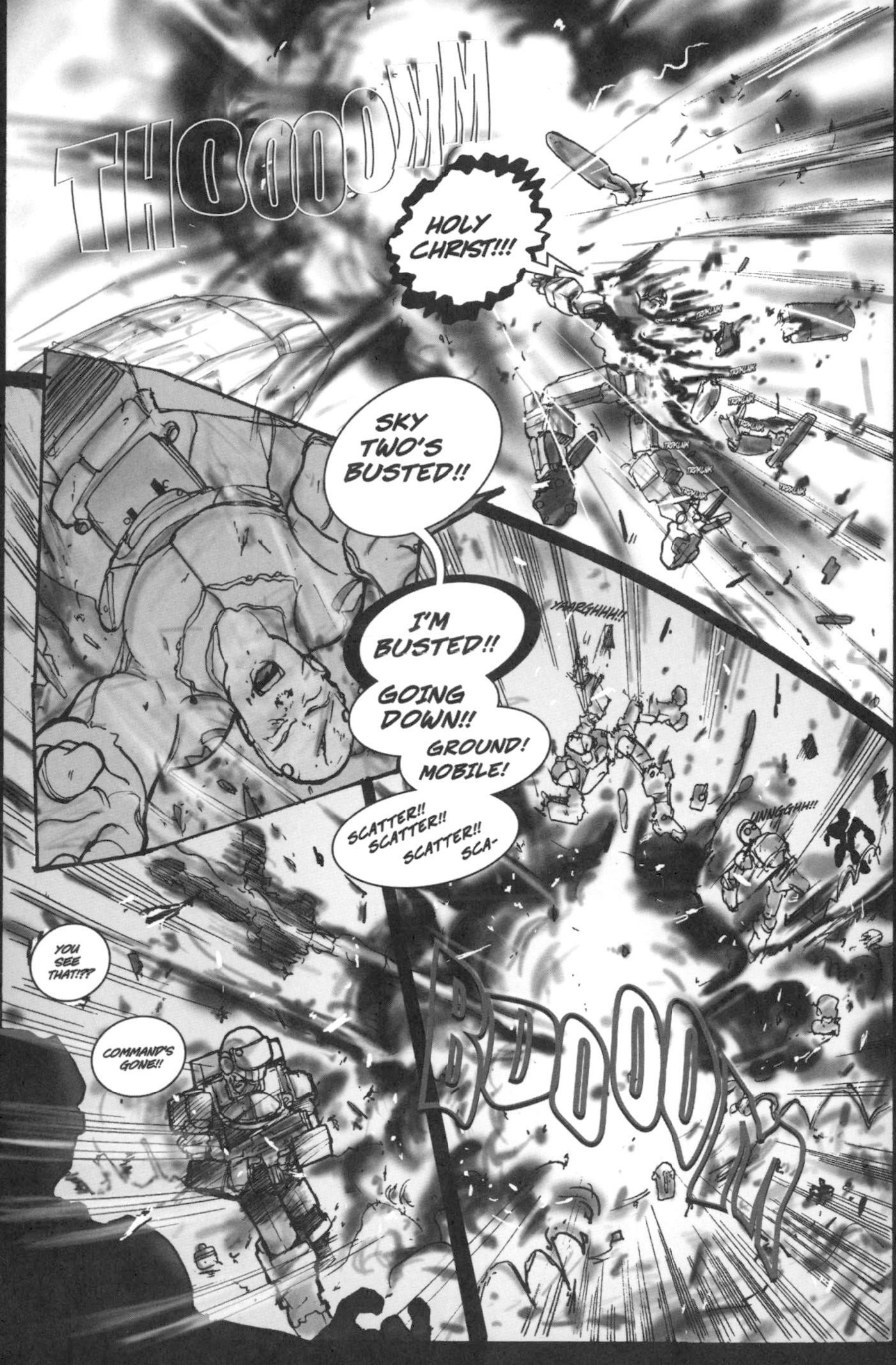
THOOOOMM
HOLY CHRIST!!!
SKY TWO'S BUSTED!!
I'M BUSTED!!
GOING DOWN!!
GROUND! MOBILE!
SCATTER!! SCATTER!! SCATTER!! SCA-
YAARGHHH!!
UNNGGHH!!
YOU SEE THAT!??
COMMAND'S GONE!!
BDOOOM

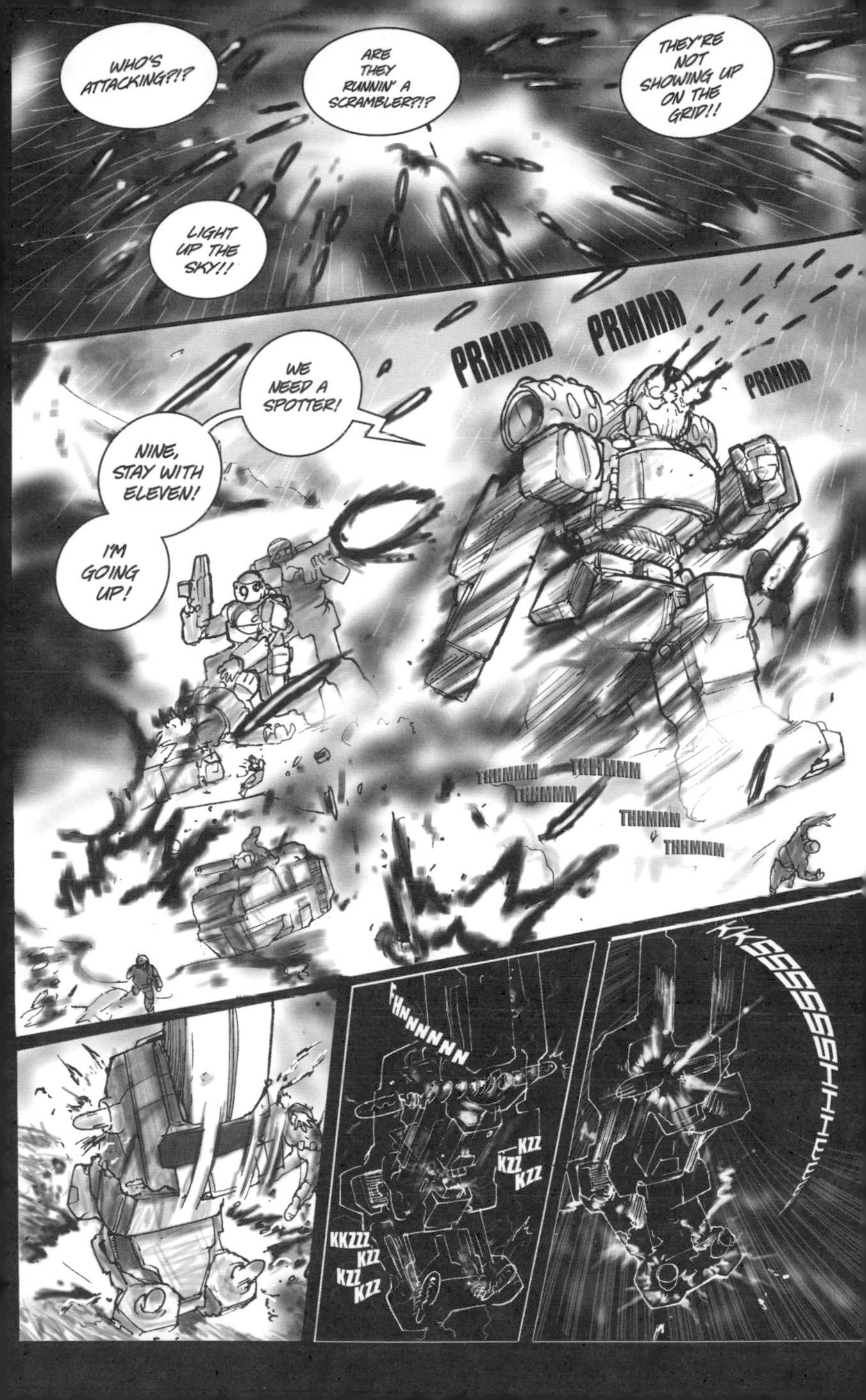
WHO'S ATTACKING?!?
ARE THEY RUNNIN' A SCRAMBLER?!?
THEY'RE NOT SHOWING UP ON THE GRID!!
LIGHT UP THE SKY!!
PRMMM PRMMM
PRMMM
WE NEED A SPOTTER!
NINE, STAY WITH ELEVEN!
I'M GOING UP!
THMMM THMMM
THMMM
THMMM
THMMM
FHNNNNNN
KZZ KZZ KZZ
KKZZZ KZZ KZZ KZZ
KKSSSSSSHHH

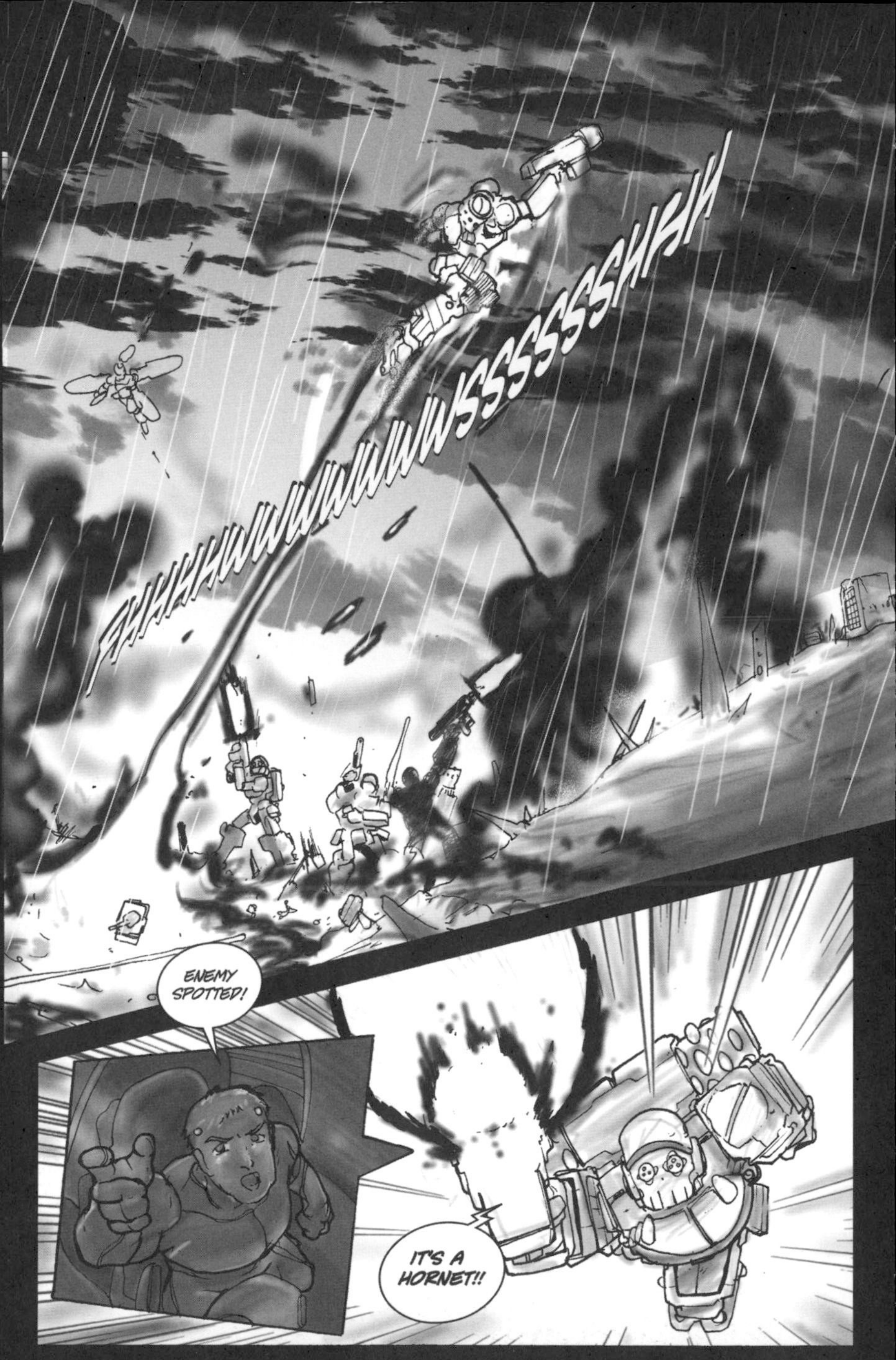
PHHHHWWWWWWWWWSSSSSSSHHH
ENEMY SPOTTED!
IT'S A HORNET!!

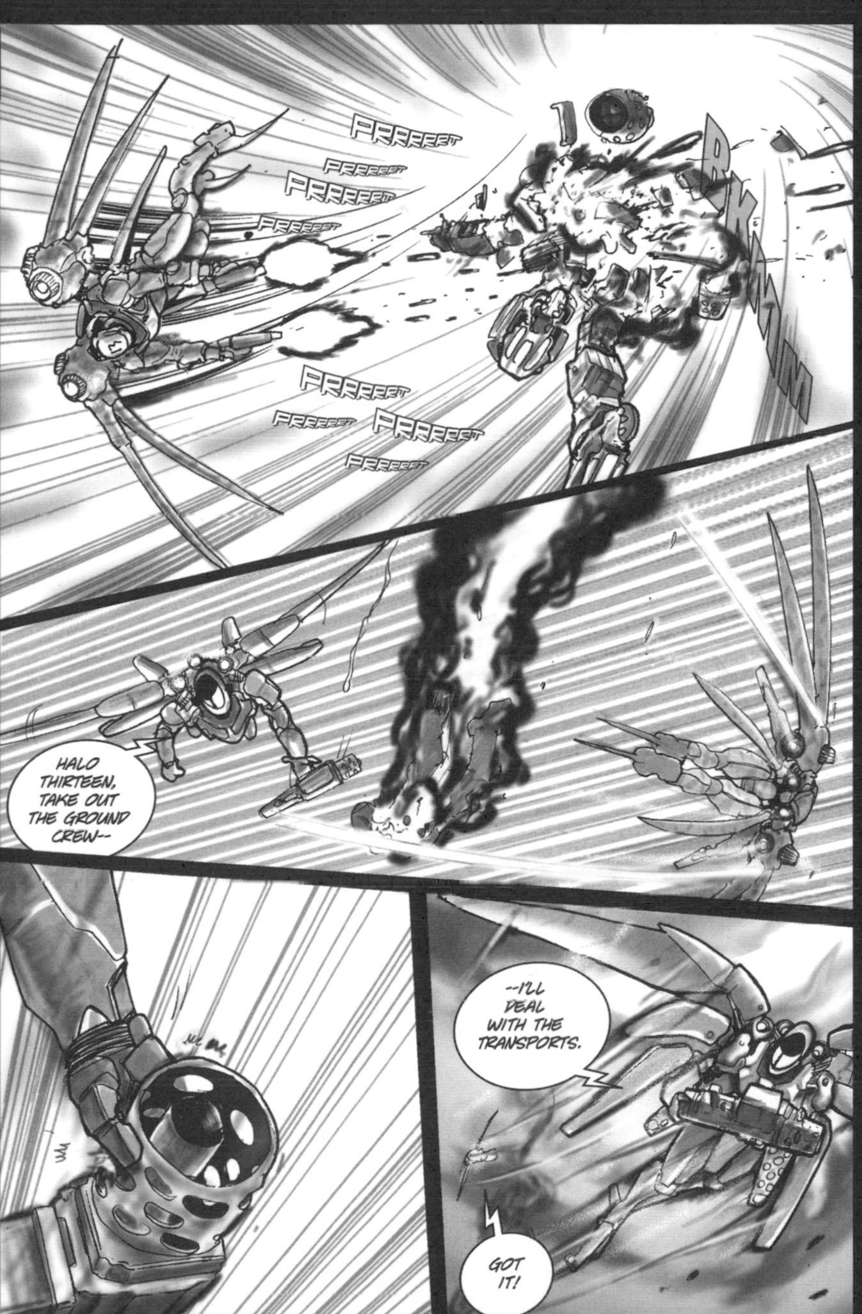
PRRREEEET
PRRREEEET
PRRREEEET
PRRREEEET
BKWMM
PRRREEEET
PRRREEEET
PRRREEEET
PRRREEEET
HALO THIRTEEN, TAKE OUT THE GROUND CREW--
--I'LL DEAL WITH THE TRANSPORTS.
GOT IT!

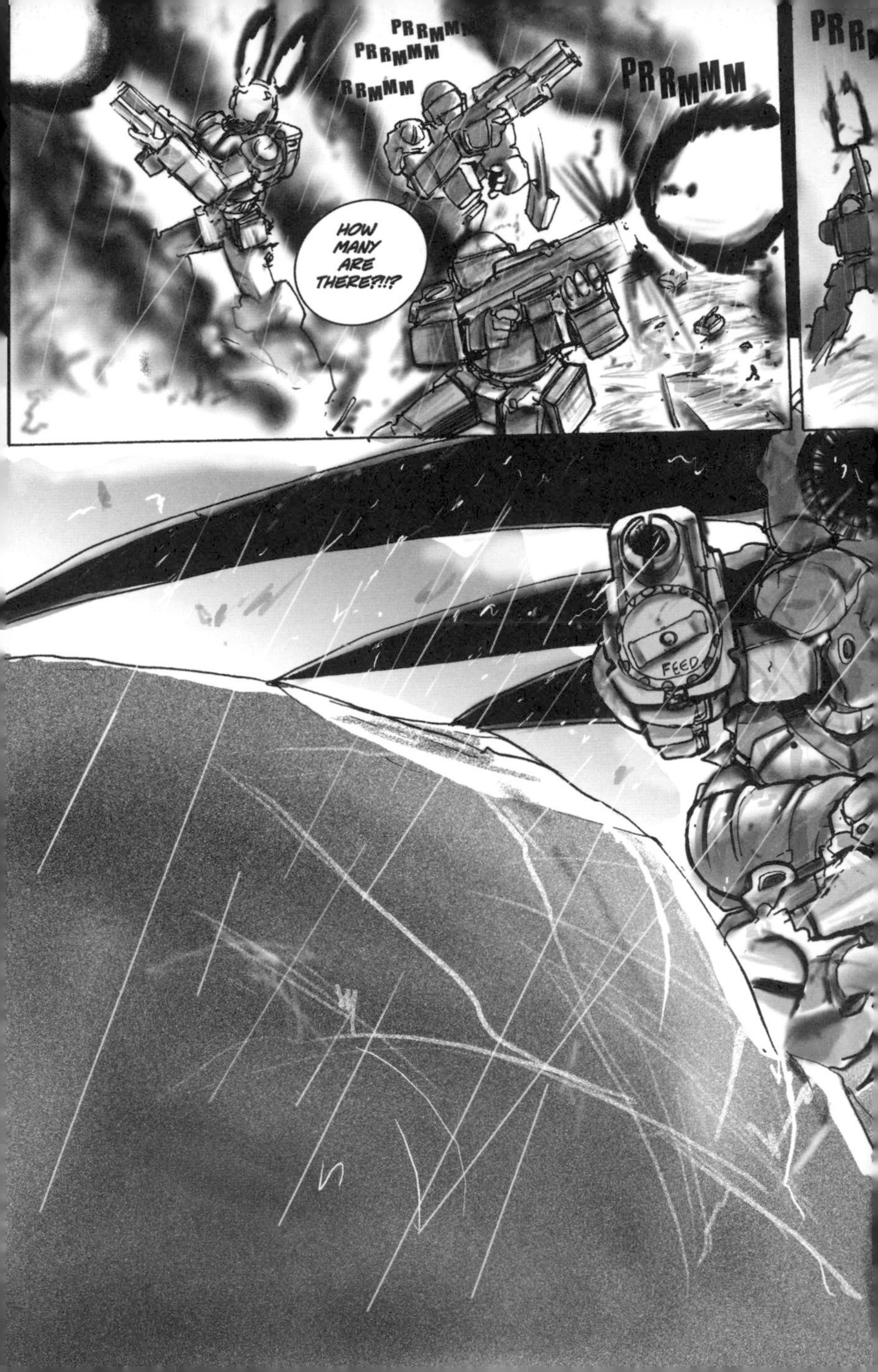
PRRMMM
PRRMMM
RRMMM
PRRMMM
HOW MANY ARE THERE?!!?
FEED

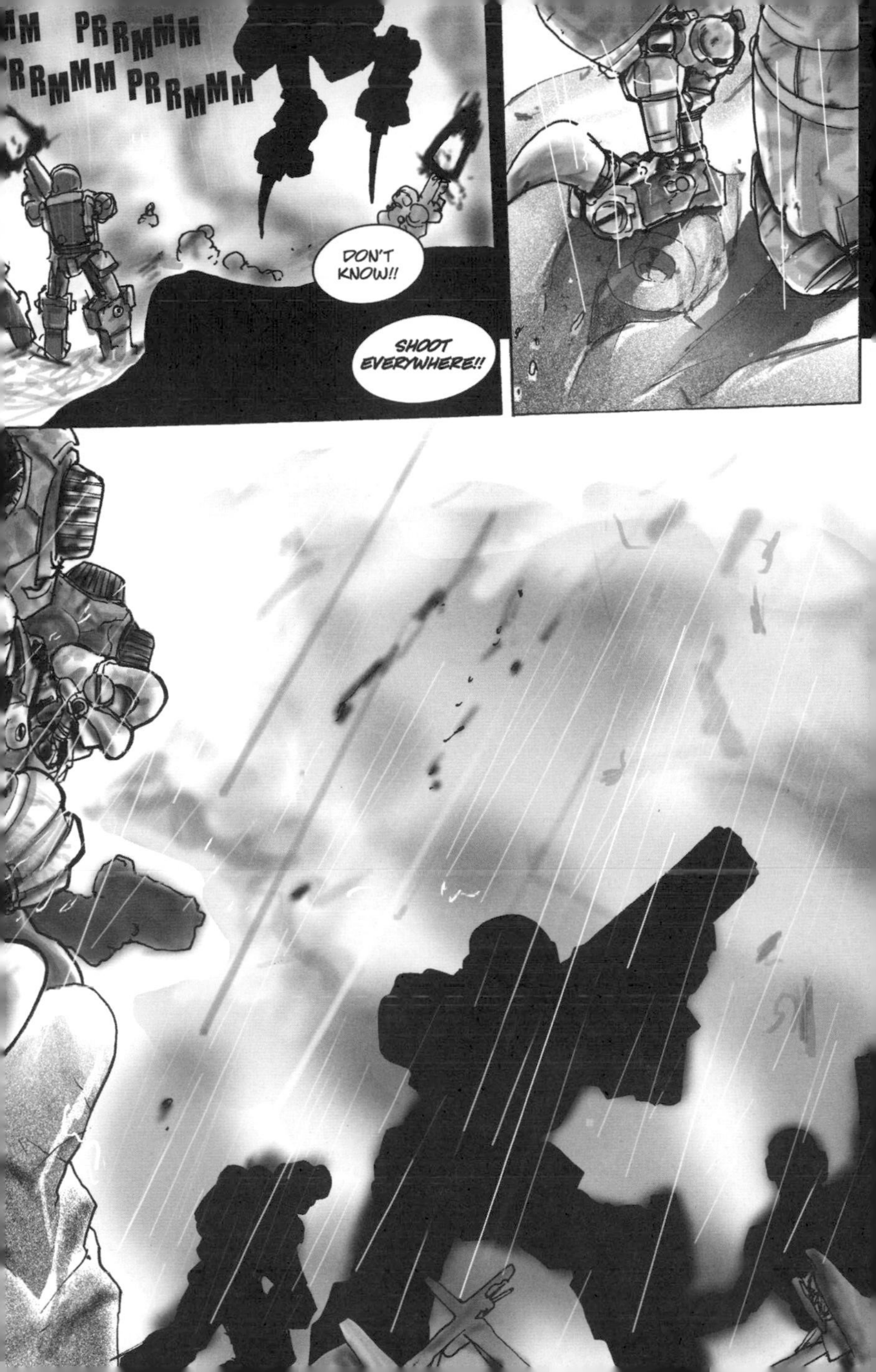

MM PRRMMM
RRMMM PRRMMM
DON'T KNOW!!
SHOOT EVERYWHERE!!

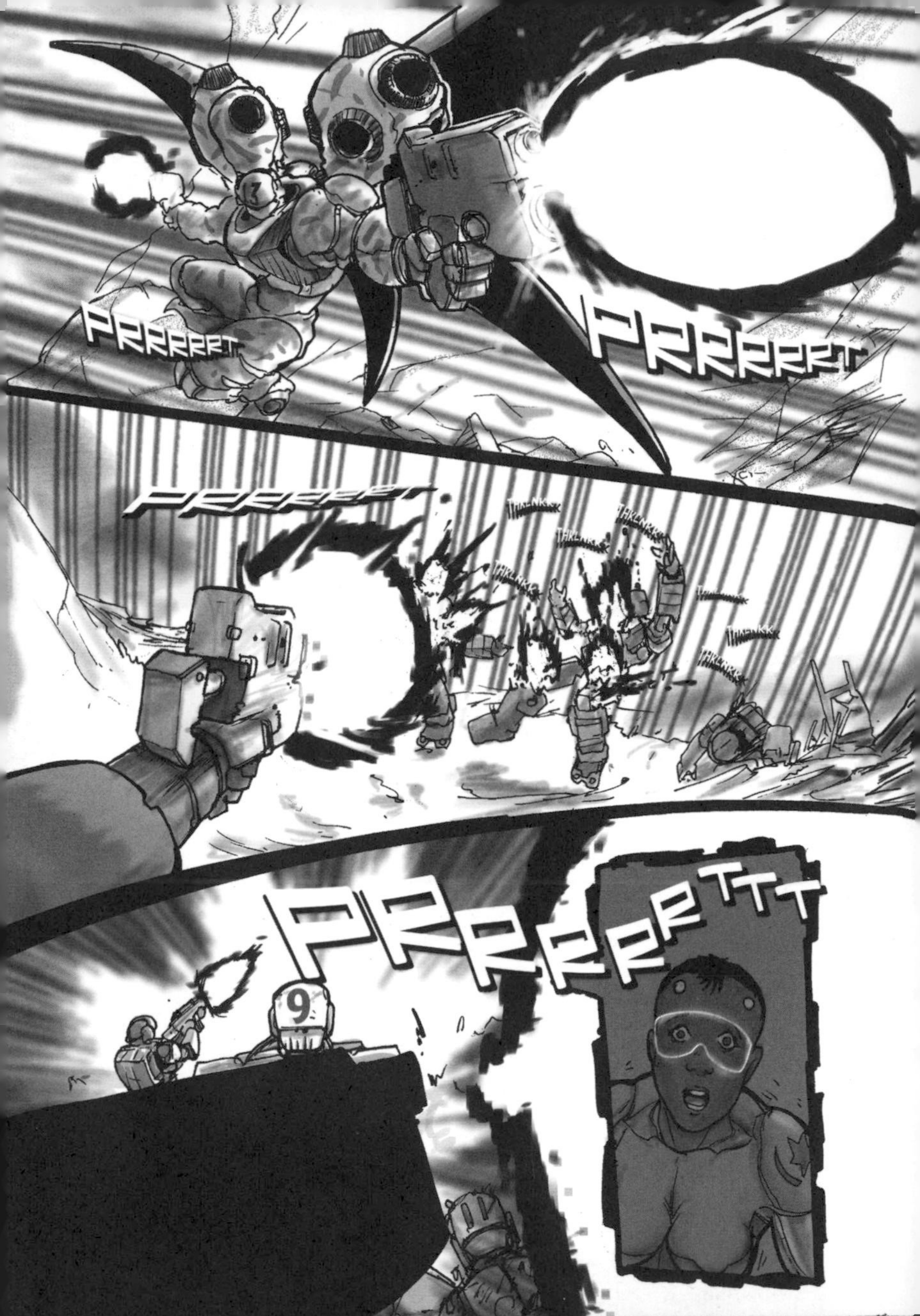
PRRRRRT
PRRRRRRT
PRRRRRT
THKLNKK
THKLNKK
THKLNKK
THKLNKK
THKLNKK
THKLNKK
PRRRRRRTTT

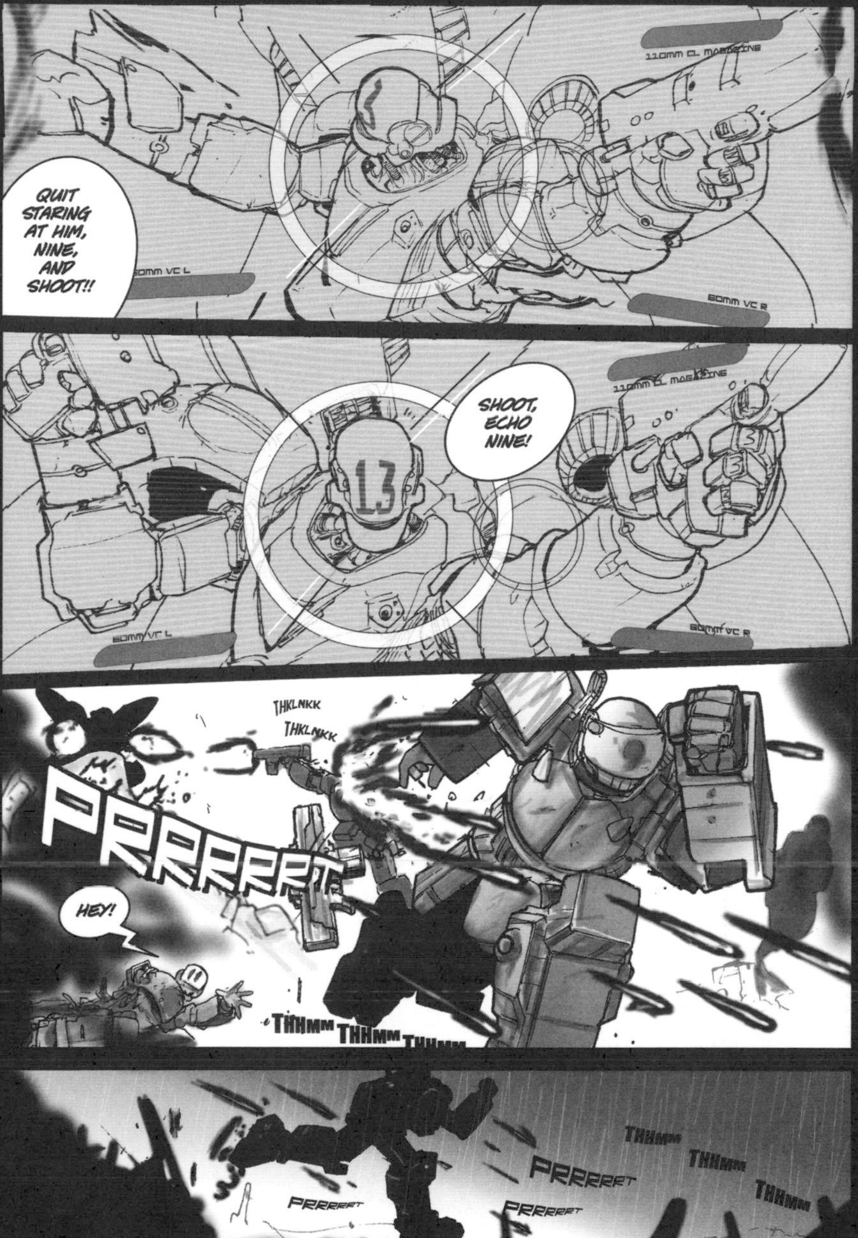
110MM CL MAGAZINE
QUIT STARING AT HIM, NINE, AND SHOOT!!
60MM VC L
60MM VC R
110MM CL MAGAZINE
SHOOT, ECHO NINE!
60MM VC L
60MM VC R
THKLNKK
THKLNKK
PRRRRRRT
HEY!
THHMM THHMM
THHMM
THHMM
PRRRRRT
THHMM
PRRRRRT
PRRRRRT

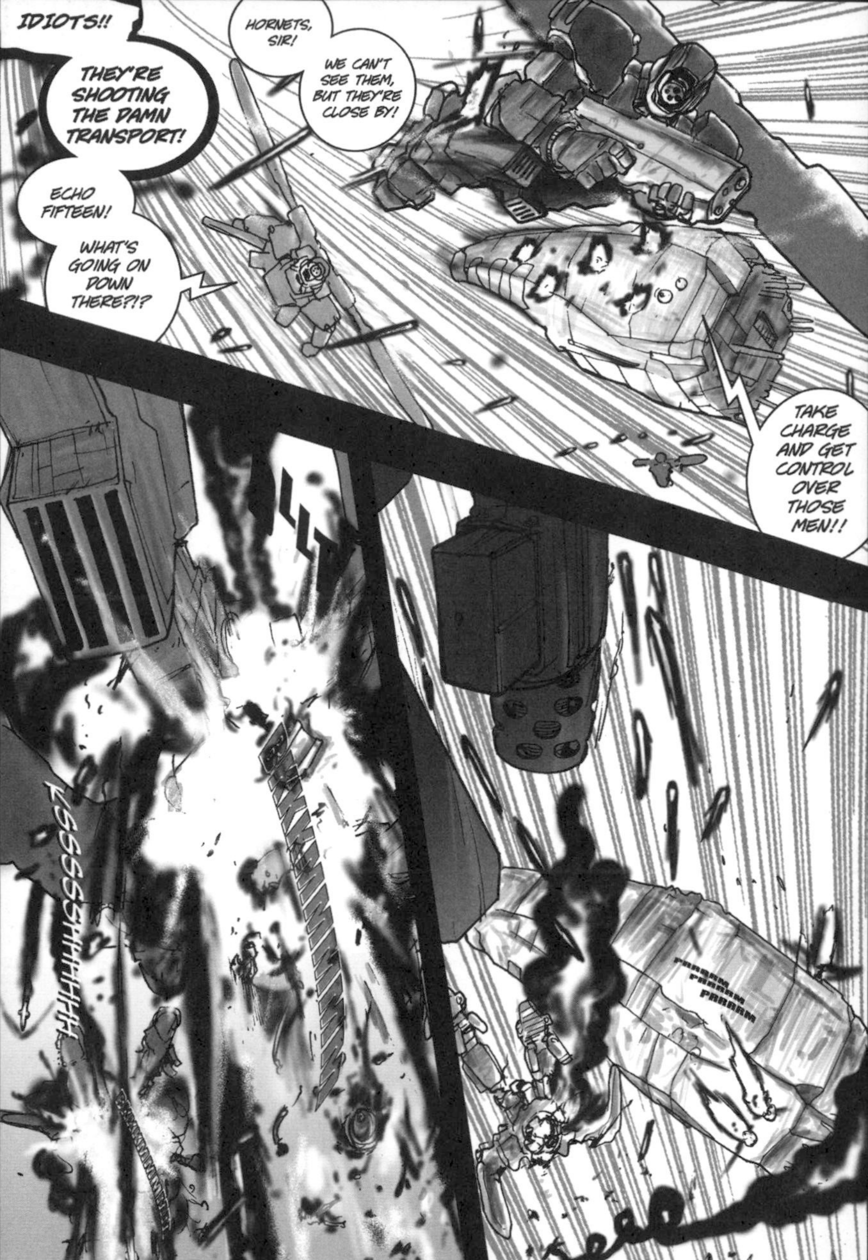
IDIOTS!!
THEY'RE SHOOTING THE DAMN TRANSPORT!
HORNETS, SIR!
WE CAN'T SEE THEM, BUT THEY'RE CLOSE BY!
ECHO FIFTEEN!
WHAT'S GOING ON DOWN THERE?!?
TAKE CHARGE AND GET CONTROL OVER THOSE MEN!!
KSSSSSHHHHHH
PRRRAM PRRRAM PRRRAM

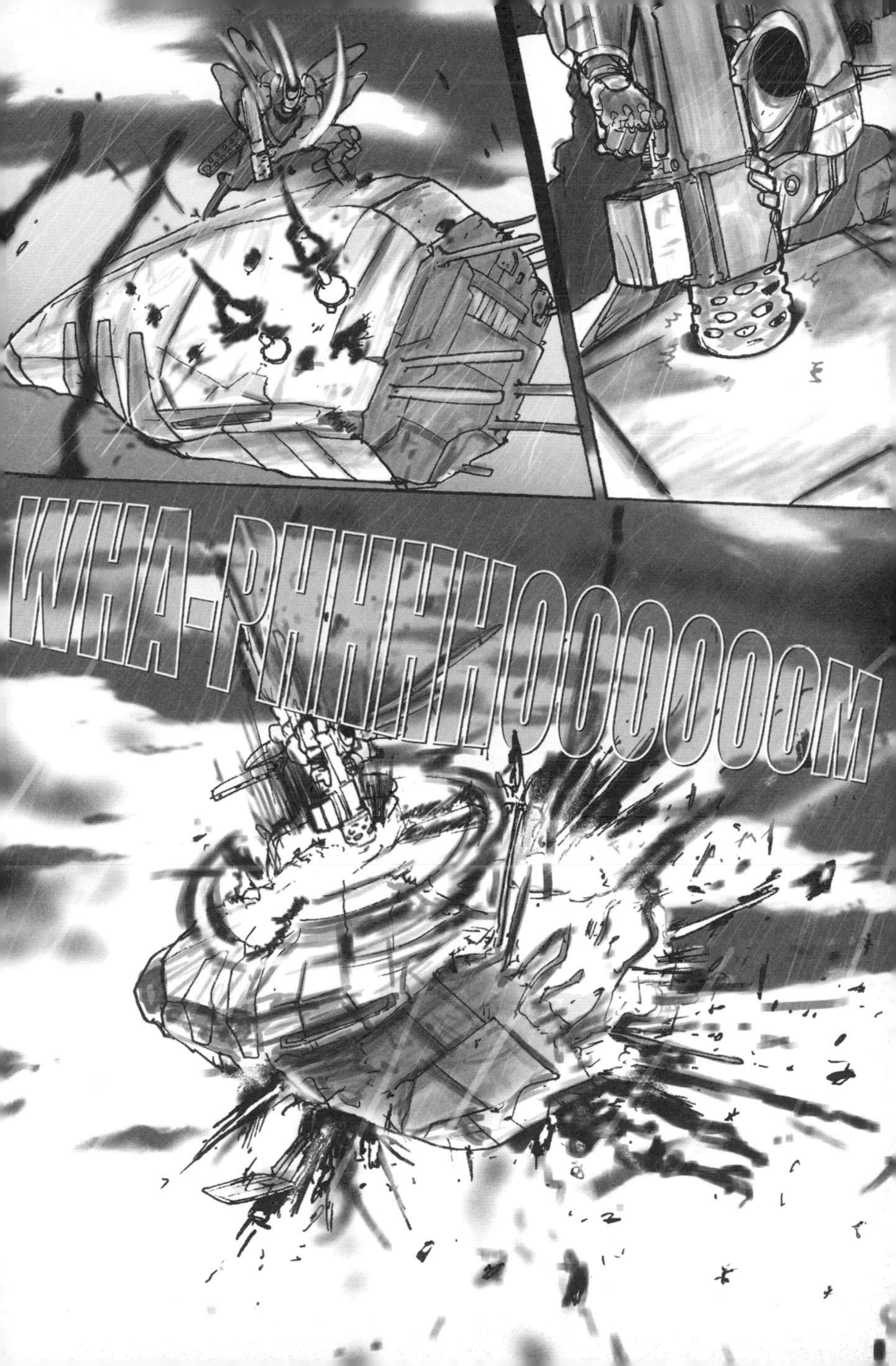
WHA-PHHHHOOOOOOM

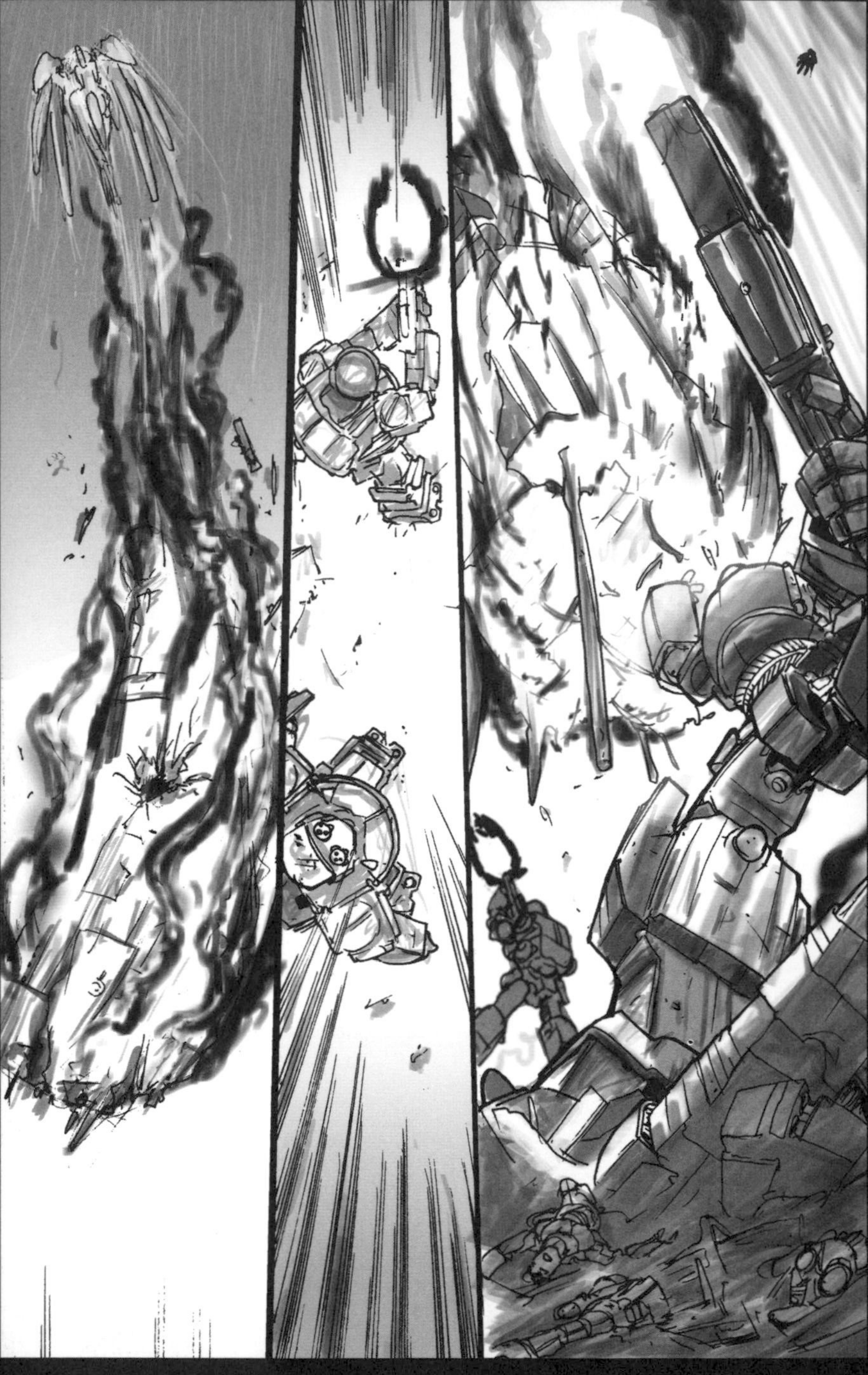

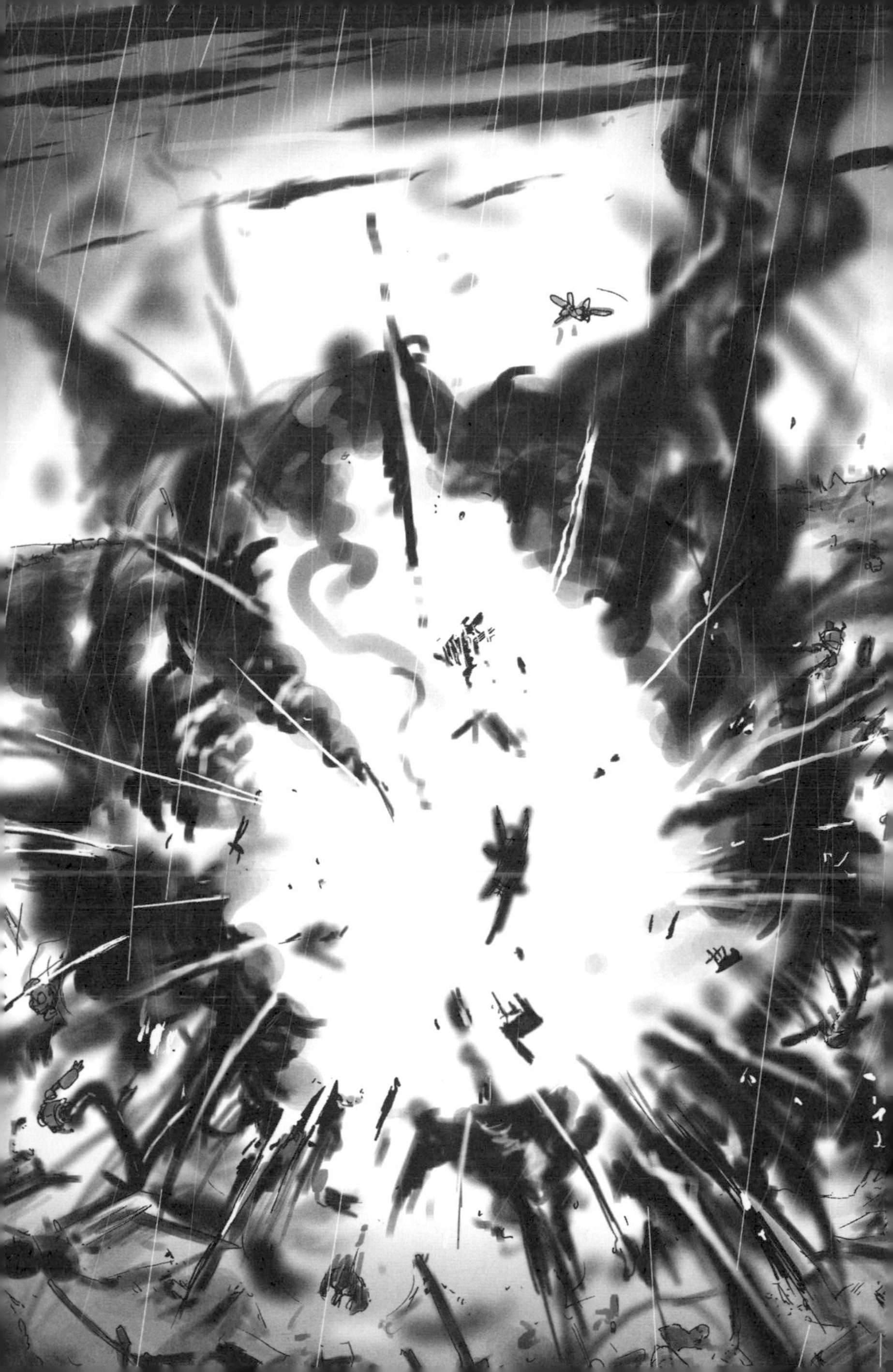

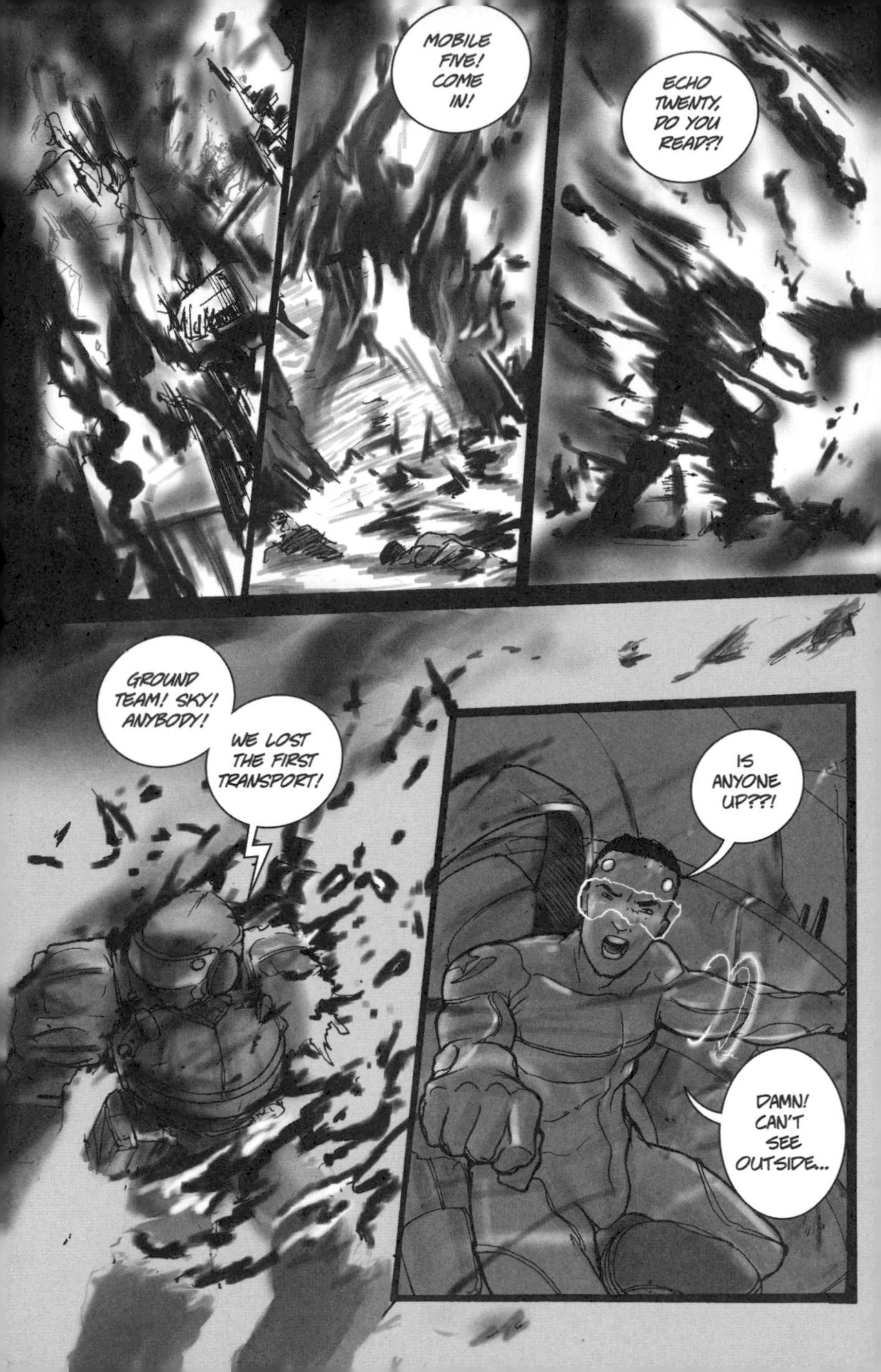
MOBILE FIVE! COME IN!
ECHO TWENTY, DO YOU READ?!
GROUND TEAM! SKY! ANYBODY!
WE LOST THE FIRST TRANSPORT!
IS ANYONE UP??!
DAMN! CAN'T SEE OUTSIDE...

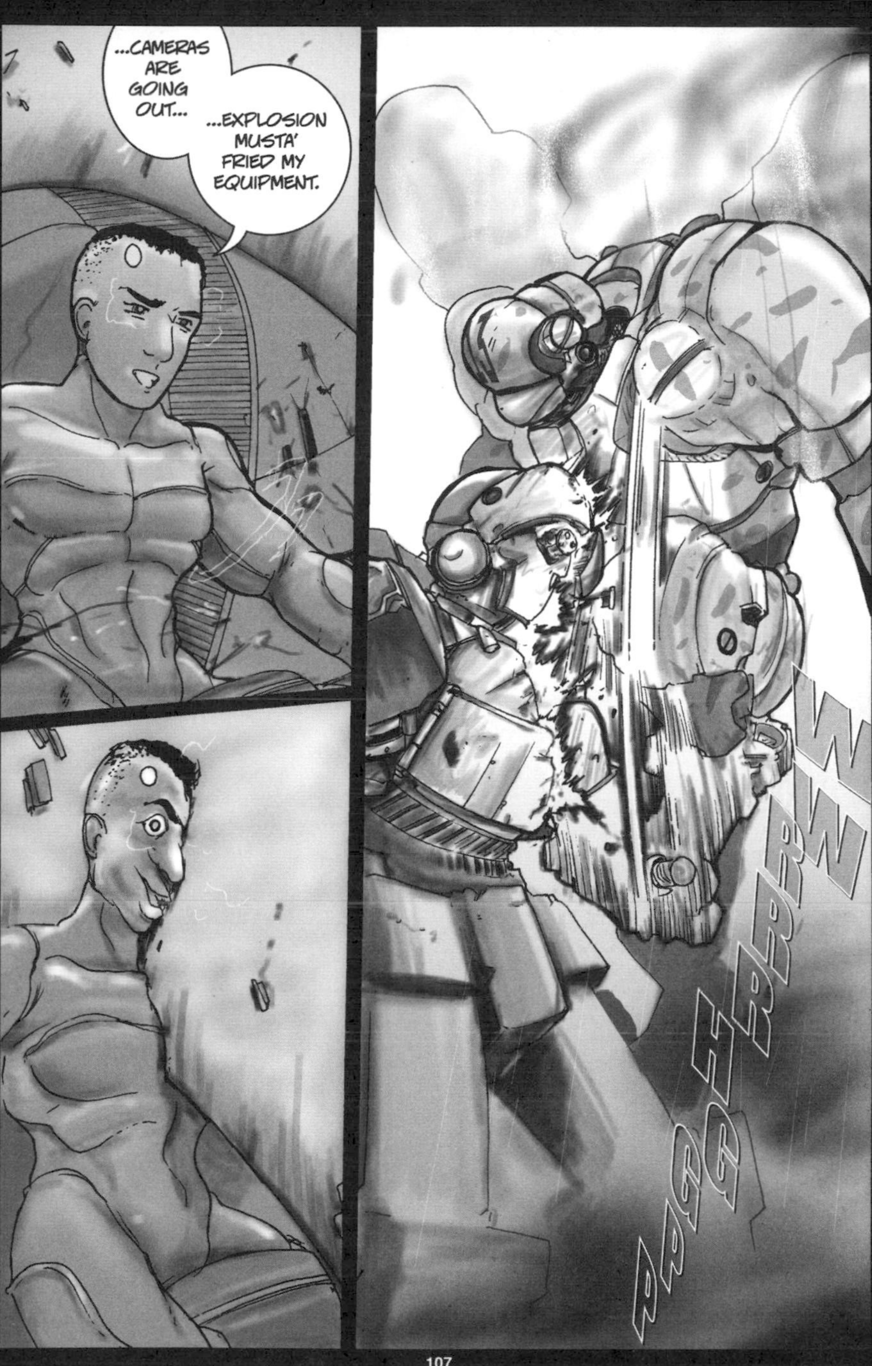
...CAMERAS ARE GOING OUT...
...EXPLOSION MUSTA' FRIED MY EQUIPMENT.
RAGGHRRRWW

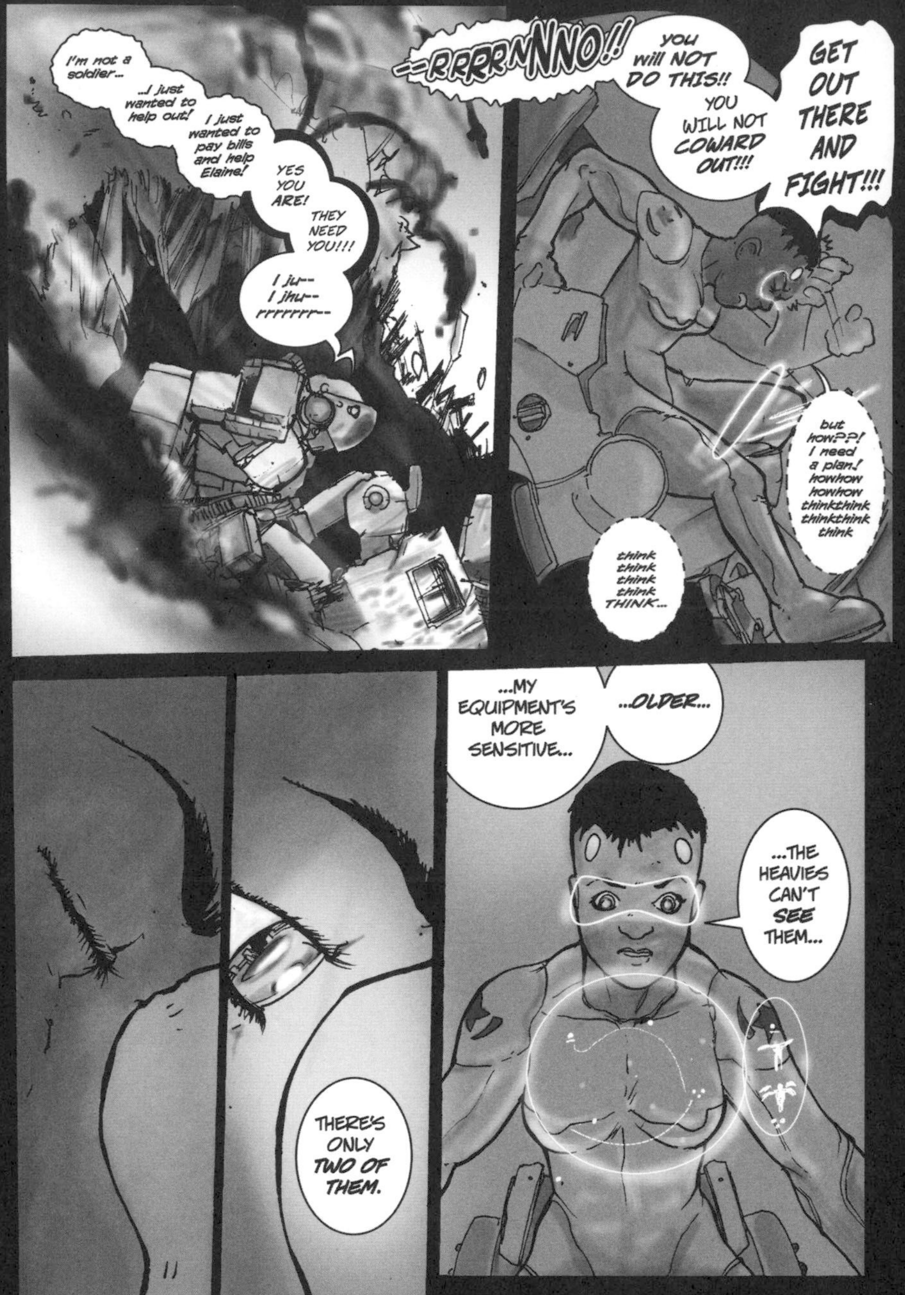
I'm not a soldier...
...I just wanted to help out!
I just wanted to pay bills and help Elaine!
YES YOU ARE!
THEY NEED YOU!!!
I ju-- I jhu-- rrrrrrrr--
--RRRRNNNO!!
YOU WILL NOT DO THIS!!
YOU WILL NOT COWARD OUT!!!
GET OUT THERE AND FIGHT!!!
but how?!?! I need a plan! howhow howhow thinkthink thinkthink think
think think think think THINK...
THERE'S ONLY TWO OF THEM.
...MY EQUIPMENT'S MORE SENSITIVE...
...OLDER...
...THE HEAVIES CAN'T SEE THEM...

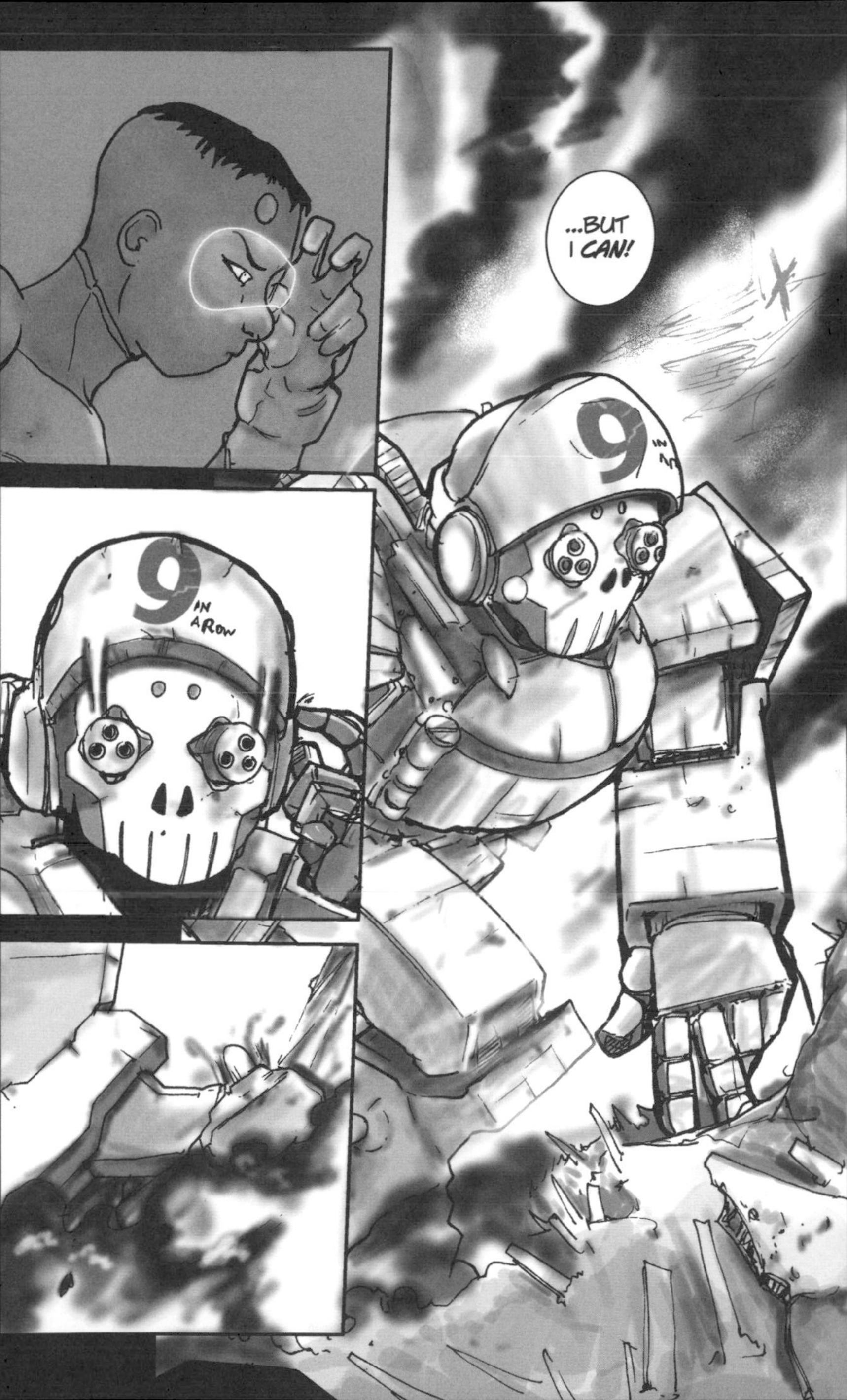
...BUT I CAN!
9 IN A ROW

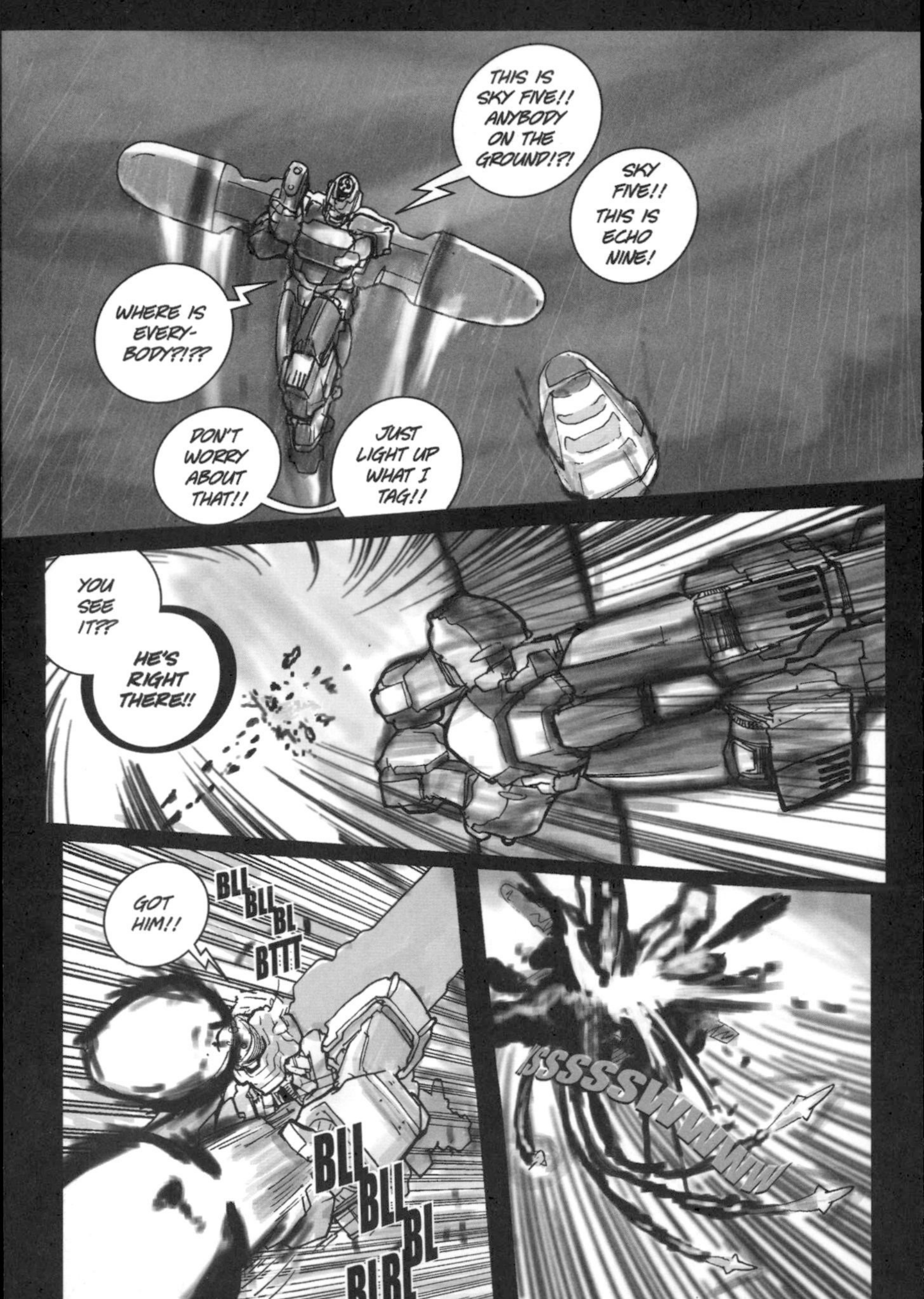
THIS IS SKY FIVE!! ANYBODY ON THE GROUND!?!
SKY FIVE!! THIS IS ECHO NINE!
WHERE IS EVERY-BODY?!??
DON'T WORRY ABOUT THAT!!
JUST LIGHT UP WHAT I TAG!!
YOU SEE IT??
HE'S RIGHT THERE!!
GOT HIM!!
BLL BLL BL BTTT
BLL BLL BL BLBL
SSSSSWWWWW

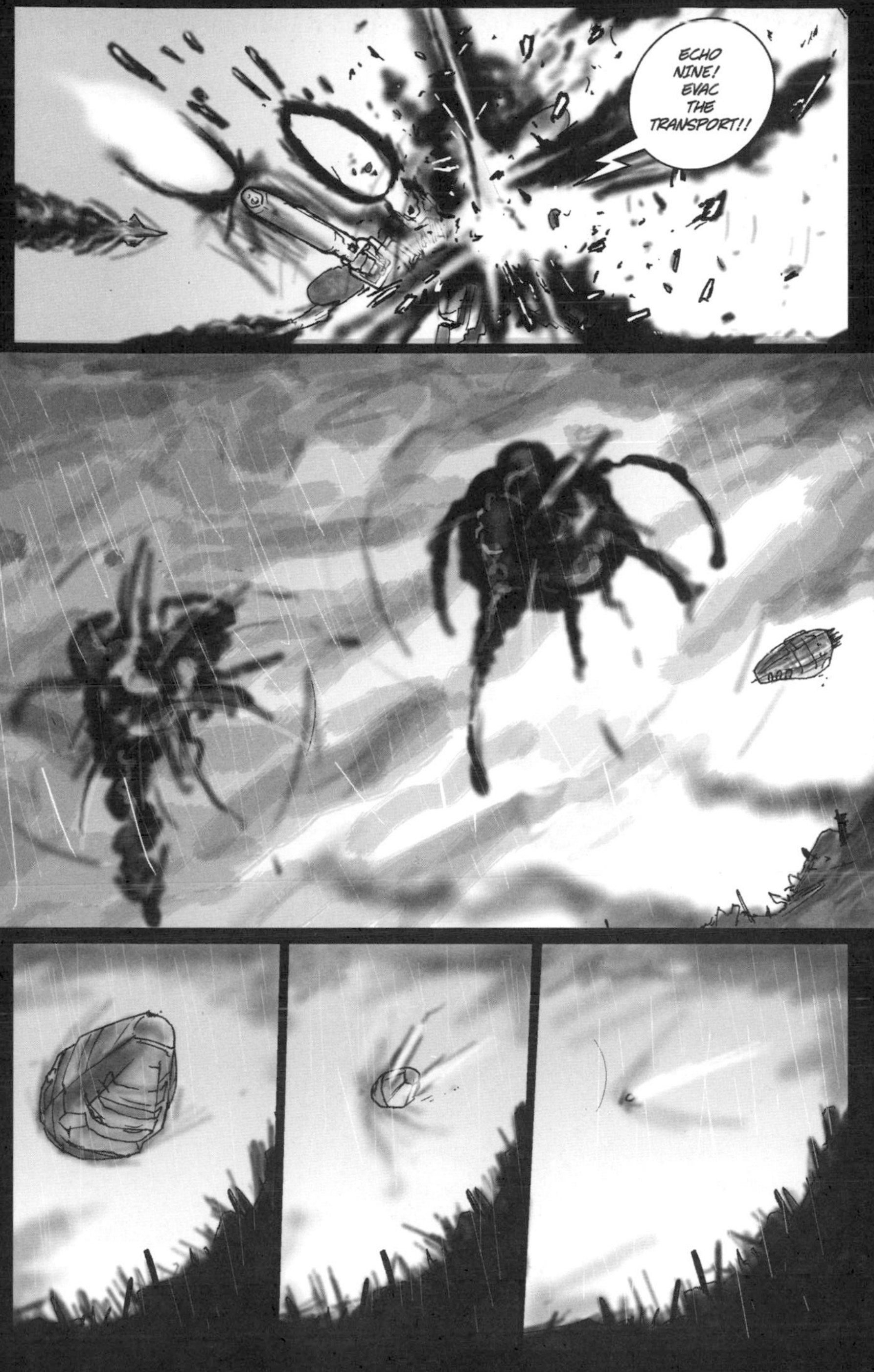
ECHO NINE! EVAC THE TRANSPORT!!

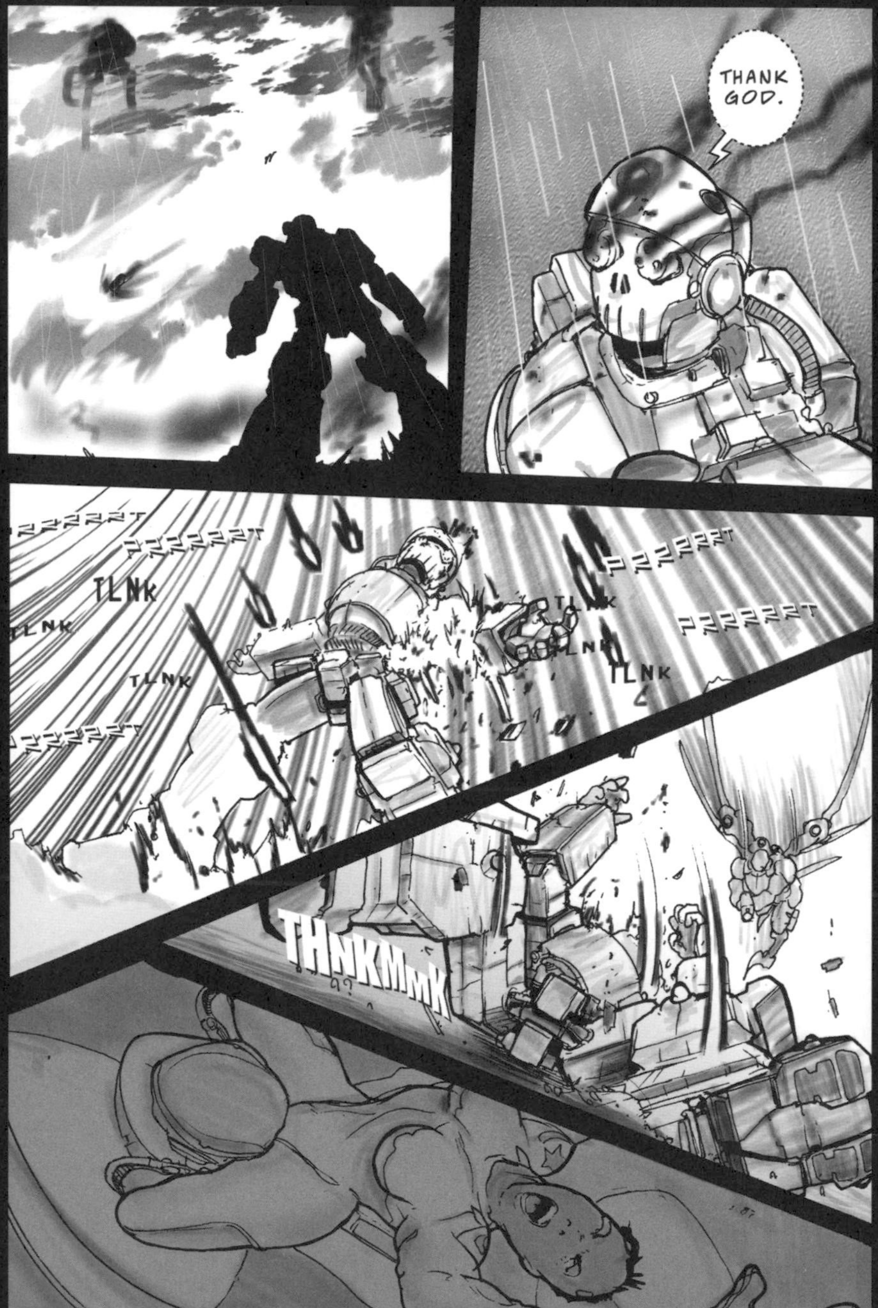
THANK GOD.
TLNK
TLNK
TLNK
TLNK
TLNK
TLNK
THNKMMMK

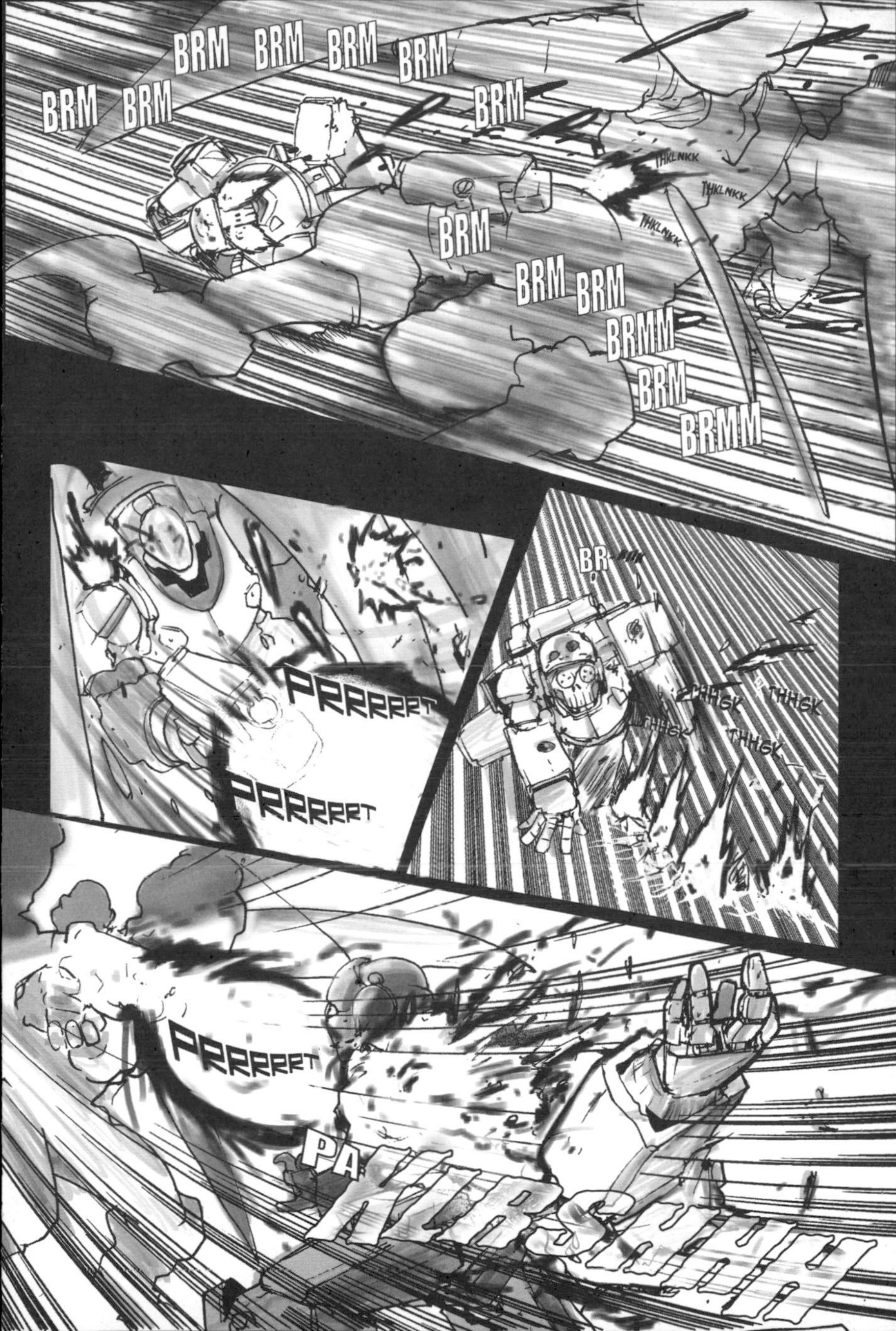
BRM BRM BRM BRM BRM BRM
BRM
THKLNKK
THKLNKK
THKLNKK
BRM
BRM BRM
BRMM
BRM
BRMM
PRRRRRT
PRRRRRT
THHGK
THHGK
THHGK
THHGK
PRRRRRT
PA

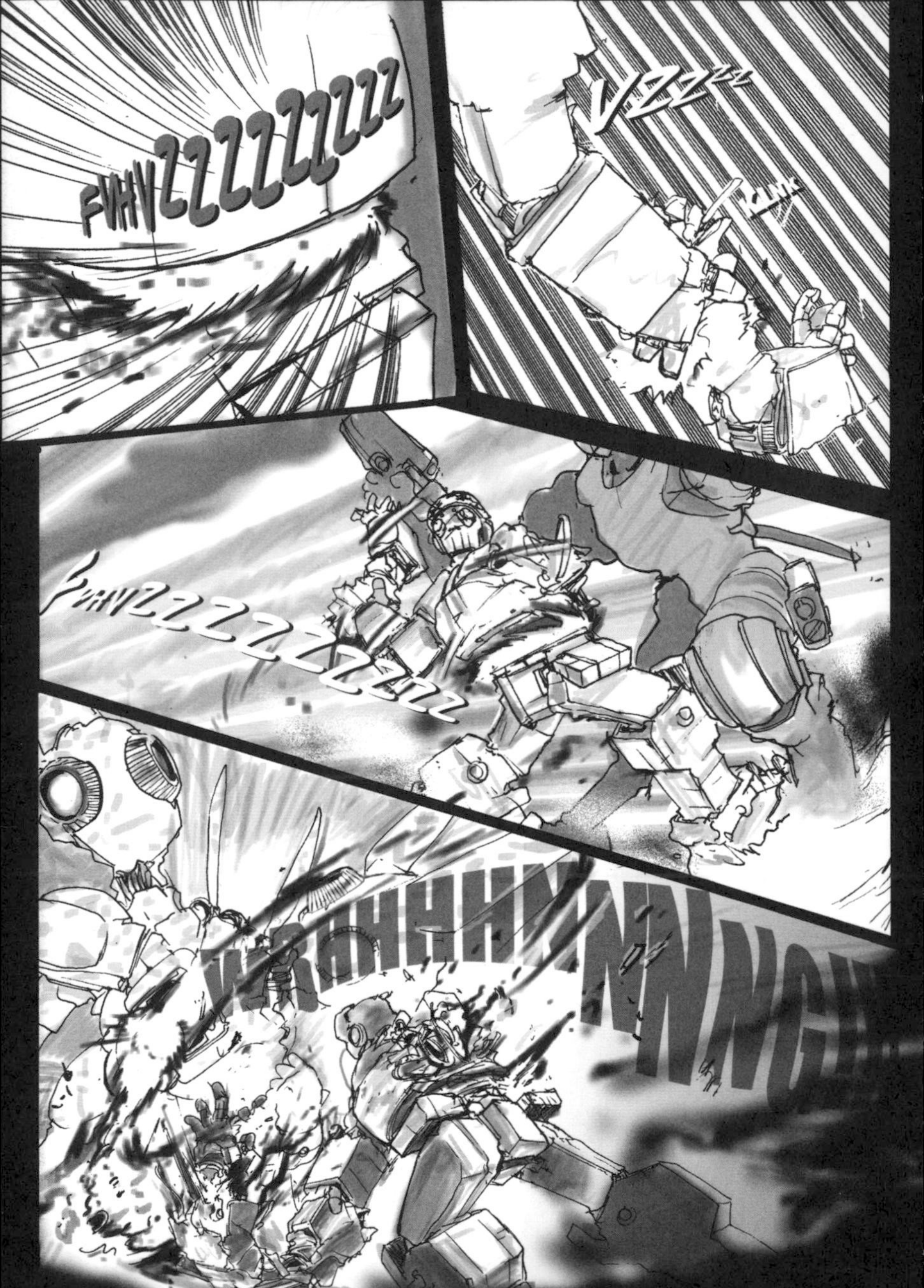

FVHVZZZZZZZZZ
VZZZZ
KLINK
FVHVZZZZZZZZZ
WRAHHHHNNNNG

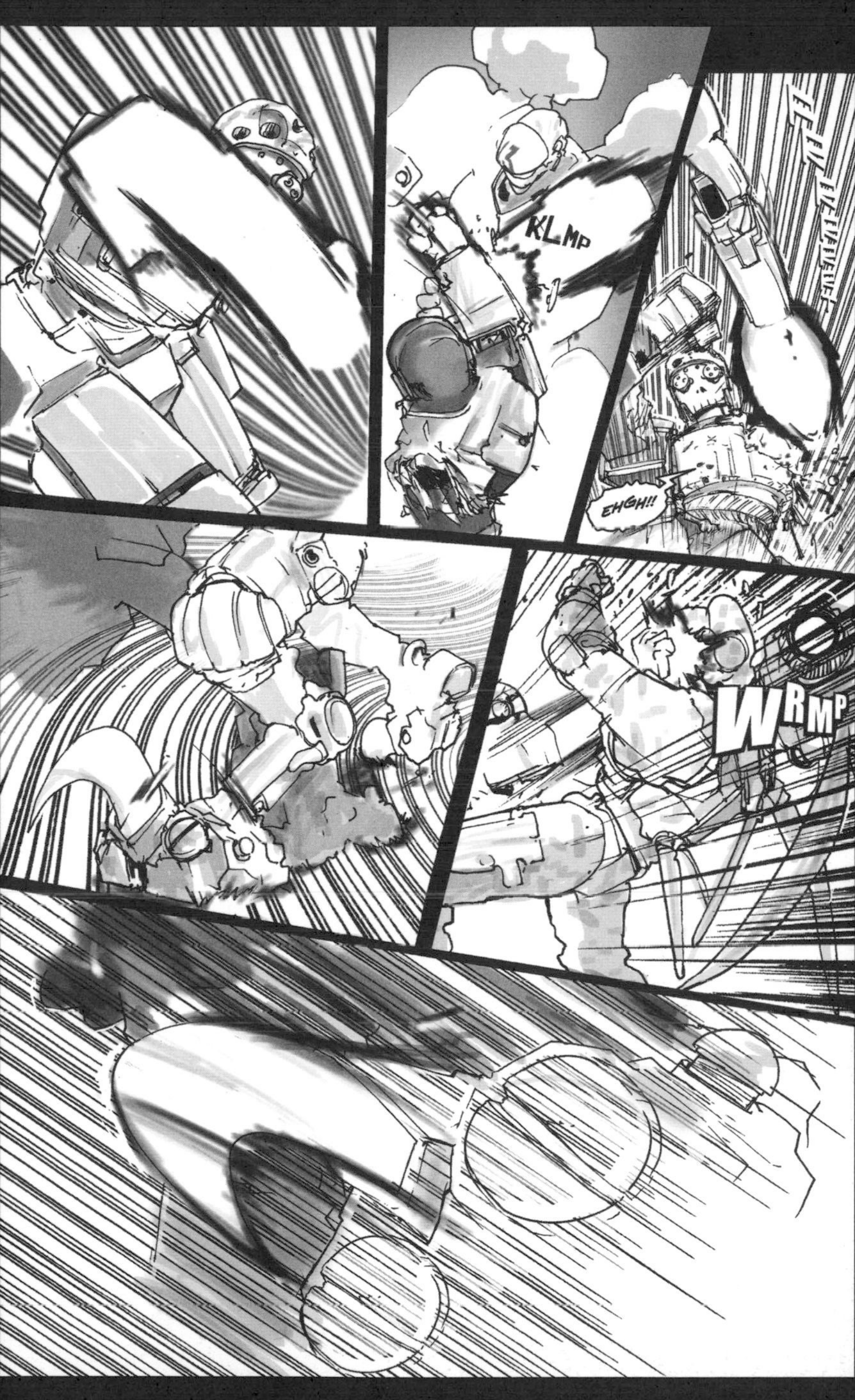
KLMP
EHGH!!
WRMP

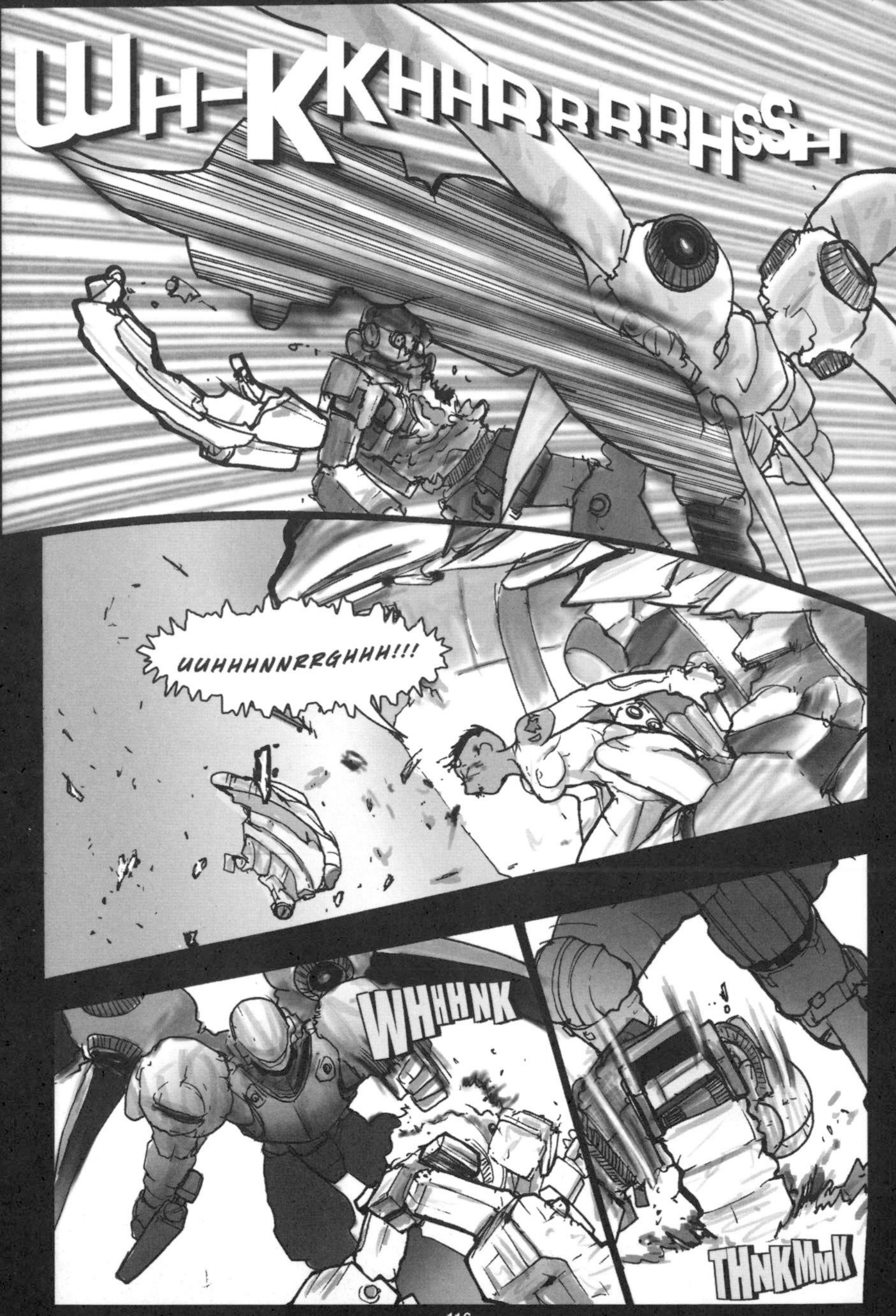
WH-KKHHRRRRRHSSH
UUHHHNNRRGHHH!!!
WHHHNK
THNKMMK

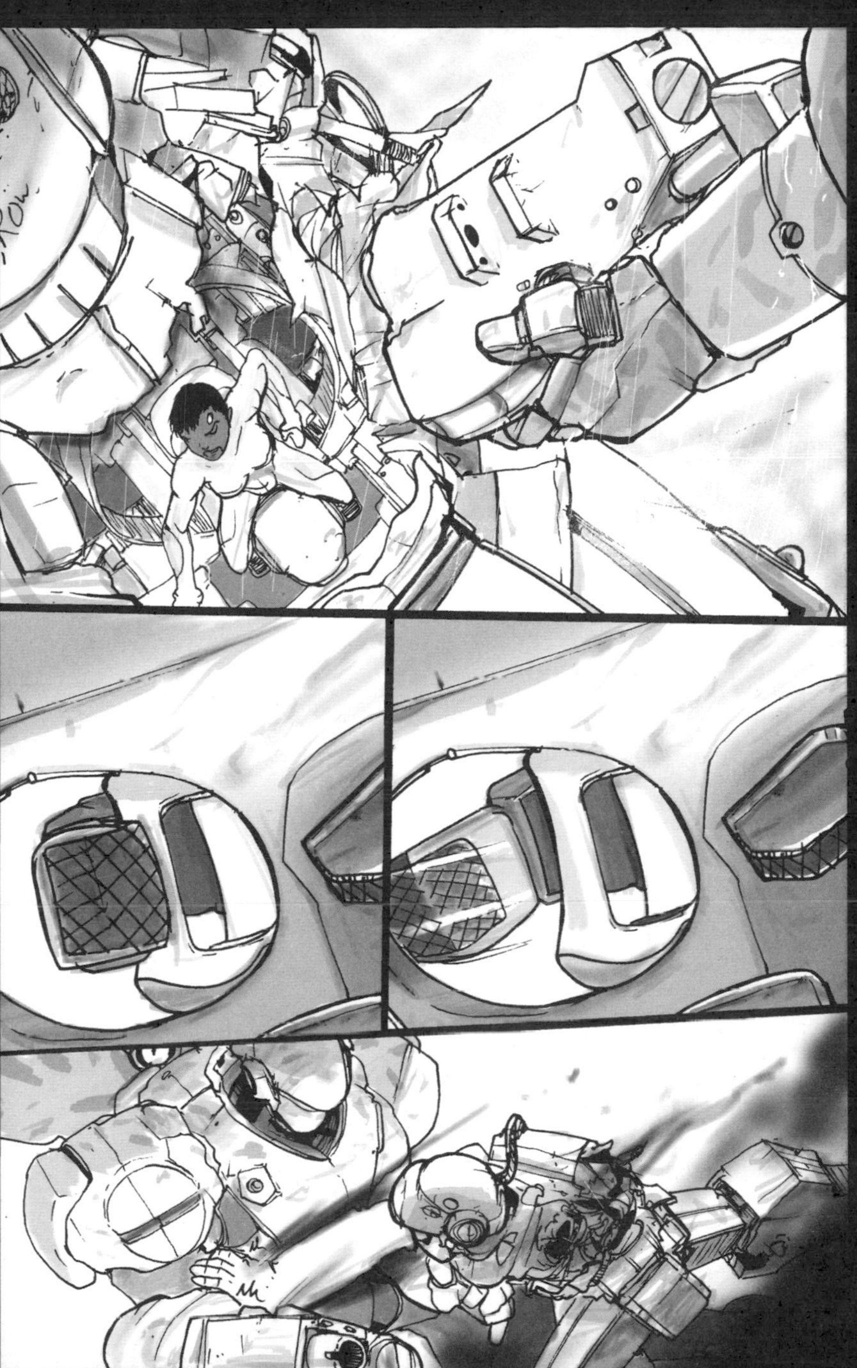

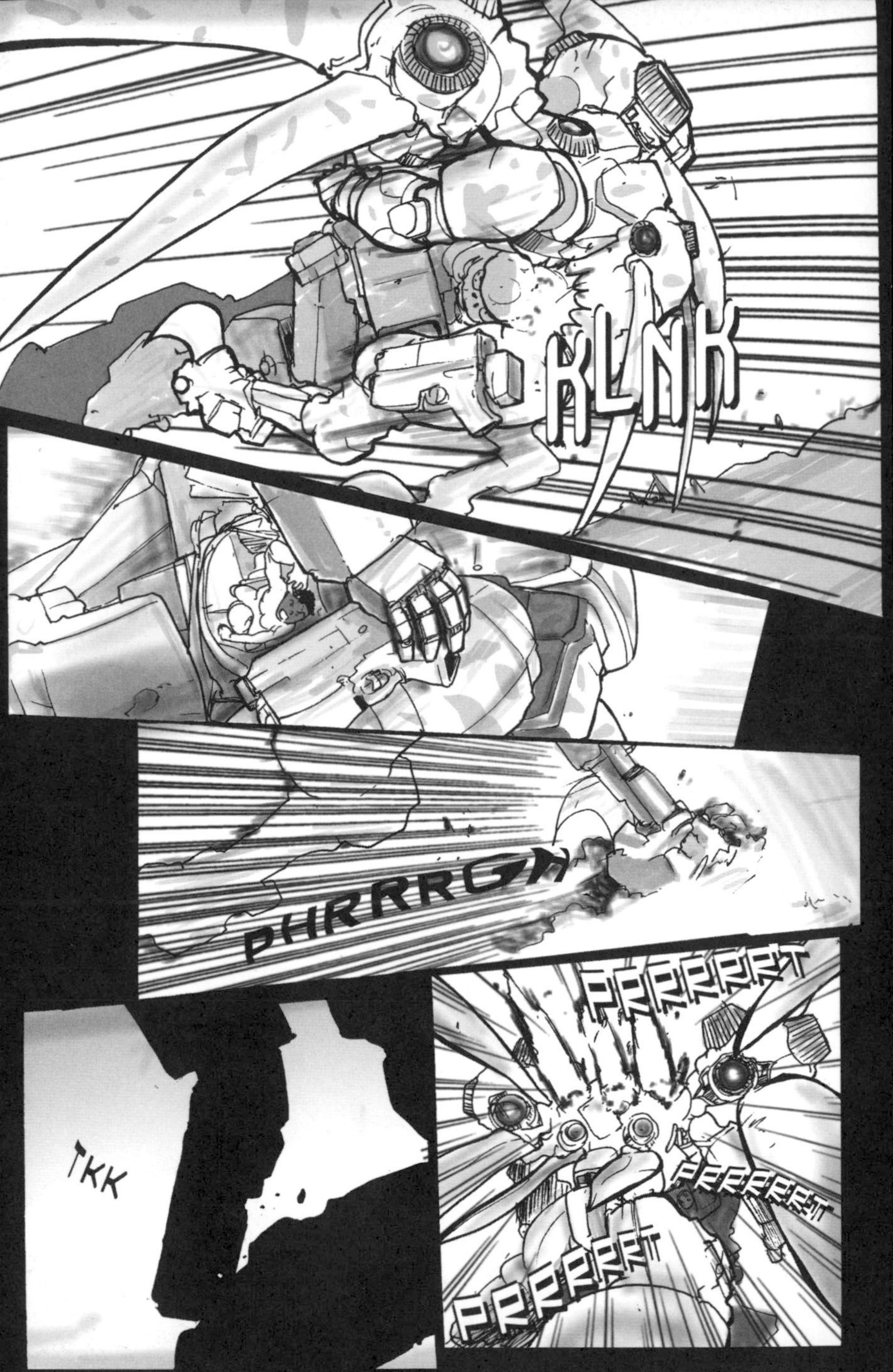
KLNK
PHRRRGH
TKK
PRRRRRRT
PRRRRRT
PRRRRRRT

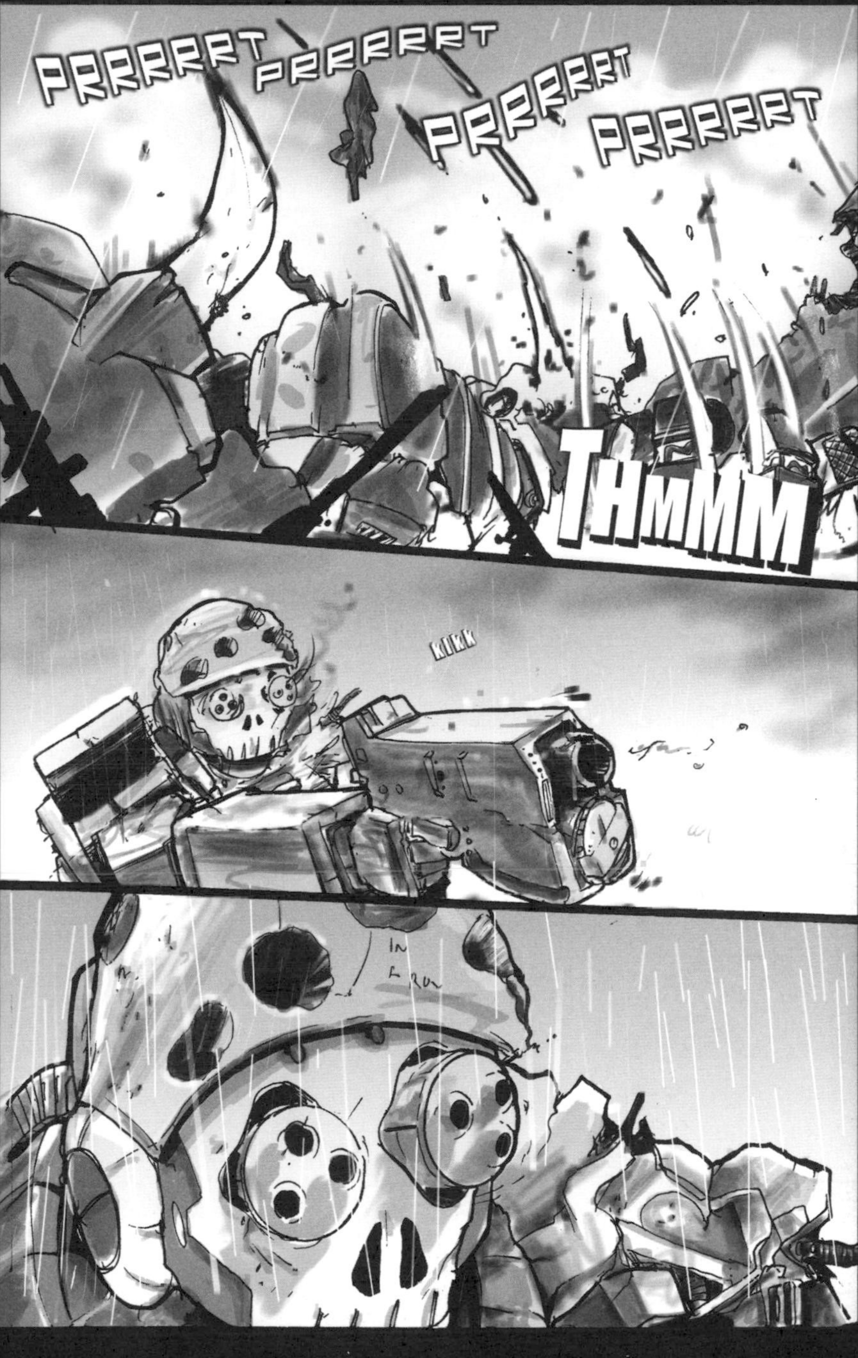
PRRRRRT
PRRRRRRT
PRRRRRRT
PRRRRRRT
THMMM
KIRK

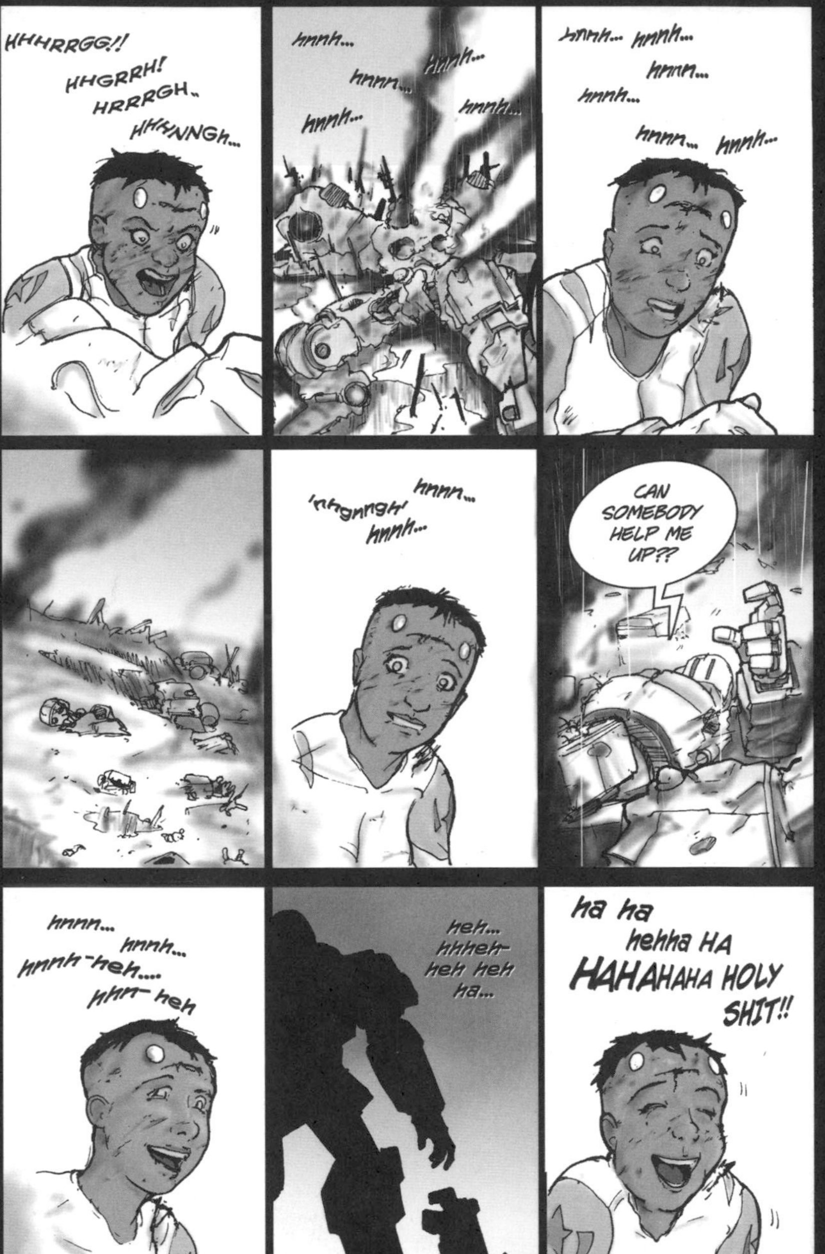
HHHRRGG!!
HHGRRH!
HRRRGH..
HHHNNGh...
hnnh...
hnnn...
hnnh...
hnnh...
hnnh...
hnnh... hnnh...
hmmn...
hnnh...
hnnn... hnnh...
hnnn...
'nhgnngh'
hnnh...
CAN SOMEBODY HELP ME UP??
hnnn...
hnnh...
hnnh-heh....
hhn-heh
heh... hhheh-heh heh ha...
ha ha hehha HA HAHAHAHA HOLY SHIT!!

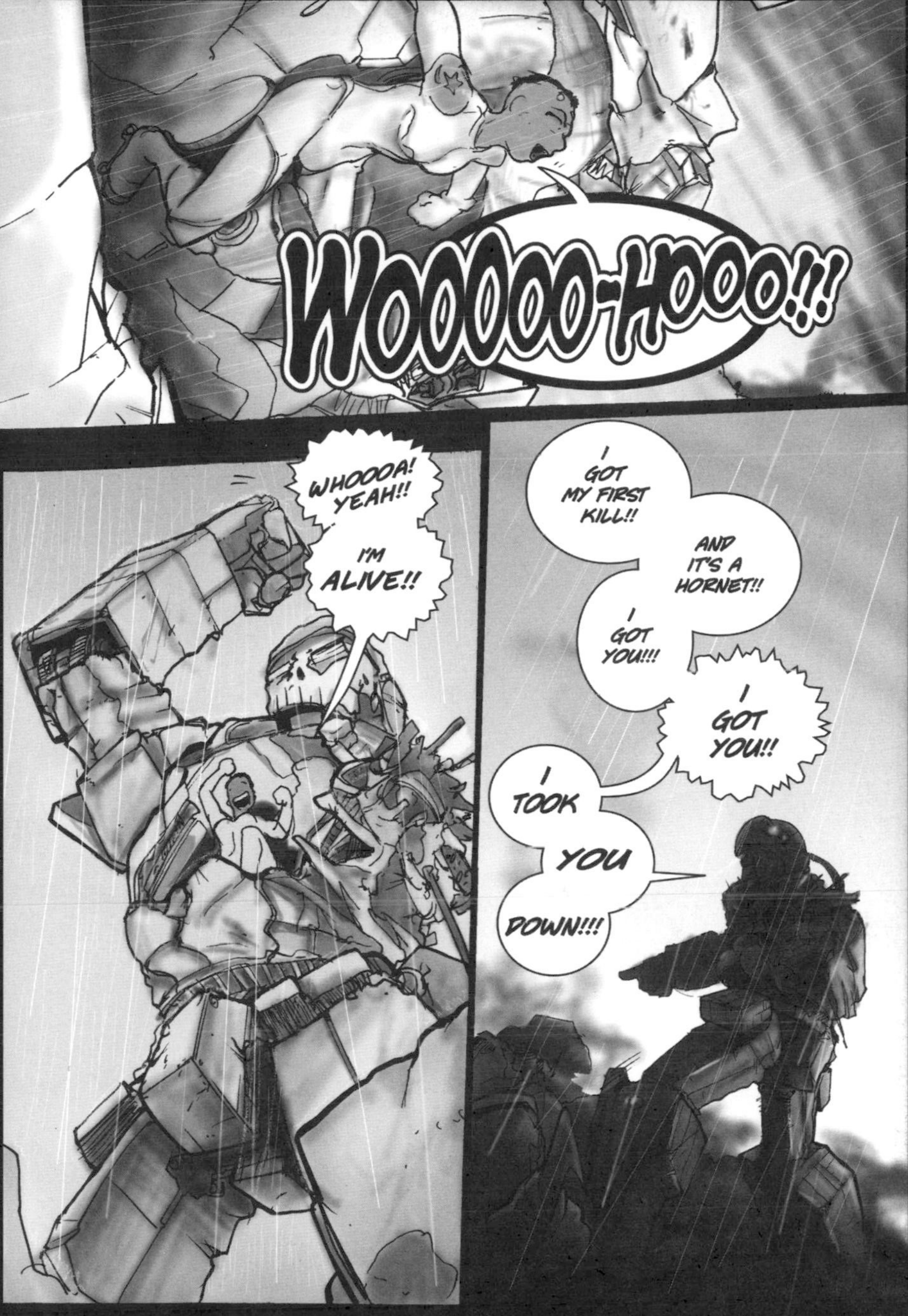
WOOOOO-HOOO!!!
WHOOOA! YEAH!!
I'M ALIVE!!
I GOT MY FIRST KILL!!
AND IT'S A HORNET!!
I GOT YOU!!!
I GOT YOU!!
I TOOK YOU DOWN!!!

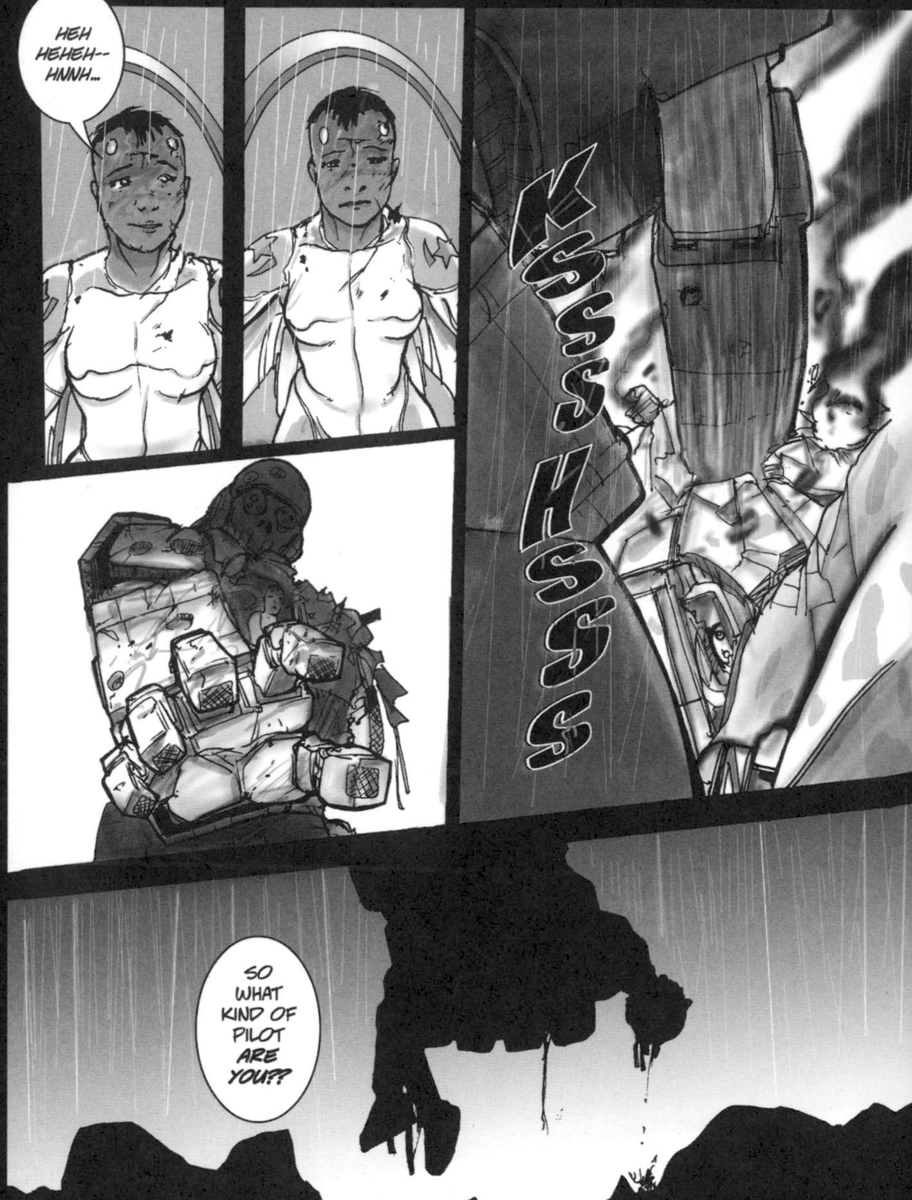
HEH HEHEH-- HNNH...
KSSSHSSS
SO WHAT KIND OF PILOT ARE YOU??

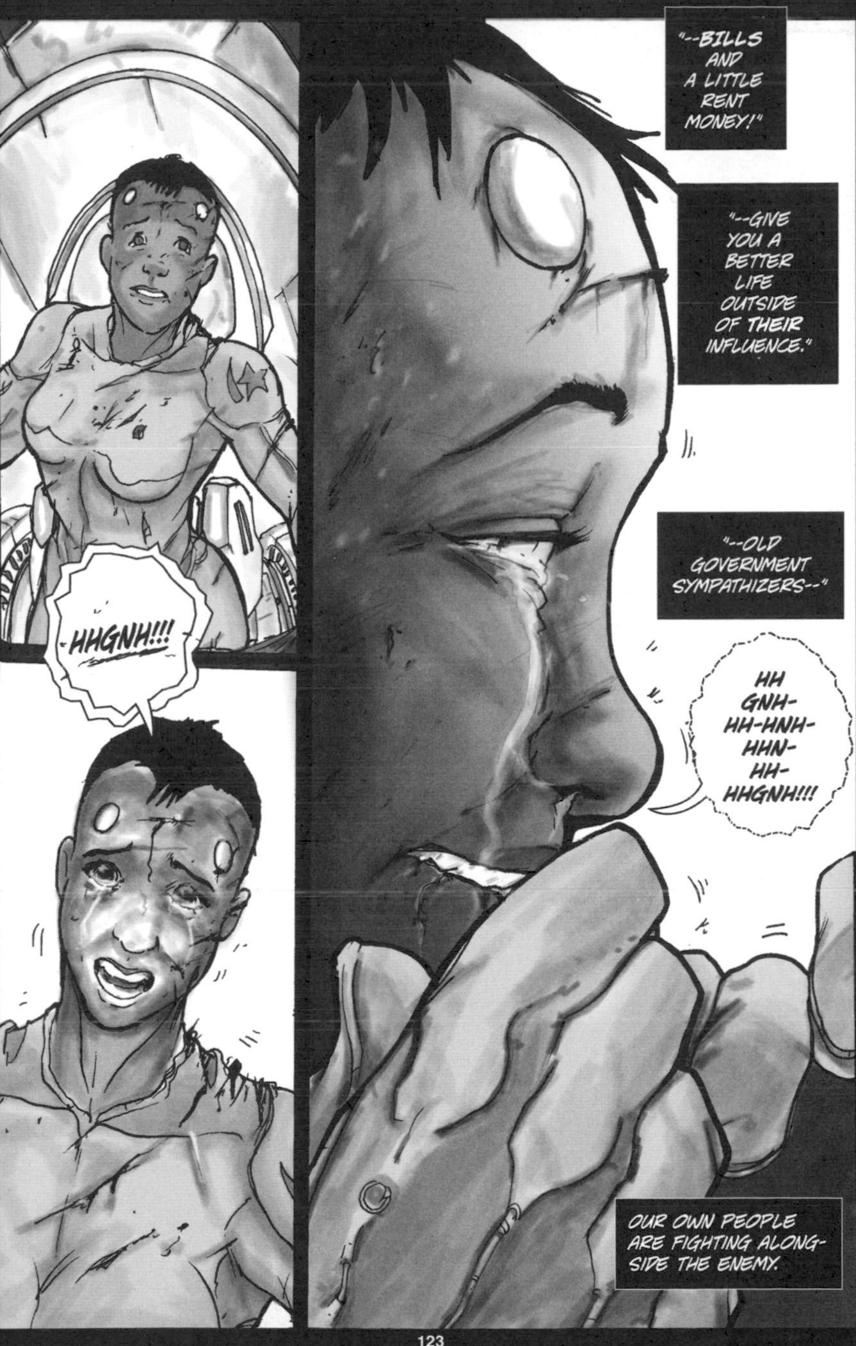
"--BILLS AND A LITTLE RENT MONEY!"
"--GIVE YOU A BETTER LIFE OUTSIDE OF THEIR INFLUENCE."
HHGNH!!!
"--OLD GOVERNMENT SYMPATHIZERS--"
HH GNH-HH-HNH-HHN-HH-HHGNH!!!
OUR OWN PEOPLE ARE FIGHTING ALONG-SIDE THE ENEMY.

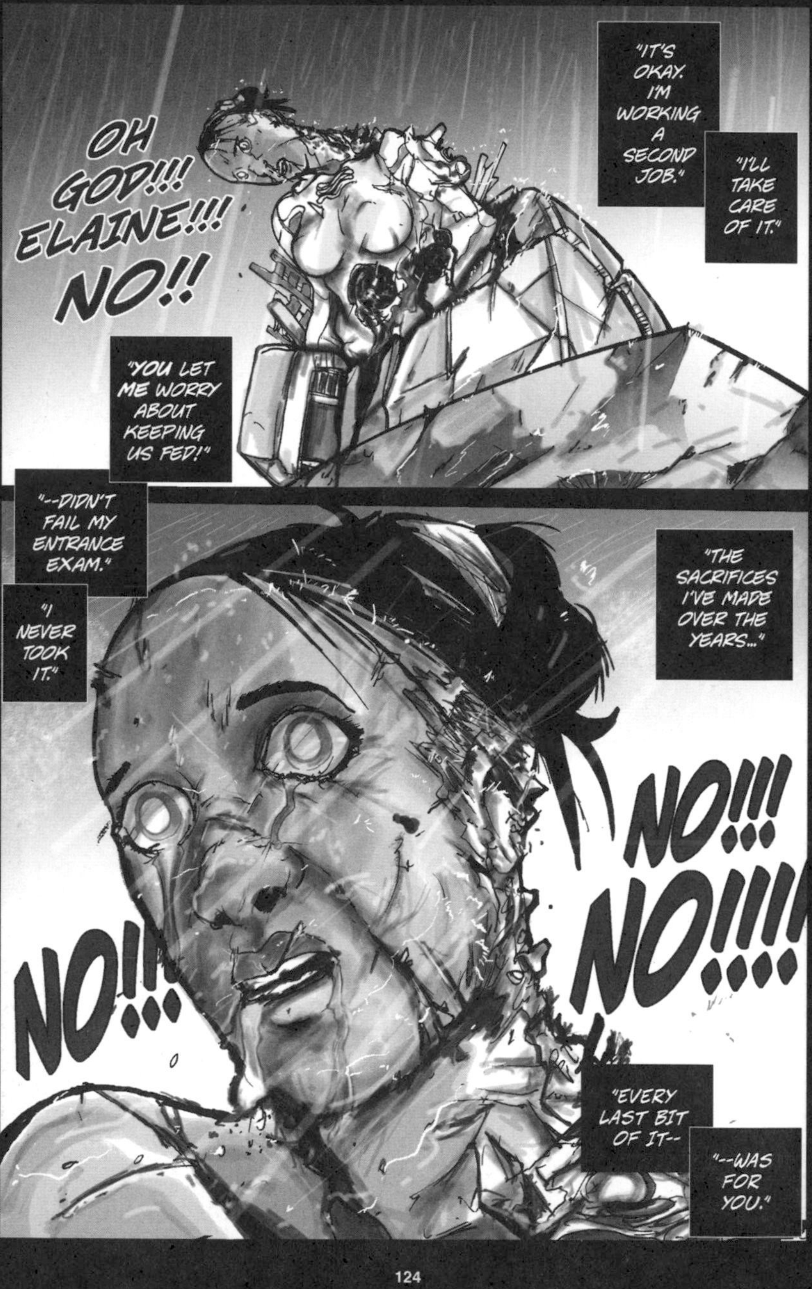
"IT'S OKAY. I'M WORKING A SECOND JOB."
"I'LL TAKE CARE OF IT."
OH GOD!!! ELAINE!!! NO!!
"YOU LET ME WORRY ABOUT KEEPING US FED!"
"--DIDN'T FAIL MY ENTRANCE EXAM."
"I NEVER TOOK IT."
"THE SACRIFICES I'VE MADE OVER THE YEARS..."
NO!!!
NO!!!
NO!!!!
"EVERY LAST BIT OF IT--
"--WAS FOR YOU."

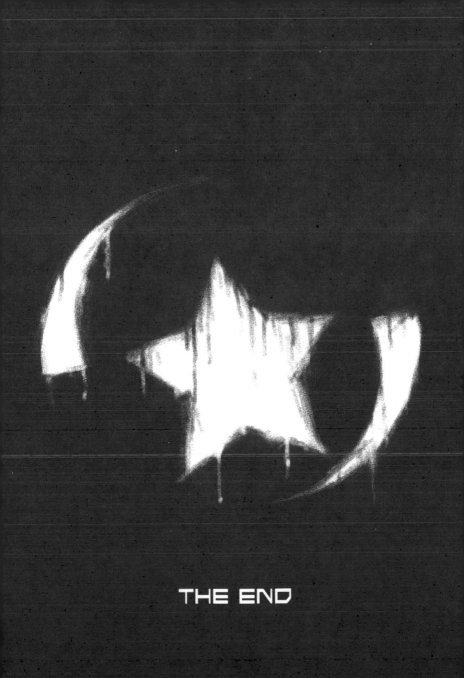

THE END

assembly

Production Sketches: Baby Shon

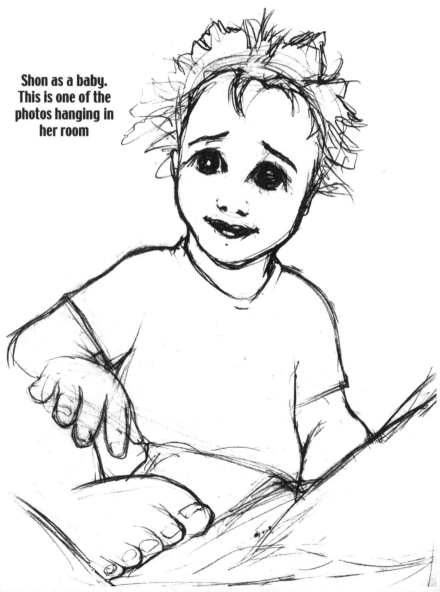

Shon as a baby. This is one of the photos hanging in her room

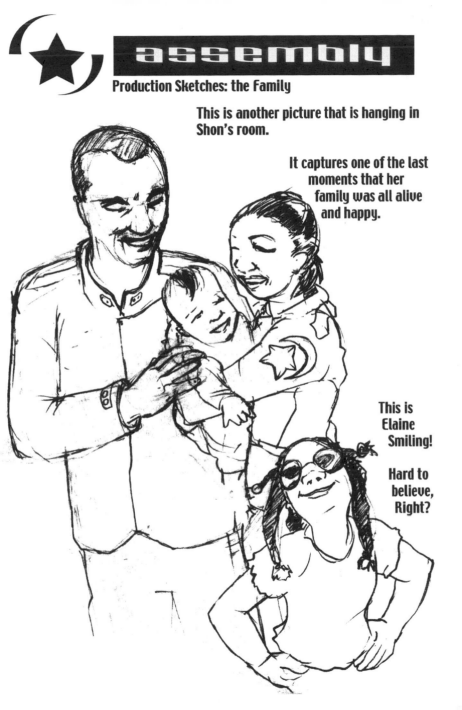

assembly

Production Sketches: the Family

This is another picture that is hanging in Shon's room.

It captures one of the last moments that her family was all alive and happy.

This is Elaine Smiling!

Hard to believe, Right?

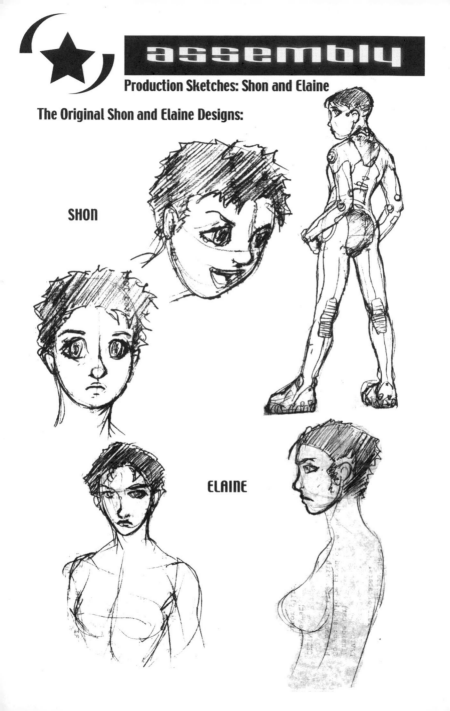

assembly

Production Sketches: Shon and Elaine

The Original Shon and Elaine Designs:

SHON

ELAINE

assembly

Production Sketches: Shon

It took a few more sketches to get Shon's look right.

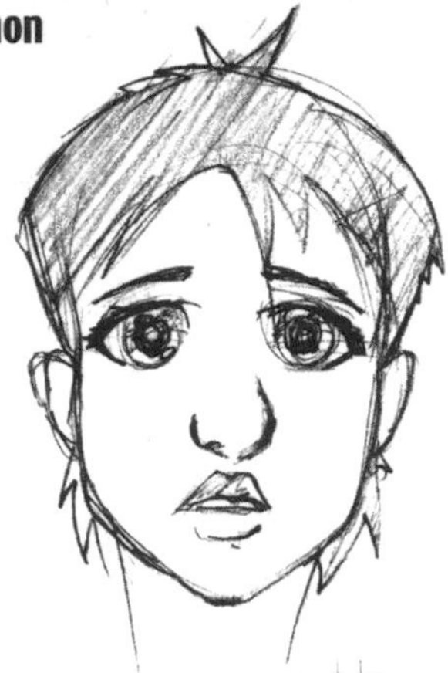

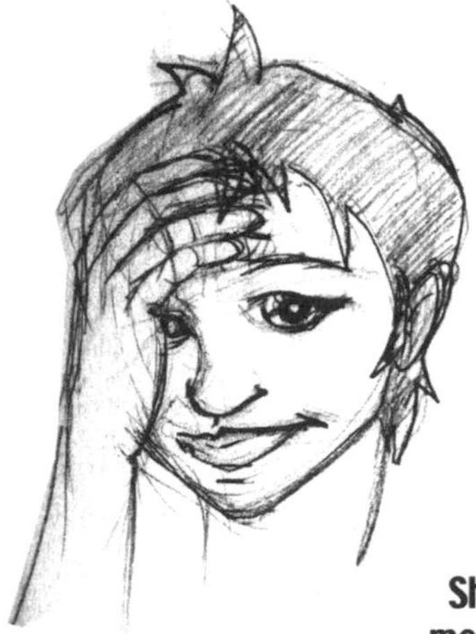

Shon in her more-or-less final design.

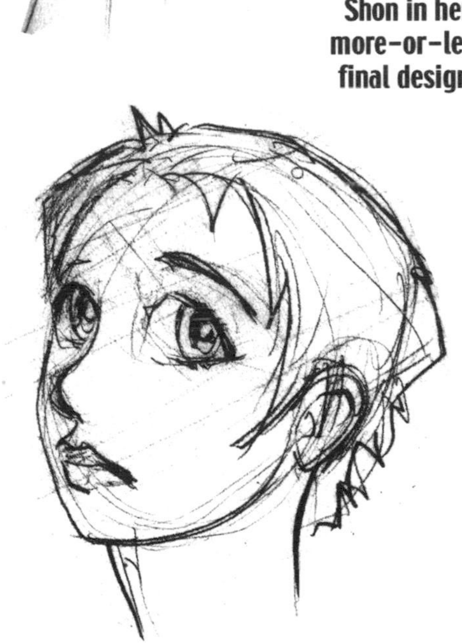

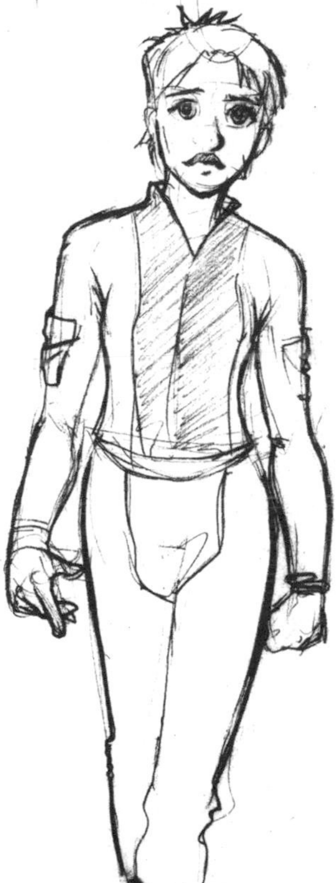

assembly

Production Sketches: Shon

Originally I thought about making her younger, around 12 or 13, then settled on the age of 16. It feels like a more practical age of consent.

I wanted to avoid the story setting of "the really young KID being the ONLY ONE who can save the world."

I like the idea of a YOUNG ADULT getting in over her head and not knowing how she'll survive.

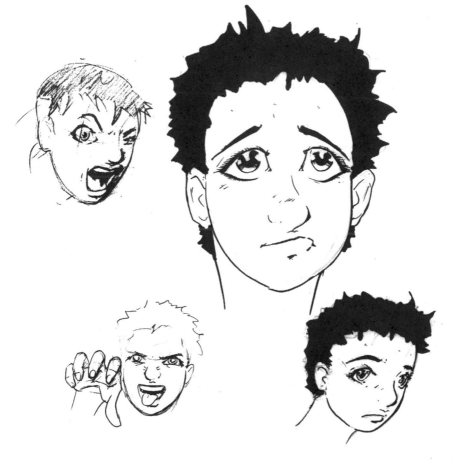

assembly

Production Sketches: Shon

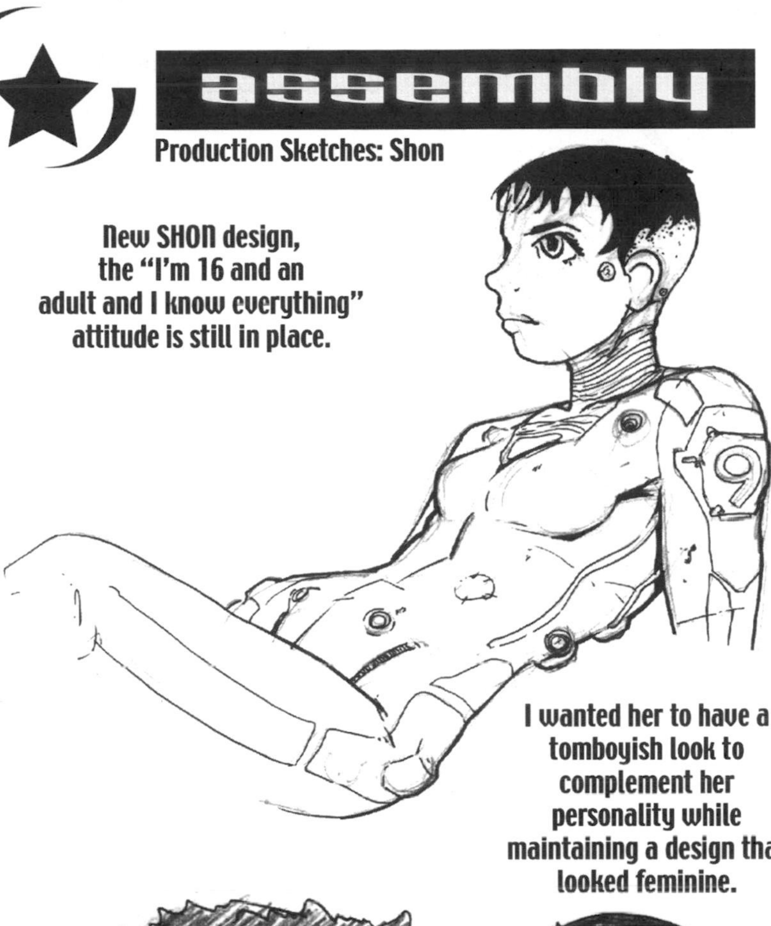

New SHON design, the "I'm 16 and an adult and I know everything" attitude is still in place.

I wanted her to have a tomboyish look to complement her personality while maintaining a design that looked feminine.

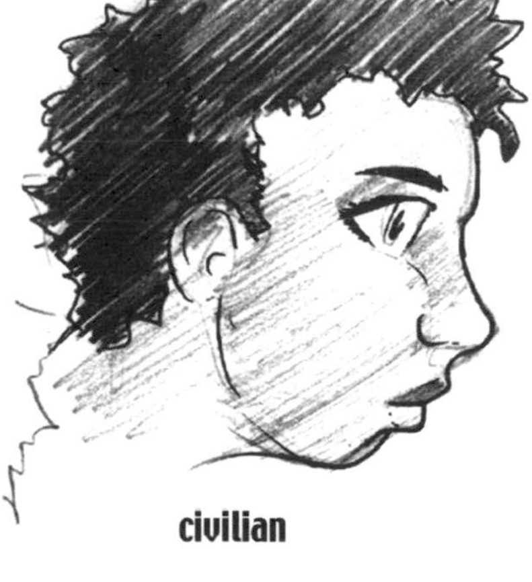

civilian

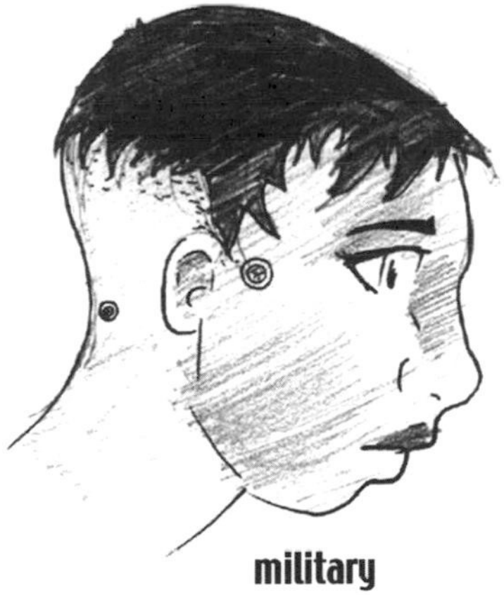

military

assembly

Production Sketches: Elaine

ELAINE

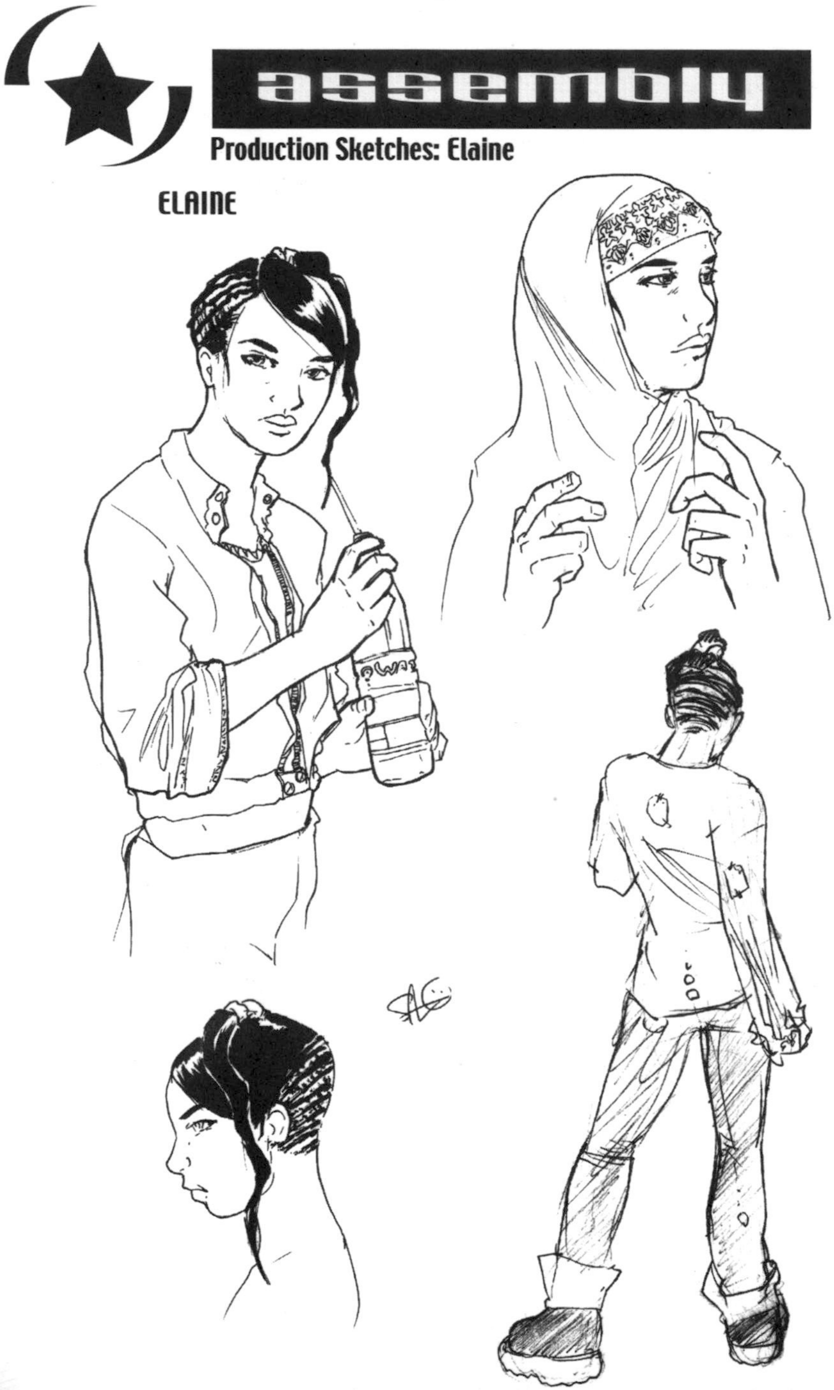

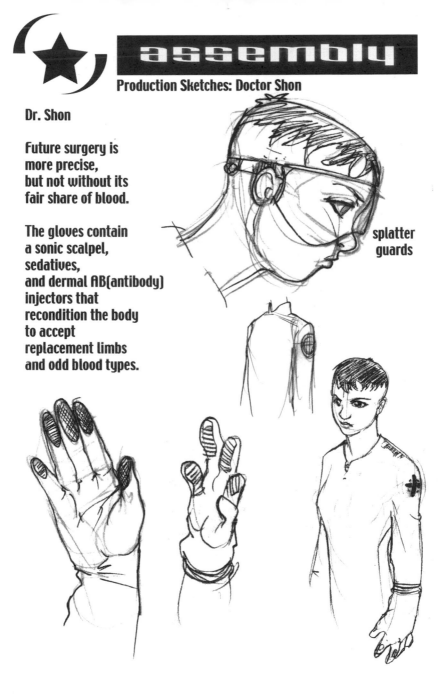

assembly

Production Sketches: Doctor Shon

Dr. Shon

Future surgery is more precise, but not without its fair share of blood.

The gloves contain a sonic scalpel, sedatives, and dermal AB(antibody) injectors that recondition the body to accept replacement limbs and odd blood types.

splatter guards

Deleted Page

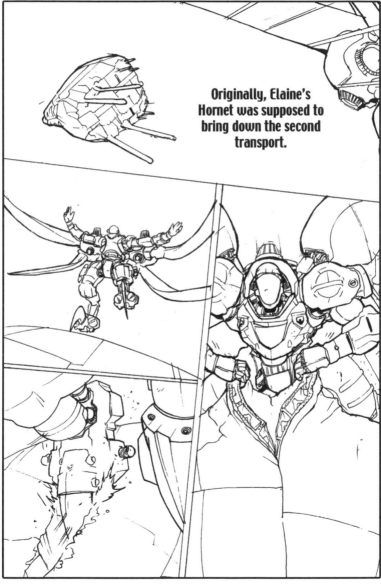

Originally, Elaine's Hornet was supposed to bring down the second transport.

assembly

Production Sketches: Heavy Moses

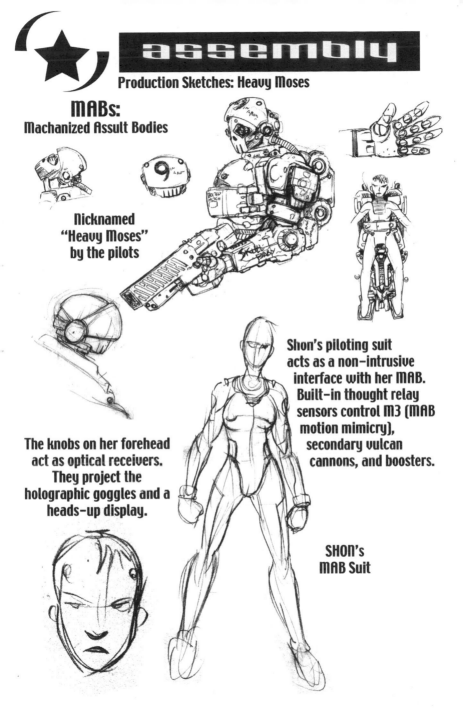

MABs:
Machanized Assult Bodies

BOLTED HATCH
SKULL BABY

Nicknamed
"Heavy Moses"
by the pilots

Shon's piloting suit acts as a non-intrusive interface with her MAB. Built-in thought relay sensors control M3 (MAB motion mimicry), secondary vulcan cannons, and boosters.

The knobs on her forehead act as optical receivers. They project the holographic goggles and a heads-up display.

SHON's
MAB Suit

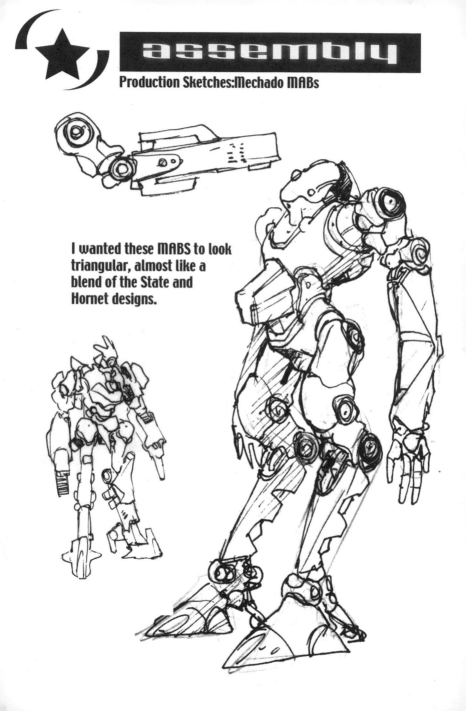

assembly

Production Sketches:Mechado MABs

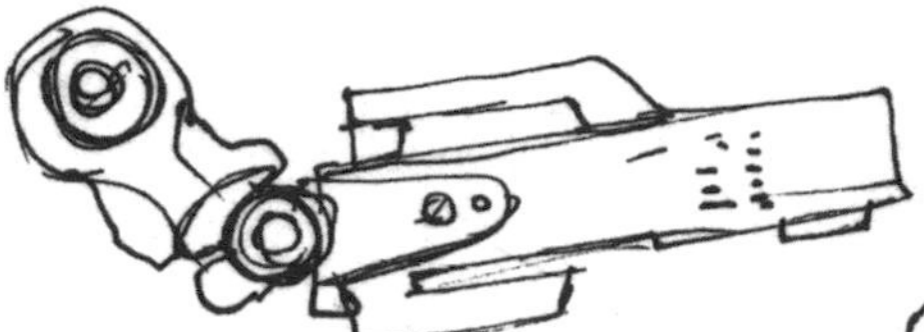

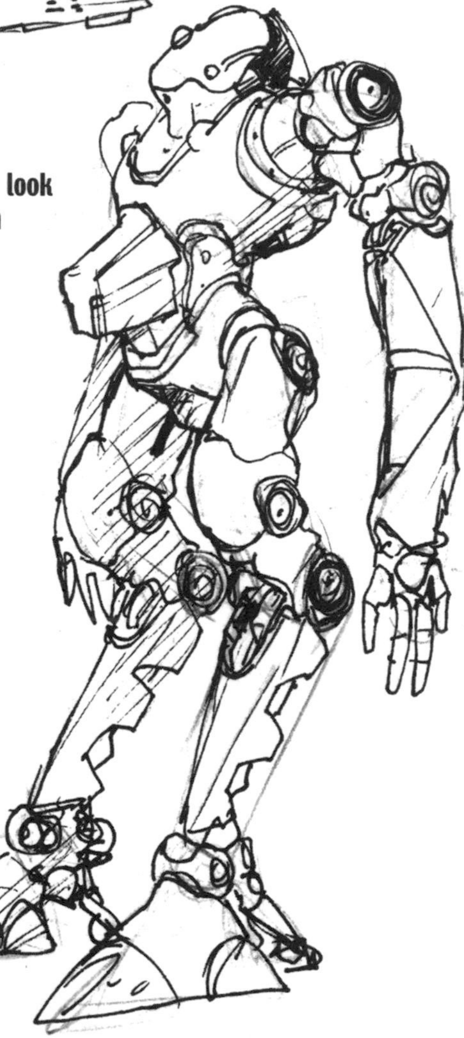

I wanted these MABS to look triangular, almost like a blend of the State and Hornet designs.

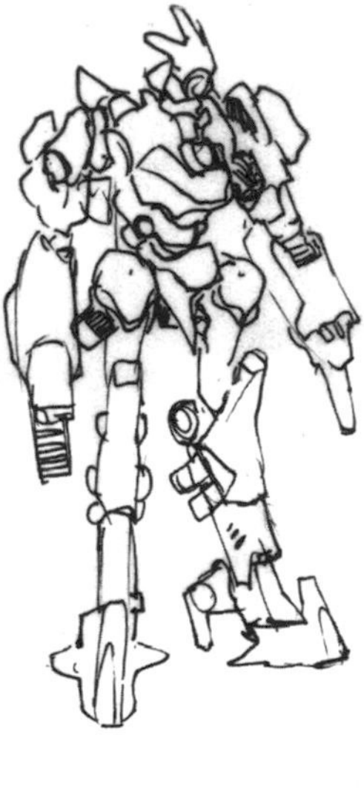

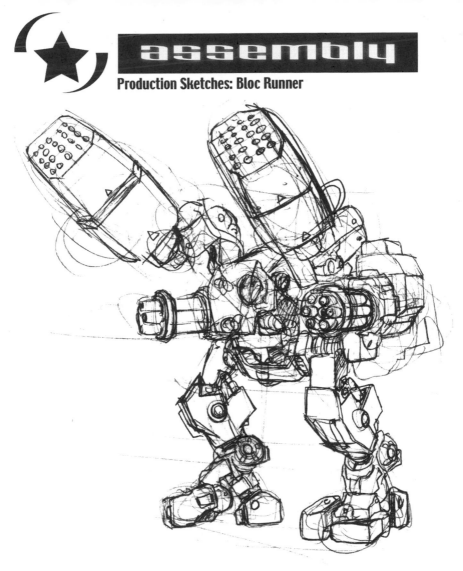

assembly

Production Sketches: Bloc Runner

These small, personal mechs turn out to be the best defense against the towering State MABs.

In designing this, I came up with something that looked and moved like an ostrich.

I wanted its look to complement the attack strategy: small, manueverable, numerous.

assembly

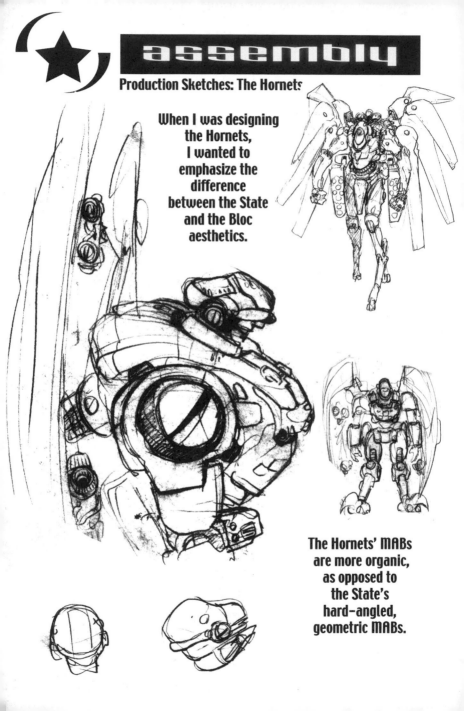

Production Sketches: The Hornets

When I was designing the Hornets, I wanted to emphasize the difference between the State and the Bloc aesthetics.

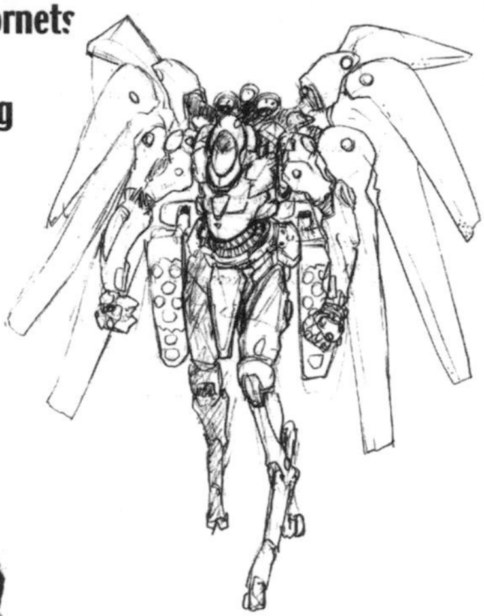

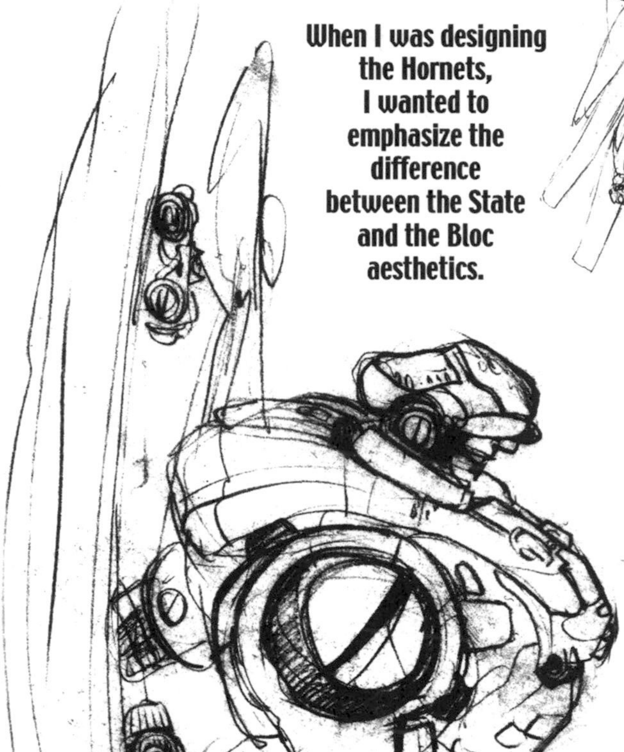

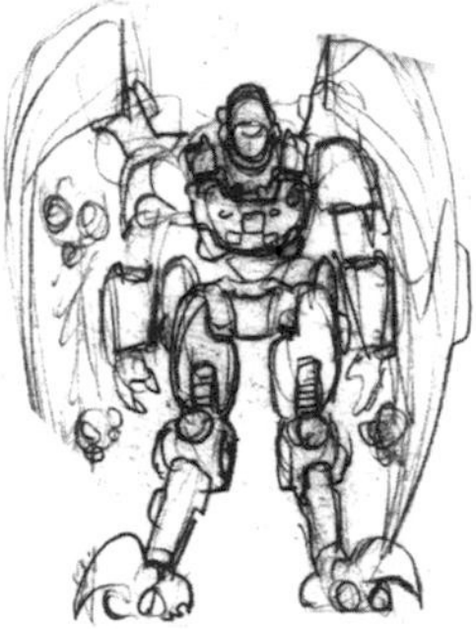

The Hornets' MABs are more organic, as opposed to the State's hard-angled, geometric MABs.

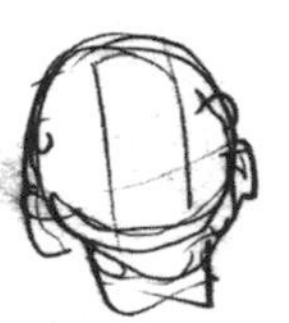

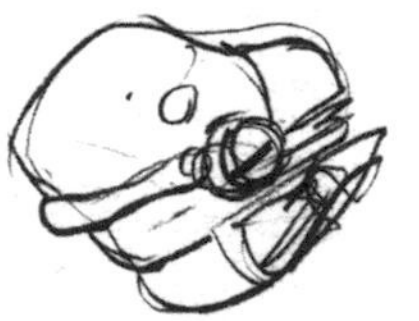

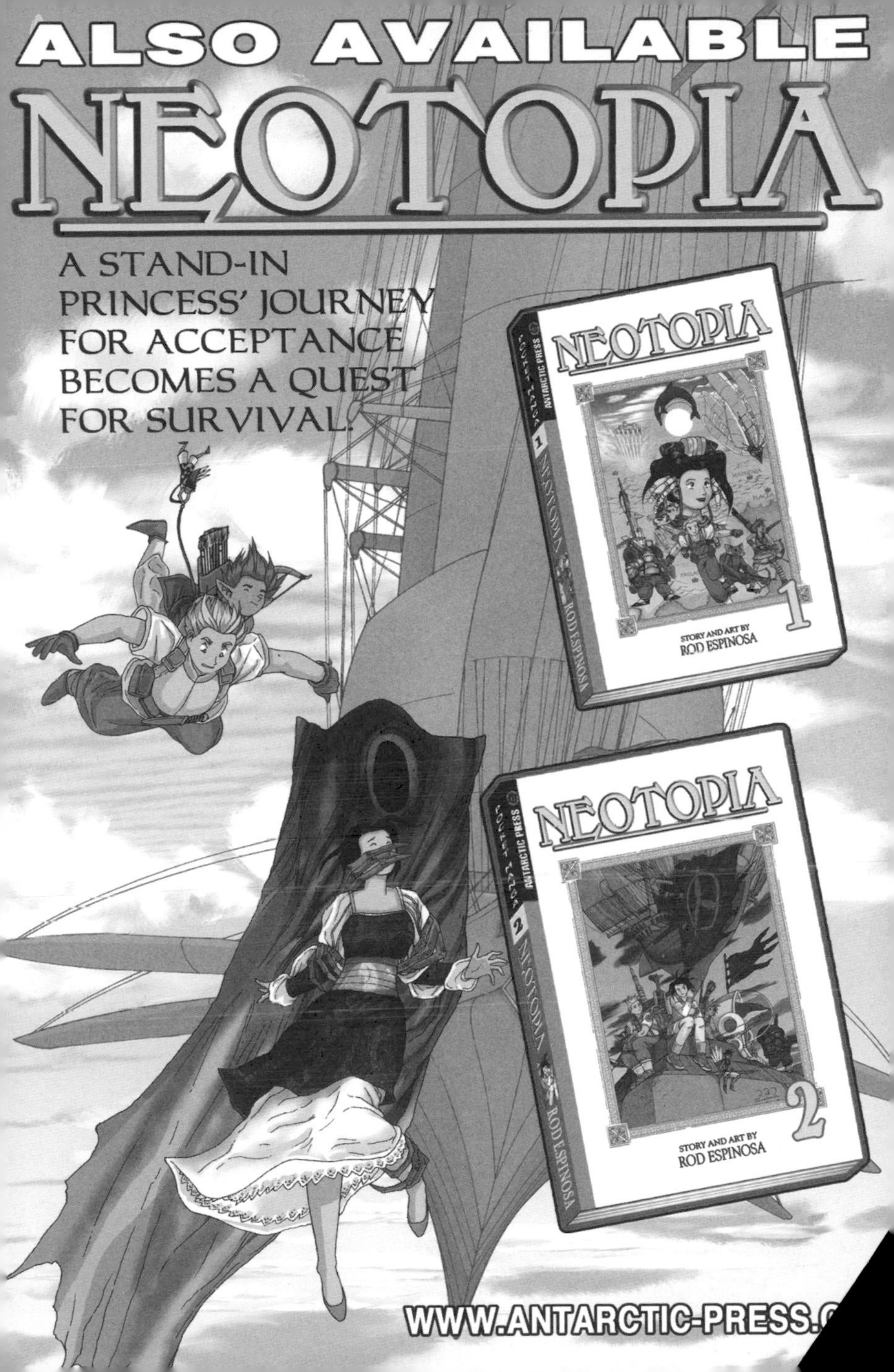
ALSO AVAILABLE
NEOTOPIA
A STAND-IN PRINCESS' JOURNEY FOR ACCEPTANCE BECOMES A QUEST FOR SURVIVAL.
ANTARCTIC PRESS
1 NEOTOPIA
ROD ESPINOSA
NEOTOPIA
1
STORY AND ART BY
ROD ESPINOSA
ANTARCTIC PRESS
2 NEOTOPIA
ROD ESPINOSA
NEOTOPIA
2
STORY AND ART BY
ROD ESPINOSA
WWW.ANTARCTIC-PRESS.C

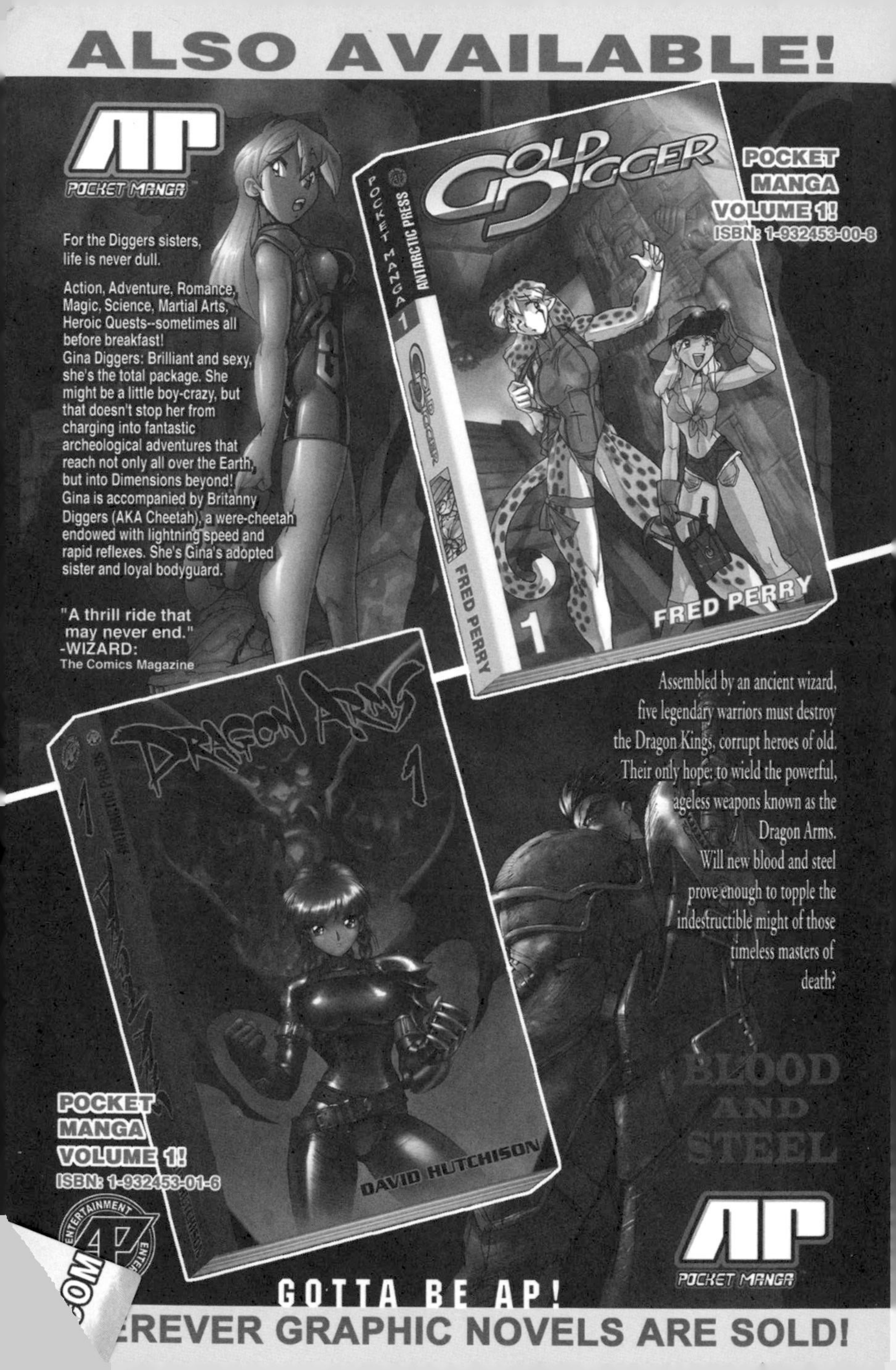

ALSO AVAILABLE!
AP POCKET MANGA
For the Diggers sisters, life is never dull.
Action, Adventure, Romance, Magic, Science, Martial Arts, Heroic Quests--sometimes all before breakfast!
Gina Diggers: Brilliant and sexy, she's the total package. She might be a little boy-crazy, but that doesn't stop her from charging into fantastic archeological adventures that reach not only all over the Earth, but into Dimensions beyond!
Gina is accompanied by Britanny Diggers (AKA Cheetah), a were-cheetah endowed with lightning speed and rapid reflexes. She's Gina's adopted sister and loyal bodyguard.
"A thrill ride that may never end." -WIZARD: The Comics Magazine
GOLD DIGGER
POCKET MANGA ANTARCTIC PRESS
1
FRED PERRY
POCKET MANGA VOLUME 1!
ISBN: 1-932453-00-8
Assembled by an ancient wizard, five legendary warriors must destroy the Dragon Kings, corrupt heroes of old. Their only hope: to wield the powerful, ageless weapons known as the Dragon Arms.
Will new blood and steel prove enough to topple the indestructible might of those timeless masters of death?
DRAGON ARMS
1
ANTARCTIC PRESS
DAVID HUTCHISON
POCKET MANGA VOLUME 1!
ISBN: 1-932453-01-6
ENTERTAINMENT AP
BLOOD AND STEEL
AP POCKET MANGA
GOTTA BE AP!
EREVER GRAPHIC NOVELS ARE SOLD!

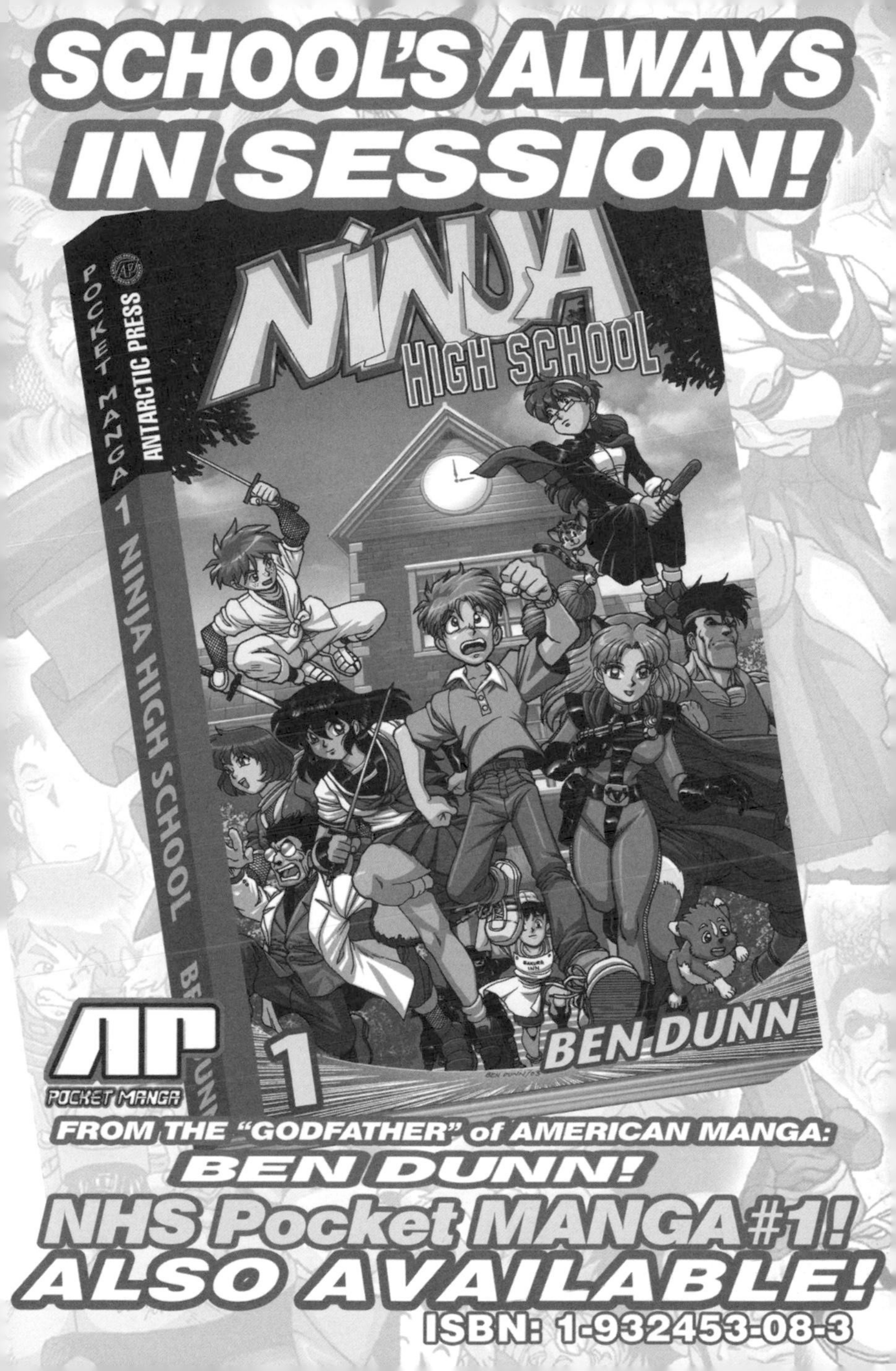
SCHOOL'S ALWAYS IN SESSION!
NINJA HIGH SCHOOL
POCKET MANGA
ANTARCTIC PRESS
1 NINJA HIGH SCHOOL
BEN DUNN
1
POCKET MANGA
FROM THE "GODFATHER" of AMERICAN MANGA:
BEN DUNN!
NHS Pocket MANGA #1!
ALSO AVAILABLE!
ISBN: 1-932453-08-3

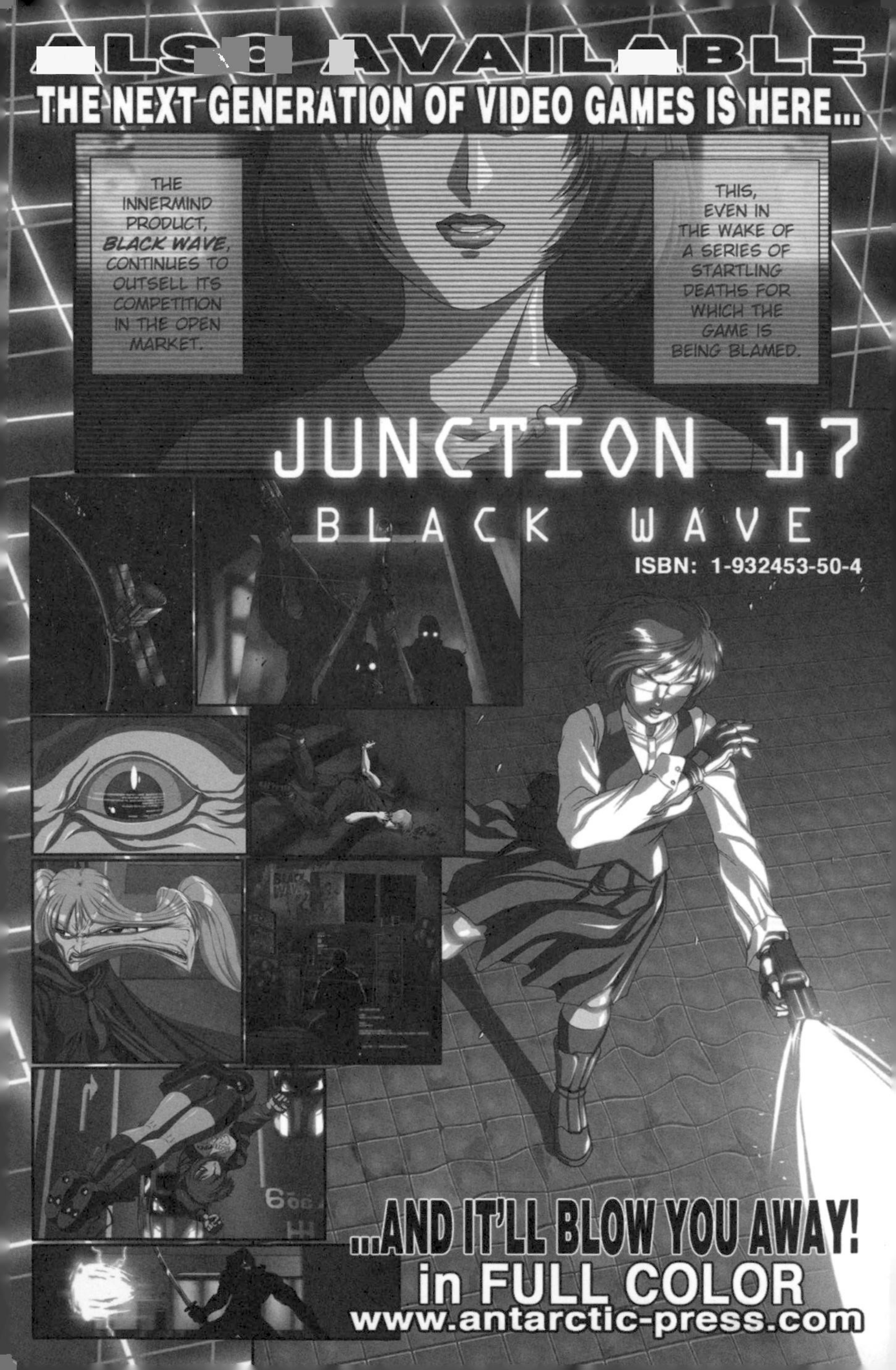

THE NEXT GENERATION OF VIDEO GAMES IS HERE...
THE INNERMIND PRODUCT, BLACK WAVE, CONTINUES TO OUTSELL ITS COMPETITION IN THE OPEN MARKET.
THIS, EVEN IN THE WAKE OF A SERIES OF STARTLING DEATHS FOR WHICH THE GAME IS BEING BLAMED.
JUNCTION 17
BLACK WAVE
ISBN: 1-932453-50-4
...AND IT'LL BLOW YOU AWAY!
in FULL COLOR
www.antarctic-press.com